SHOCK OF THE OLD:
Christopher Dresser's
DESIGN REVOLUTION

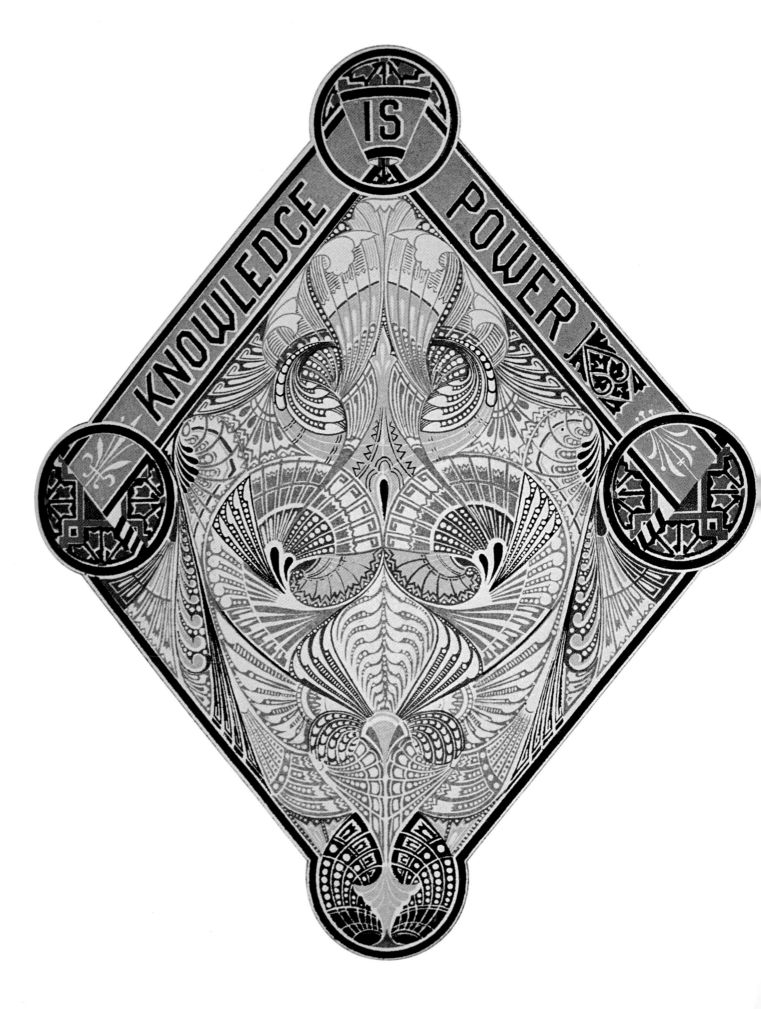

SHOCK OF THE OLD:
Christopher Dresser's
DESIGN REVOLUTION

EDITED BY MICHAEL WHITEWAY

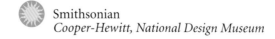

Smithsonian
Cooper-Hewitt, National Design Museum

IN ASSOCIATION WITH
V&A PUBLICATIONS

DISTRIBUTED BY
HARRY N. ABRAMS, INC., PUBLISHERS

Published in conjunction with the exhibition 'Shock of the Old:
Christopher Dresser', organized by Cooper-Hewitt, National
Design Museum, Smithsonian Institution, New York:
5 March to 25 July 2004

Victoria and Albert Museum, London:
9 September to 5 December 2004

Published by V&A Publications in association
with Cooper-Hewitt, National Design Museum, 2004

V&A Publications
160 Brompton Road
London
SW3 1HW
UK

Distributed in North America by Harry N. Abrams,
Incorporated, New York

ISBN 0-8109-6658-1 (Harry N. Abrams, Inc)

Library of Congress Control Number 2003110745

Designed by Harry Green

JACKET ILLUSTRATIONS
Front: Teapot, electroplate with ebonized wood, *c*.1879 (see plate 6).
Back: Electroplated conical sugar bowl (plate 276) with two teapots
by James Dixon & Sons (plates 3 and 5).

FRONTISPIECE: Christopher Dresser. 'Knowledge is Power',
pl. XXIV from *The Art of Decorative Design* (London, 1862).
Michael Whiteway.

Unless otherwise credited, all photographs taken by Michael Whiteway.

Printed in Hong Kong

HARRY N. ABRAMS, Inc
100 Fifth Avenue
New York, N.Y. 10011
www.abramsbooks.com

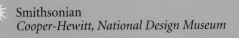

1. Christopher Dresser.
Watercolour design from
an album of designs,
c.1885. Metropolitan
Museum of Art, New York.

Contents

Christopher Dresser at Cooper-Hewitt, National Design Museum

PAUL WARWICK THOMPSON, DIRECTOR

Why should Christopher Dresser be the subject of a major retrospective exhibition? His is hardly a household name, but his position as the first professional designer for industry has made him one of the most influential figures of the nineteenth century as seen through twenty-first-century eyes. The road to full recognition of his importance has been long and slow. In 1937, at the very moment when a fragment of handsome, but unattributed, Lincrusta wallpaper (see detail, left) entered the collection of Cooper-Hewitt, its unknown designer was the subject of a pioneering article by the distinguished architectural historian Nikolaus Pevsner.[1] Pevsner's article was eventually to bear fruit, but meanwhile the Second World War intervened and much of the archival material that Pevsner had been shown, and on which he had based his article, was destroyed. When Pevsner championed Dresser in 1937, it was still some time before museum curators acknowledged his importance; meanwhile another – still unattributed – wallpaper came to Cooper-Hewitt in 1941 (see page 114). Dresser was represented in the seminal show of *Victorian and Edwardian Decorative Arts* at the Victoria and Albert Museum in London in 1952, but as the organizers admitted, little of his work had been traced.[2] Museums tended not to collect Dresser's work because it was mass-produced and so was not considered as 'precious' as works crafted by other designers. It was dealers and private collectors who recognized his remarkably modern spirit and radical approach, and consequently collected and preserved his work. John Jesse and Richard Dennis, specialist dealers and enthusiastic pioneers of nineteenth-century design history, curated the first exhibition devoted to Dresser, which was held in 1972 at the Fine Art Society in London.[3] The best collections of Dresser's work are still in private hands in Europe and America.

As the Smithsonian Institution's National Design Museum, it is appropriate that Cooper-Hewitt should give this outstanding innovator his first museum retrospective, to re-introduce the breadth, variety and innovation of Christopher Dresser's work. Dresser was an inspiring teacher and lecturer, and the author of numerous books that influenced designers on both sides of the Atlantic. His life and career, and his position in the artistic hierarchy of the time as well as his invention of the new profession of commercial designer, are the subject of the essay by Charlotte Gere and Michael Whiteway. Promoting highly modern ideas for his time, his stylized and eclectic approach to design was based on an abstracted reinterpretation of historical patterns and natural forms rather than direct transcriptions. Having studied botany before taking up a full-time career as a designer, he adopted a theoretical approach to pattern and ornamentation, which is examined in detail by Stuart Durant. Least known among his productions are his innumerable designs for textiles and wallpaper, his activities as an 'ornamentist' as he described them and the field in which he was, ironically, the most prolific. Much new material, the result of painstaking detective work, is presented by Harry Lyons in his essay. Dresser promoted a form of 'international eclecticism' in English design. His myriad sources, in historicism as well as non-Western cultures, are the subject of an essay by Judy Rudoe. David Taylor tackles the unexplored impact of Dresser on the United States, which he visited in 1876, one of the first in a small-scale migration of design talent from Britain. As Widar Halén demonstrates, Dresser was a leading figure in the introduction of Japonism to the West and was the first officially commissioned designer to pay a state visit to Japan, in 1876–7, to view indigenous craft and design techniques and to report on them to the British government.

Dresser saw himself as a tradesman; he came from the lower rather than upper middle class, unlike his famous contemporary, William Morris. His most essential divergence from other nineteenth-century designers springs from his understanding of industrial production and consumer culture. Simon Jervis points concisely to the differences between Dresser and Morris. Despite their socialist theories, Morris and the English Aesthetic movement artists' handcrafted works were ironically so expensive that relatively few middle-class clients could actually afford them. In embracing new technologies and mass production, Dresser's work had tremendous geographic and demographic impact across social classes. He was among the first product designers fully to understand and embrace mass production, and to acknowledge the importance of the machine in raising standards of beauty and design for a mass market. In 1899 *The Studio* magazine observed that Dresser was 'Perhaps the greatest of commercial designers imposing his fantasy and invention upon the ordinary output of

British industry.'[4] Jervis pleads for caution when referring to Dresser as a proto-modernist, arguing that we should review the entire eclectic body of Dresser's oeuvre. That said, in the twenty-first century, it is impossible not to view the geometric, minimal and abstract forms produced by Dresser on his return from Japan as startling precursors to the Bauhaus metalwork of Marianne Brandt and Wolfgang Tümpel; and his combinations of materials and new metal processes as presaging the twentieth-century 'Machine-Age' aesthetic.

The use of manufacturing technology contributed to an explosive development of consumer culture. Suddenly fine design was no longer relegated to commissioned work for the elite, but was accessible to anyone with the means to purchase goods. At the same time, the development of decorative art and design museums in Europe and the United States reflected a widespread interest in educating the taste of the public as well as the trade. The impetus for establishing the first design museum in the United States was the educational institution that nurtured Dresser himself, the South Kensington Museum (the Victoria and Albert Museum or V&A, as it was known from 1899). The development of the Smithsonian's Cooper-Hewitt National Design Museum is deeply rooted in the late nineteenth-century industrial art museum movement, led by the V&A, which was effectively the first design museum in the West. Both were initially established in collaboration with schools, and both were formed to educate future designers and raise standards of design and manufactures. In 1836, after lobbying and a parliamentary inquiry, the British government established a School of Design; although not very successful at first, it was the only publicly funded art school attempting to train designers for the new industrial age. It was appropriate, then, that Dresser became, at a very young age, a product of this new form of education.

Some 15 years after the establishment of the school, opinion in Britain was still agitated about design standards, especially after the Great Exhibition of the Industry of All Nations in 1851 had exposed British products to comparison with those of other countries. The Great Exhibition had been promoted and steered to success (it was visited by 6.2 million people) by Prince Albert, who, as the consort of the monarch, was pleased to find in 'the application of art and science to industry' a nonpolitical project through which he could benefit his adoptive country. He ensured that the profits of the exhibition were devoted to the establishment of an educational campus in South Kensington. One of his most energetic lieutenants in the Great Exhibition was an unusually entrepreneurial civil servant, Henry Cole.[5] After the exhibition, Cole was put in charge of the ailing School of Design. He relaunched it in new premises, with a new syllabus, and used its collections of artifacts, plus others bought from the exhibition, to create a public museum of design. After a few years in Marlborough House, the school and the museum (which together formed a government agency called the Department of Science and Art) moved to the South Kensington campus. They rapidly expanded under Cole's dynamic direction, and the museum formed the nucleus of what is today the V&A.

Dresser saw all of this from the inside, so to speak. He was faithful to the school that had trained him, and sympathetic to Cole's ideas on design reform. He was quite outspoken, however, in criticizing the new museum for its continuing adherence to neo-Renaissance, which he saw as debased, rather than seeking out examples of international design styles and forms. He wrote extensively, promoting the importance of contemporary design and the need to raise the status of design as high as or higher than that of pictorial art. Dresser's writings also had an influence on American design. During his visit to the Philadelphia Centennial in 1876 he registered 13 wallpaper designs with the United States Patent Office; a number of American wallpapers from this period are believed to derive from Dresser's patterns. In the 1880s, John D. Rockefeller decorated his New York city house with Dresser pattern Lincrusta wall-covering; the sample in the Cooper-Hewitt collection is one of the first twentieth-century museum acquisitions of Dresser's work. Dresser's ideas on ornament, pattern and decoration influenced American architects including Frank Furness and Louis Sullivan, and his books on Japan influenced Walter Burley Griffin, Charles Sumner Greene and Henry Mather Greene, and Frank Lloyd Wright. In 1876 Dresser was invited to address public audiences at the Philadelphia Centennial. In one of his lectures, he urged American designers to establish a formal museum of design in the United States, like London's South Kensington Museum, in order to inspire future designers.

While it is not known whether they specifically knew of Dresser's lecture, two decades later Sarah Cooper Hewitt and Eleanor Garnier Hewitt established the Cooper Union Museum for the Arts of Decoration in New York. The first design museum in the United States, this was the genesis of the Smithsonian's Cooper-Hewitt, National Design Museum.[6] Its creation was very consciously crafted according to Dresser's precepts, and those of his British design compatriots. The Hewitt sisters were granddaughters of Peter Cooper, who founded The Cooper Union for the Advancement of Science and Art and planned to include a museum for the exhibition of mechanical devices and a Cosmorama in the main building. Like Dresser, Cooper believed that beauty in design should be accessible to everyone and not just the elite. On the seal of the university Cooper placed the words 'Founded by a Mechanic of New York', indicating that this tuition-free school would enable lower-class workers to receive a higher education in design. Recalling their grandfather's dream, the sisters asked that a room at Cooper Union be set aside as a museum, noting

> Perhaps the most interesting thing to be seen in the Musée des Arts Décoratifs [in Paris] is the earnest attention and pleasure in the faces of the workmen who frequent it, and who are measuring, copying, or giving general study to the masterpieces of their own trades ... it is upon the same lines that the new Museum for the Arts of Decoration at the Cooper Union is endeavoring to carry out its work.

The Hewitt sisters' father, Abram Hewitt, was in the iron trade. He travelled widely throughout Europe, immersing himself in the industrial arts of Britain and France before marrying Peter Cooper's daughter. Hewitt was an ardent Francophile, and he served as the American Commissioner at the Paris Exposition of 1855. In addition to taking his two daughters to many exhibitions and galleries in London and Paris (including the South Kensington Museum and the gallery of Henry Duveen), he gave them free run of his personal library where they had access to the *Illustrated London News*, the *London Graphic* and illustrated books on design by Owen Jones among others. By the age of 16 the sisters shared their father's love of design and were already building their collections. Whether consciously or not, the Hewitt sisters fulfilled Dresser's call to action at the Philadelphia Centennial, establishing a design museum in the United States. The museum's intended audience was not limited to designers and artisans, however, for the sisters hoped it would allow 'an intending purchaser ... [to] familiarize himself with the best that has been done in any one of these departments ... it is as an educator of the public standard of taste that this museum hopes to do its best work.' As the sisters specified, the objects in the museum were arranged in sections inviting 'much comparison and discussion as to material, workmanship, and design, and gives an insight into the artistic work of each epoch all over the world'. The range of objects in this exhibition, which starts at Cooper-Hewitt, National Design Museum, before travelling on to the Victoria and Albert Museum, demonstrates that these qualities are also the hallmarks of Christopher Dresser's work.

Organizing an exhibition on Christopher Dresser would not be possible without calling upon Michael Whiteway's assistance and expertise. He is a published authority on nineteenth-century architect-designers.[7] His connoisseurship and instinctive 'feel' for Dresser's work place him in a league of his own. Through their knowledge of Dresser, Whiteway and the other contributors to the book – Stuart Durant, Charlotte Gere, Harry Lyons, Judy Rudoe, David Taylor, Simon Jervis and Widar Halén – have, over the last 30 years, reminded us of Dresser's significance. We are all indebted to their deep knowledge of the field. Charlotte Gere has been remarkably generous with her scholarship and time, both in terms of editorial guidance and in writing all the text accompanying the manufacturers' sections for this book. Cynthia Trope, Collections Manager in the Product Design and Decorative Arts department of Cooper-Hewitt, has been invaluable in organizing and researching this exhibition and book. We also owe a great deal of thanks to the many museums, archives and private lenders to the exhibition. Their response and assistance have been invaluable, and allowed us properly to demonstrate Dresser's singular vision and importance.

We would also like to thank David Bonsall, John H. Bryan, John H. Bryan III, Constance R. Caplin, Sophie Cox, Isabelle Grey, Joseph Holtzman, James Joll, Chris Morley and Brian Cargin, Andrew McIntosh Patrick and The Fine Art Society, Peter Rose, Sheri Sandler, John Scott, Mr and Mrs Lee Smith, Ellen and William Taubman, Massimo Valsecchi and Paul Walter.

For editorial insights, we are grateful to Helen Dunstan, Dr Cathy Gere, Joanna Asquith-Langhorne and Mariko Whiteway.

We are indebted to our many generous sponsors, without whom the exhibition and accompanying programs would never have been possible: Enid and Lester Morse, Connie and Harvey Krueger, Barbara and Morton Mandel, Deedee and Barrie A. Wigmore, Esme Usdan and James Snyder, Kay Allaire, John H. Bryan. Furthermore: a program of the J.M. Kaplan Fund, Stephen McKay, Inc., Mr. and Mrs. Arthur Ross, Susan and Jon Rotenstreich, and anonymous donors.

A number of museum professionals on both sides of the Atlantic contributed enormously to the exhibition and book, including Linda Lloyd-Jones, Emma Kelly, Suzanne Fagence Cooper, Rupert Faulkner, Mark Haworth-Booth, Jennifer Opie, Eric Turner, Stephen Calloway and Anthony Burton of the Victoria and Albert Museum in London, and Mary Butler, Frances Ambler and Ariane Bankes of V&A Publications, as well as the book's editor, Slaney Begley, and designer, Harry Green, Mario Aleppo of the National Archive, Ruth Harman of Sheffield Archive, Joan Jones of the Minton Archive, Sally Dummer of the Ipswich Museum, James D. Draper and Lori Zabar of the Metropolitan Museum, and the late Augusto Morello of Milan. At Cooper-Hewitt, the exhibition and book would not have been possible without the extraordinary efforts of Barbara J. Bloemink, Ph.D., Stephen Van Dyk and his interns, and the work of Konstanze Bachman, Jill Bloomer, Elizabeth Broman, Jocelyn Groom, Allison Henriksen, Gregory Herringshaw, Chul R. Kim, S. Jordan Kim, Steve Langehough, Larry Silver and Scott Wilhelme. Lastly, many thanks to exhibition designers Sandra Wheeler and Alfred Zollinger of Matter Practice.

Christopher Dresser's career perfectly articulates the Hewitt sisters' intention in forming the first American design museum, and the museum's current mission: to explore the impact of international design both historically and in contemporary life. It is therefore with pride and a sense of indebtedness to the founders of this museum that Cooper-Hewitt, National Design Museum has organized the first truly comprehensive museum exhibition on Christopher Dresser; and that the exhibition is continuing on to the Victoria and Albert Museum, whose historic beginnings so closely integrate with Dresser's life and philosophy.

MAULL & POLYBLANK   LONDON

Introduction

MICHAEL WHITEWAY

Christopher Dresser was the first independent industrial designer, in the sense that he worked for a large and varied number of manufacturers. He was an exact contemporary of his fellow design reformers William Morris and E.W. Godwin, but he differed from them in that instead of specializing in the traditional fields for architect-designers of interior decoration and furniture design, he designed for the new breed of industrially based manufacturers. During his working life Dresser was employed by scores of different clients not only in Britain but also in France, Japan and the USA. Both as a designer and as an art adviser for the textile, carpet and wallpaper industries, he helped to bring modernity and order to their artistic direction. Early in his career he worked for some of the most prestigious names of the Industrial Revolution – Wedgwood, Minton and Coalbrookdale – but later he was to choose to work with manufacturers over whom he could exert more control; some of these makers combined in 1881 under Dresser's art direction to supply the Art Furnishers' Alliance, a store in which everything was either designed by or approved of by him.

An archetypal Victorian, Dresser benefited from opportunities not available to previous generations. He came from a socially modest, Non-conformist background (as did many of the other innovators of the Industrial Revolution). From the age of 13 he studied at a Government School of Design. These schools had been recently established to help improve the dismal standards of design in the new category of industrial- rather than craft-based manufactures that was dominating production during the nineteenth century.

During Dresser's formative years in the 1840s and '50s the structure of the modern world was being formed. The rapidly growing population was moving increasingly to the sprawling towns forming around the new industries; by 1850 the railway system had connected most of the major towns in England. Scientific and industrial advances were becoming everyday events; this was the age of Brunel, Faraday, Stephenson and Darwin, an age when it seemed as if science and technology could provide the solution to any need.

Dresser had begun to study botany – then a modern and exciting science – while at the School of Design, and this intellectual discipline perhaps encouraged

2. Christopher Dresser.
Carte-de-visite portrait photograph.
Courtesy of the Linnean Society, London.

3. James Dixon & Sons, Sheffield. Teapot, electroplate and ebonized wood, designed *c*.1878, made *c*.1878–85. © The British Museum, London.

4. James Dixon & Sons, Sheffield. Teapot, electroplate with ebonized wood, no. 2276, 25 November 1880. Württembergisches Landesmuseum, Stuttgart.

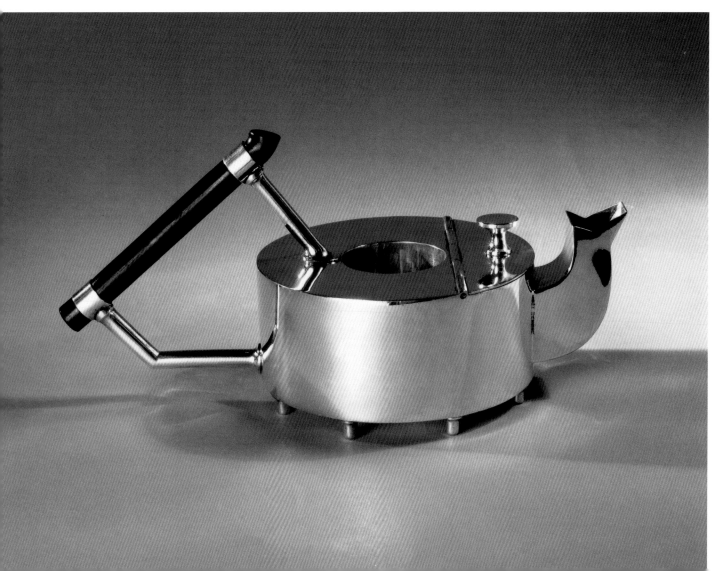

5. James Dixon & Sons.
Teapot, electroplate with
ebonized wood.
© The Trustees, National
Museum of Scotland,
Edinburgh.

6. James Dixon & Sons.
Teapot, electroplate
with ebonized wood,
no. 2274, *c*.1879.
Andrew McIntosh
Patrick Collection.

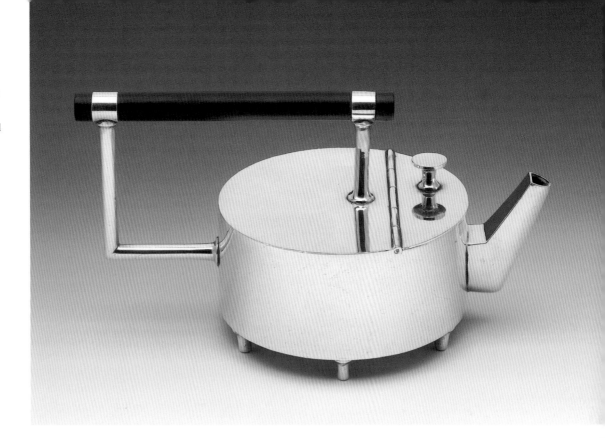

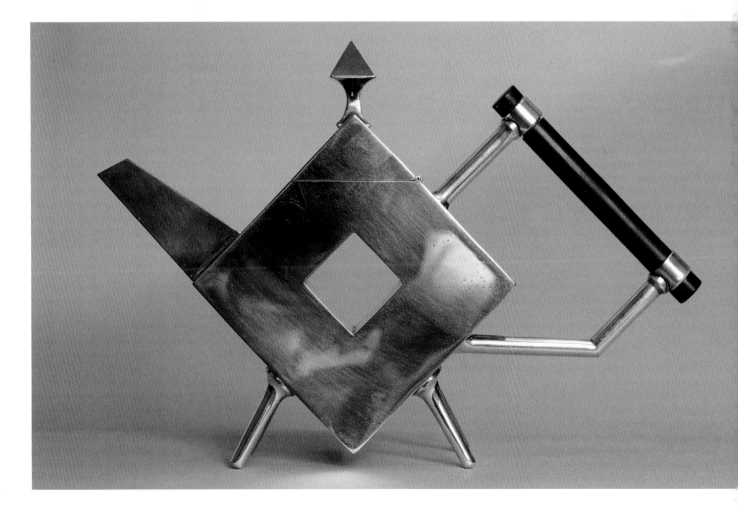

him to believe that design could be approached in a similarly systematic way. Certainly Dresser's development of his principles of design based on the abstraction of plant forms would have been the obvious approach for a botanist to take.

Dresser's other great source of inspiration was the world beyond the arid Classical and self-righteous Gothic styles that dominated at the time. The Great Exhibition of 1851 had introduced the public to the artistic riches of the wider world. Dresser was particularly impressed by the Indian exhibits, which were in a great contrast to the moribund pastiches displayed by British and European industry. He would also have found visual stimulation in the great museums that were then being founded and expanded, as well as the new excavations and discoveries that were constantly being made.

Colour printing – chromolithography – enabled other cultures and eras to be presented in much more realistic detail than ever before. Dresser contributed a plate to the greatest colour book on the decorative arts produced in the nineteenth century, the magnificent *Grammar of Ornament* published in 1856 by his mentor Owen Jones. This was to be the standard pattern book on world ornament well into the next century.

Dresser appreciated the importance of reputation and status to his career; after he was awarded a doctorate from Jena University he always used the title 'Doctor'. Following his three books on botany, published between 1859 and 1860, he produced in 1862 a most original book that established his claim to be taken seriously as a designer: *The Art of Decorative Design*. This was followed in the 1870s by *Principles of Decorative Design* (originally published as a series of articles in a self-improvement magazine, the *Technical Educator*) and his prestige full-colour book *Studies in Design*. By 1870 Dresser had established his career as a designer to such an extent that he could claim: 'As an ornamentist I have much the largest practice in the Kingdom; so far as I know there is not one branch of art manufacture that I do not regularly design patterns for.' His reputation was such that most of his designs from the mid-1870s onwards bore his signature or the inscription 'Designed by Dr Chr Dresser', thus establishing his name as a brand, and reassuring uncertain consumers that they were buying aesthetically approved objects.

Dresser maintained a studio of assistant design-

---

the material with which we have now to deal differs in character widely from that of which those vessels already considered have been formed, yet that many principles which have been enunciated are equally applicable to the objects now under consideration. Silver objects, like those formed of clay or glass, should perfectly serve the end for which they have been formed; also, the fact that ornament applied to rounded surfaces should be adapted for being viewed in perspective remains as binding on us as before; but herein the works of the silversmith differ from those already considered ——they are formed of a material of intrinsic value, which is not the case with articles of earthenware or glass. Silver and gold being materials of considerable worth, it is necessary that the utmost economy be observed in using them, and in order to effect this a

Besides this, works in silver and in gold are always in danger of being destroyed, owing to the intrinsic value of these metals; and if stolen, the theft is promptly hidden in the melting-pot. Now if we form the vessels of thin metal, we render the money value of the material less, and thus our works are to a smaller degree tempting to the avaricious, and their chance of longevity is greater. The precious metals are at all times perilous materials for the formation of works of art; but while we do use these worthy materials, let us so employ them as to give to our works every possible opportunity for long existence. If a work is to be so formed that it may exist for many years, it becomes of the highest importance that those objects which we create be well considered as to their utility, and at the same time beautiful in form. Long existence is an evil in the

Fig. 122.

Section of Fig. 119.   Fig. 119.   Section of Fig. 120.   Fig. 120.

Fig. 123.

special mode of construction must be resorted to. If we propose to ourselves the formation of a sugar-basin of semi-circular shape, of what thickness must the metal be in order that it may not bend when lifted? It is obvious that

case of an ugly object, or an ill-considered vessel; that which is not refining in its influence is better blotted out. Let that man who will not seek to embody beauty in his works make them heavy with metal, so that they may

the vessel must not yield its shape to ordinary pressure, nor be subject to alterations of form when in ordinary use; but if it is to be so formed throughout of metal of such thickness as will secure its retaining its shape, it will be costly and heavy, and

tempt the thief, and thus sooner blot out his works, as they tend only to debase and degrade; but he who loves refinement, and seeks to give chasteness of character to the objects which he creates, may well strive to secure to them length of duration.

---

ers, which under his direction was immensely productive, working on designs in a wide variety of materials. For example, in 1869, according to Nikolaus Pevsner, Dresser supplied 158 textile designs to just one client – Ward of Halifax. At different times Dresser described himself as an 'ornamentist', an 'art advisor' and an 'architect'. His roles seem to have been first as a designer in his own right, secondly as a supplier of designs by his studio and thirdly as an art advisor who guided the artistic direction of a manufacturer. He describes his studio system in *Modern Ornamentation* (1886):

> The patterns now published are all original designs which are the work of the Author, his Assistants, and his Pupils collectively. All are the result of the Author's suggestions, or have been produced under his observation, but some are from the pencil of those who have passed beyond the condition of the tyro.

These varied roles can make the absolute attribution of some designs difficult, if not impossible, for today's historians. However, Dresser's approach made him very useful to the new breed of carpet, textile and wallpaper manufacturers who had both a customer base greatly expanded by the growth of the urban middle-class population and the vast

7. 'Principles of Design' from *The Technical Educator*, p. 104, showing the Elkington sugar basin at plate 8. Michael Whiteway. The design is included among the sketches on p. 25 of the 'Ipswich' sketchbook.

production capacities enabled by new technologies. Their appetite for new designs was insatiable, but they often lacked any design direction; as long as Dresser's work remained popular with their public he remained invaluable to these manufacturers.

Since his time as a student at the School of

8. Elkington, Birmingham. Sugar basin, electroplate. Private Collection.

Design, Dresser had enjoyed a close collaboration with the circle associated with the South Kensington Museum (now the V&A), and particularly with Owen Jones. From 1873 Dresser also developed a close friendship with the director of the museum, Sir Philip Cunliffe Owen. Dresser acted as official representative for the museum on his trip to Japan in 1876–7; indeed Tiffany & Co., in their catalogue of the goods that Dresser bought on their behalf in Japan, describe Dresser as 'of the South Kensington Museum'. However, Dresser moved in a different social circle to many of his more illustrious contemporaries, and indeed the field of design itself was widely unappreciated until after the Second World War.

One of Dresser's great strengths as a designer was his ability to understand the properties of materials and the processes of production, and to adapt his designs and ideas on aesthetics to them. Of course the principles of fitness for purpose and honesty of construction go back to Pugin, but Dresser's scientific training gave him a particular insight into the use of materials. This ability, along with a very obvious change in attitude towards ornament, became particularly apparent on his return from Japan.

Throughout his career Dresser had been endeavouring to develop a language of design based not on literal representation but on a kind of botanical abstraction, and a global eclecticism that avoided conventional historicism – he even notes that some of the art of ancient Egypt was too representational. On his return from Japan in 1877 Dresser's perceptions changed. From previously describing himself as an 'ornamentist', he almost rejects ornament. Japan taught him that often form is enough to entertain and please the eye; that ornament can distract from rather than enhance form. He came to understand that even the humblest object could benefit from the attentions of a designer, writing in his book on the arts of Japan in 1881:

> There is as much pride in Japan manifested by the maker in completing a little cup, a lacquer box, a sheet of leather paper, or even a pair of chopsticks and by perfect work any handicraftsman may attain the celebrity enjoyed here by a Landseer, a Turner or an Owen Jones.

The post-Japan designs emphasize the qualities of the materials from which they are made, and revel in the methods of their manufacture. They no longer have the pomposity of High Victorian style, and instead predict the egalitarianism of modern design. Unfortunately what should have been Dresser's greatest triumph, the Art Furnishers' Alliance, a store financed and supplied by his many clients, was a failure financially, and closed after two years. From this point on Dresser's career declined and with a few notable exceptions he seems to have largely reverted to his previous role as a supplier of pattern designs to the wallpaper and textile industries.

Dresser's achievement was that he pioneered the profession of industrial designer, creating radical solutions to the design problems of his age far in advance of those of any of his contemporaries. It is hard to judge Dresser's contribution to the history of design. His influence on the purity of form lived on in industry after his death, but the initiative in design passed to the ideas of the Arts and Crafts movement. The reputation of Dresser's exact contemporary William Morris had somehow eclipsed that of all other design reformers of the nineteenth century. We can only speculate about what might have happened if Dresser's approach to design had triumphed, an approach that was optimistic about the industrialized future, embraced the machine and made no excuses for the modern world.

Nº 13 GLOSOCOMIA CLEMATIDEA

Nº 5. ONION Nº 3 DAFFODIL Nº 8 HONEYSUCKLE Nº 4 NARCISSUS Nº 18. LEYCESTERIA FORMOSA

Nº 11. SPEEDWELL Nº 10 LADIES SMOCK

Nº 12 HAREBELL Nº 2. WHITE LILY Nº 1. IRIS Nº 7 MOUSEAR

Nº 16 PERIWINCKLE Nº 14 CONVOLVULUS

Nº 6 DOG ROSE

Nº 9 MALLOW Nº 17 CLARKIA Nº 15. PRIMROSE C. DRESSER. DEL

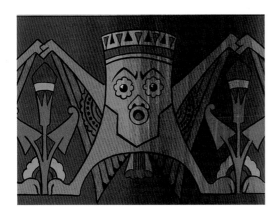

Dr Christopher Dresser :
His Life and Career

CHARLOTTE GERE AND MICHAEL WHITEWAY

Childhood and education, 1834–54

Christopher Dresser was born in Glasgow on 4 July 1834, the third child of Christopher Dresser (1807–69) and his wife, Mary (née Nettleton). Dresser's parents, who had married in 1829, were Methodists, both from Yorkshire yeoman families, and his father, grandfather and eldest brother were all excise officers. Dresser senior was moved around in the course of his official duties, to Stockton in 1839, briefly to London in 1841, Bandon, County Cork, in 1842, Hereford in 1847 and Halifax from 1852 to 1860.[1] Dresser would claim that all the education he received was during the four years of his childhood spent in Ireland. From an early age he showed a precocious artistic talent, and remembered spending a large part of his childhood drawing and painting. He also recalled being in trouble for exchanging a little box with a lock, given to him by his father to keep his treasures in, for an 'old-fashioned two-penny paintbox'.[2] In 1847 the boy Christopher was enrolled, at the age of 13 – two years earlier than usual – to study applied design and botany at the recently established Government School of Design at Somerset House in the Strand. His parents must have had considerable faith in his abilities to send him to London at such an early age and to support his very prolonged training, which lasted for seven years, until 1854.[3]

The Government Schools of Design were set up to train designers for industry.[4] The deplorable state of art education in the manufacturing sector was seen as limiting the competitiveness of British industry internationally, and the need for trained designers was accepted by the government as a priority. Dresser's education and subsequent career were the outcome of reforming liberal policies that opened up new opportunities to the under-privileged. Among the leading spirits was Sir William Ewart, a barrister and progressive politician, who was responsible for the parliamentary Bill establishing public libraries and an advocate of the widest access to museums and galleries for the working classes. Sir William set up the 1835 select committee to 'enquire into the best means of extending a knowledge of the Arts and of the principles of Design among the people (especially the Manufacturing Population) of the Country'. The resulting Schools of Design were 'for the purpose of affording Instruction to those

9. Watercolour design for pl. XCVIII of the *Grammar of Ornament*, 1856, drawn by Christopher Dresser. V&A: Jones Q16 (box) 1671.

engaged in the practice of ornamental Art, and the preparation of Designs for the various Manufactures of this country'.[5]

The schools were for 'artisans', who paid very small fees supposedly within their means, in order to be trained in the principles of applied design. Dresser's father was not, in fact, an artisan, but his earnings as a minor government official were probably little more than those of a skilled craftsman. Predominantly concerned with practical training in ornamentation, the very indifferent instruction in the school specifically barred study of the human figure. The authorities believed that teaching fine art would qualify the students 'beyond their stations'.[6] Dresser evolved his own design principles that were against using the human figure, but the fact remains that his training was deficient in this respect. He later wrote: 'That I was intended by nature as an artist, I do not doubt; but let it ever be remembered that, with a view of causing me to become one, my parents placed me at a "school of design"; as a consequence, I may not be an artist'.[7]

One of the chief defects of the school when Dresser arrived was the lack of practical skills among the instructors. The classes were large and the students learned to draw simply by copying; however, things greatly improved with the programme of reform pushed through from 1852 by Sir Henry Cole (1808–82) and Richard Redgrave (1804–88) – the latter had arrived to teach botany at the time Dresser enrolled at the school. The teacher of architectural drawing was C.J. Richardson, one-time pupil and assistant to Sir John Soane. John Bell, the sculptor who worked on designs for the Coalbrookdale Iron Foundry, was also attached to the school. William Dyce, author of the influential *Drawing Book of the Government School of Design* (1842) and first director of the school who had left in 1843, returned for a year in 1847 to teach design. Dresser declared that his 'love for the natural sciences' came from attending lectures by Lyon Playfair at the School of Mines in Jermyn Street in 1851 and 1852. He decided to specialize in botany. Redgrave believed that plants should be studied from nature before being transformed into symmetrical decorative ornament.[8] Dresser studied plants from Kew Gardens under the supervision of the keeper, Joseph Dalton Hooker. Hooker and his father, Sir William Hooker, director at Kew, were to be valuable supporters of Dresser the botanist. If it

were not for the fact that Dresser was exceptional in every sense, he would have been an outstanding advertisement for the new system of art education offered by the school. He won three prizes for applied design in 1851, a £15 scholarship in 1852 and a further scholarship, three prizes and three medals in 1853 (below).

10. Schools of Design bronze medal awarded to Christopher Dresser. Collection of Ellen and William Taubman.

During his years of training, Dresser was able to observe from within the Cole circle – which included the architects Augustus Welby Northmore Pugin (1812–52) and Owen Jones (1809–74) (plate 255) as well as Redgrave and Cole himself – debates about ornamentation and pattern and their relation to industry, and these probably contributed more to his education than the narrow regime of the school.[9] As one of the significant steps on the road to design reform, Cole had set up Felix Summerly's Art-Manufactures in 1847, a scheme for uniting the fine arts to manufactures in the form of a co-operative of artists – a number of whom were connected with the School of Design – designing articles in good taste to be produced inexpensively for domestic use.[10] Among the firms involved were Wedgwood and Minton for ceramics, Coalbrookdale for cast iron, Elkington for electrotypes and James Dixon of Sheffield for plate (the relevance of these to Dresser's later career will shortly become apparent). Nearly a hundred of the 'Art-Manufactures' were shown at the Society of Arts in 1848, and some again at the 1851 Great Exhibition. Meanwhile, in 1849 Cole started the *Journal of Design and Manufactures,* a publication designed to propagate his ideas and publicise the Summerly products. Although short-lived it had a considerable impact, with polemical statements on design, including a summary of Redgrave's lectures on the use of natural forms in the applied arts. The 1851 Great Exhibition in London was the main focus of the *Journal of Design* for its duration. The magazine, which was fully illustrated, carried inserts of textiles and wallpapers in stylized naturalistic designs printed in a range of muted colours (right).

11. Owen Jones. Textile sample, *Journal of Design and Manufactures* (1849–52). Courtesy of Smithsonian Institution Libraries, Washington DC.

1851 and the Great Exhibition

The genesis of popular interest in the arrangement and embellishment of the home can be traced to the early years of the nineteenth century, but its spread from within a cultured and moneyed elite to the prosperous – and increasingly influential – middle classes can be explained in broad terms by the phenomenon of the 1851 Great Exhibition. The brainchild of Prince Albert, ably assisted by Cole and Playfair, it brought all the most exciting aspects of the modern world under one roof. A vast audience from every walk of society was introduced to modern technology and manufactured goods from all over the world. For Cole the main point of the exhibition, apart from its global ambitions, was its financial independence and profitability. He wrote,

> The history of the world, I venture to say records no event comparable in its promotion of human industry, with that of the Great Exhibition of the Works of Industry of All Nations in 1851. A great people invited all civilized nations to a festival, to bring into comparison the works of human skill. It was carried out by its own private means; was self-supporting and independent of taxes and employment of slaves, which great works had enacted in ancient days. A prince of pre-eminent wisdom, of philosophic sagacity, with power of generalship and great practical ability, placed himself at the head of the enterprise, and lead it to triumphant success.[11]

It is hard to overstate the importance of the Great Exhibition. The organizers of this hugely successful event inaugurated an era of international exhibitions – literally trade shows – across the world,

effectively demarcating the design history of the second half of the nineteenth century. Working machinery was one of the greatest sights of the show, conveying the might of the industrialized world (plate 12). The great Victorian naturalist Professor Richard Owen worked on the sections of the Great Exhibition relating to Animal Products and the Animal Kingdom. Jones devised a colour scheme for the interior of the Crystal Palace based on theories of harmonious juxtaposition, an influential example of the Victorian taste for polychromy in architecture. Pugin's 1851 Mediaeval Court offered Gothic as a modern decorative style; it was treated with respect, but warily by a public still in love with the upholstered, curvilinear comfort of the rococo. It was Pugin's swansong; he was already ill and he died the following year aged only 40. Without his guiding hand, his successors perpetuated an old-fashioned, over-elaborate Gothic style that he would probably have abandoned. The way forward, as he saw it, through paring away all

the ornament to leave the structural elements as a pure design statement on their own, had to wait for Dresser and Godwin to unveil Egyptian-, Japanese- and Greek-inspired designs in the 1870s.

It goes without saying that Dresser visited the Great Exhibition, since his most cherished mentors were involved, and he later recalled that his attention was directed to the Indian and Oriental displays by them. Oriental art provided a major source of new ideas for the group around Cole and Jones. Among Dresser's earliest surviving drawings are 'Indian Ornaments from the Great Exhibition', a turban ornament and an ornamental dagger and sheath (right). Specimens of art and ornament were being collected specifically to inspire the students at the Schools of Design (and for the soon-to-be-founded South Kensington Museum) and the collection was greatly enlarged by purchases of Oriental material from the Great Exhibition by a committee including, as well as Redgrave and Cole, Owen Jones and Pugin. In their choices, they stress the similarities of technique and design among objects from different cultures, as inspiration for applied art and manufactures. Jones and Redgrave were particularly keen on the Asiatic purchases, and Dresser continued to recommend these decorative traditions in his design writings (see chapter 2). Dresser constantly reiterated his debt to Redgrave, and to Jones, whom he admired above all others.

The many deficiencies of the 1851 displays were noted and pondered by the promoters. Attempting to distinguish the main lapses in taste, Cole mounted an exhibition of 'False Principles in

12. *Machinery Hall in the Great Exhibition of the Works of Industry of All Nations, 1851.* From *Dickinson's Comprehensive Pictures of the Great Exhibition of 1851* (1854), 2 vols. Michael Whiteway.

13. Christopher Dresser. Watercolour drawing of an Ornamental Indian Dagger, 1851. V&A: 979 (EP6).

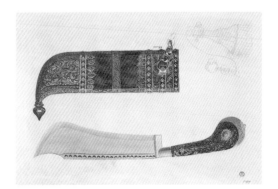

Design' at the Museum of Ornamental Art in Marlborough House. The catalogue took an uncompromising stance on 'the chief vice in the decoration common to Europe in the present day ... the tendency towards *direct imitation of nature*'. This was an unambiguous hit at the 1851 exhibits with their swags of flowers and fruit, fish and game, rose-scattered carpets, flower-encrusted porcelain and wallpapers featuring perspectives of a railway station or the Crystal Palace. Even 25 years later Dresser remembered some of the horrors:

> scissors formed as birds, which separated into halves every time the scissors were opened; candle-sticks formed as human beings, with the candle fitting into the top of a chimneypot hat or into the head; egg-cups formed as birds' nests; ... carpets upon which ponds of water were drawn with water-lilies floating upon them; and other absurdities equally offensive to good taste.[12]

Dresser certainly took these lessons to heart; he believed that the flat patterns in a room, particularly the wallpaper, should act simply as a background to the people in it (see chapter 3).[13] The 'False Principles' display had to be withdrawn, after objections by the manufacturers, and a number of the objects went on to be long-term best-sellers in the Victorian marketplace. The 'bird' scissors are still available today.

Dresser's enthusiasm for the Great Exhibition contrasts with William Morris's famous reaction – he remarked to his mother that it was all 'wonderfully ugly' – and his disdain probably prevented him from taking in either the modern colour scheme or the originality of the furniture, metalwork and tiles displayed in Pugin's Mediaeval Court. Although he abandoned his architectural training in the office of G.E. Street, with his moneyed background Morris was able to put his ideas on domestic design into practice immediately. In 1859 he built his own house at Bexleyheath in Kent, with his friend Philip Webb as architect. 'Red House' has been judged as the first modern domestic house; it was to be the template for the 'Palace of Art', one of the achievements of the 'art' movement, and much imitated by artists and patrons alike. When he established his decorating firm, Morris, Marshall, Faulkner & Co., in 1861, he understood that the way forward must depend on a choice of articles for the ordinary home. The firm made its début at the 1862 International Exhibition in London, with two stands, showing stained glass, painted tiles, jewellery and furniture. When it was fully up and running the Morris firm made a complete 'look' available to people of modest means with 'artistic' inclinations. However chequered the fortunes of the Victorians in the twentieth century – and Dresser himself was particularly slow to emerge from obscurity – the reputation of Morris never faltered. When the interest in Victorian design began in the 1950s he was the only designer whose work was preserved across the whole sphere of his activity.[14]

Dresser and Morris (1834–96) shared a birth date, and their careers were spent pursuing the same aims. However, Morris's achievement was seen as completely independent from South Kensington influence: Thomas Armstrong, director for art in the 1880s, wrote:

> No impetus has been given to decorative art in our time, to compare with that which had its origin some thirty years ago, in dingy Red Lion-square, where a few young men, unknown to the public, but warmed by real enthusiasm, and as the result has shown, led by the light of genius, set to work quietly, and without advertisement, to apply art to industry, with results known to you all, which are associated with the name of, and are in the main due to, William Morris.[15]

Dresser was obliterated from the story of nineteenth-century design from within the very institution that nurtured him.

In a sense the two were alike. Both wished to improve domestic design and to make it available cheaply. Access to the 'working man' is a theme running through their writings. Neither really achieved their aims, and the main beneficiaries were the moneyed middle classes – and, in Morris's case, the 'swinish rich' (his own epithets). However, the differences between them vastly outweigh the similarities. Morris never abandoned a Ruskinian faith in the supremacy of 'nature' as the inspiration for design. He was, for various reasons, not all of them ideological, wedded to hand-craftsmanship, and his philosophy for interior decoration was prescriptive – less is better. Morris campaigned incessantly against the consumerist instincts of the age. Dresser on the other hand took the consumer culture seriously; he was pragmatic and a committed heir of the Industrial Revolution who never lost

sight of the demands of machine production and the modernity of materials.

He believed in subsuming natural forms in near-total abstraction. In a lecture to the Society of Arts in 1871 he insisted: 'True ornamentation is of purely mental origin, and consists of symbolized imagination only. ... Ornamentation is ... even a higher art than that practised by the pictorial artist, as it is of wholly mental origin' (above). He employed such new processes as embossing, gold blocking – like Pugin he favoured book-bindings of cloth impressed and decorated with gold-blocking (plate 39), whereas Morris chose vellum – and electro-plating; he liked terracotta, linoleum, anaglypta, japanned tin, cast iron, riveted brass and copper. His mission was to improve design in manufactures, but he did not expect the public to abandon their cruet-sets, claret-jugs, toast-racks, coal-scuttles, picnic-sets and ornaments. All he hoped was that they would be made according to the principles, laid down by Pugin and Jones, that he preached throughout his career.

Pugin and Owen Jones

Pugin died when Dresser and Morris were only 18, but his great work of fitting out the new Houses of Parliament – the Palace of Westminster – was already well advanced. The furnishing and decorating of the Palace of Westminster forced commercially viable solutions to problems of interpreting the Gothic Revival – and by extension, other revivalist or exotic styles – in terms of modern living that might otherwise have taken far longer to emerge. Pugin's procedure at the Palace of Westminster, of gathering around himself a group of hand-picked manufacturers, had set a pattern that became the prototype for 'art furniture' and decorating schemes in the future, the first being, of course, Cole's 'Summerly' venture. Pugin dismissed the Palace of Westminster as 'a sham' in terms of archaeologically correct Gothic architecture, but its legacy was all the elements for the fashionable domestic interior, from writing desks, dining tables, chairs, sofas, beds and washstands; from chandeliers to lights, locks, handles, hinges, clocks, ink pots, silverware; from tiled floors to dinner and tea-services, right down to coat hooks and umbrella stands. It is not without significance that Dresser's design practice encompassed a similar range of household goods.

Given the splendour and importance of the project, many of Pugin's designs were practical, even severe. Minton's ceramic table wares, variants of Cole's prize-winning 'Summerly' shapes and named 'Pugin Gothic', are simply decorated with trefoil or flower-and-leaf borders and lettered mottoes (plate 15). His long-lasting contribution to pattern design was to introduce geometric and stylized heraldic and floriated forms in place of illusionistic pictorial designs, an outmoded legacy of the Romantic movement, thus paving the way for the modernism of Owen Jones and Dresser himself. The fact that he showed that this could be done freed commercial design from mere copying and imitation.

The Great Exhibition and its successors generated a vast amount of print, in the form of catalogues and official reports as well as press reports, much of it illustrated. The publication in 1856 of Owen Jones's colour-illustrated *Grammar of Ornament* codified the decorative messages of the exhibition into a system of pattern and motif. Jones advanced Pugin's ideas about stylization and flat-patterning, proposed in *Floriated Ornament* in 1849. Plate XCVIII of the *Grammar*, concerning 'the geometrical arrangement of flowers', was Dresser's first published work (plate 9). He was probably assisting Jones in other ways at this date. At the

LEFT

14. Christopher Dresser. *Studies in Design* (London, 1874–6), pl. 19. Michael Whiteway.

OPPOSITE ABOVE

15. A.W.N. Pugin. Ceramic plate with lettered scroll and Gothic motifs, made by Minton & Co., 1851, V&A: 459/460-1852. Bought from the 1851 Great Exhibition for the South Kensington Museum.

OPPOSITE BELOW

16. Owen Jones. *Design for the Chinese Court at the South Kensington Museum*, watercolour, 1856. V&A: Jones box 205, D.122 1905. Bought by Dresser from the sale of Jones's effects, 1874 and then acquired from Dresser's posthumous sale by the V&A in 1905.

sale after Jones's death in 1874 Dresser bought drawings by him for the 'Oriental' Courts (Indian, Chinese and Japanese) in the South Kensington Museum, implying a special affinity for this aspect of Jones's work (below). In their turn, the V&A bought these drawings in 1905 from Dresser's estate, and a note on the acquisition file records his involvement with Jones over the period covered by the work on the South Kensington courts.[16] The implication may be that Dresser had some hand in these designs; crossover between Jones and Dresser is particularly apparent in their flat-pattern designing in the 1860s and '70s (see chapter 3).

Little remains of Jones's decorative work; some striking designs for silks and wallpaper and one remarkable house – Alfred Morrison's townhouse at 16 Carlton House Terrace – survives, this last item with much of the Alhambresque decoration and fittings intact. The gilded and painted rooms, with coffered ceilings inspired by the Alhambra, influenced Dresser's decorating and architectural projects in the 1870s. Morrison's outstanding collection of Chinese art – much of it featured in

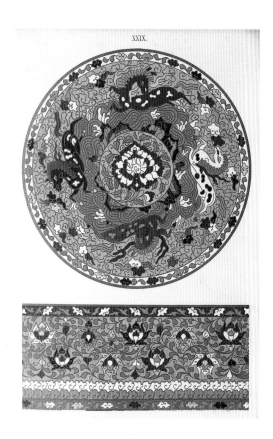

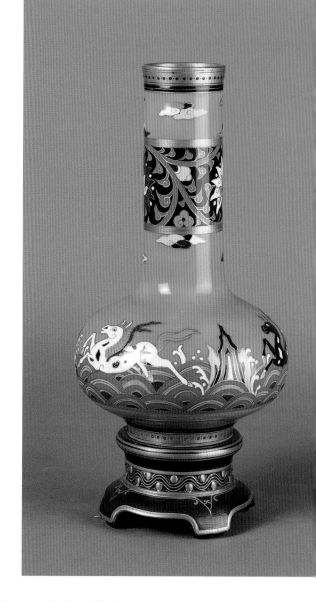

Jones's *Examples of Chinese Ornament Selected from Examples in the South Kensington Museum and Other Collections* (1867) – must have been the inspiration for the Chinese-style ceramics produced under Dresser's guidance at Minton's in the 1860s (above and right).

Jones's inspiration is found in its most unmediated form in Dresser's two surviving architectural projects: Allangate, Halifax, for Thomas Shaw MP, 1869–70 (plate 167), and Bushloe House, Leicester, 1874, for his solicitor Hiram B. Owston.[17] Bushloe House mixes elements of Japanese with Persian and Egyptian styles. The geometric elements in the design give it the boldness that was characteristic of Dresser's pattern-making, and makes his work so easy to pick out. The furniture was mainly ebonized with stencilled or incised gold decoration. At Allangate (opposite) effective use was made of stained glass, and the furniture was again of ebonized wood with incised ornament. The black and gold is particularly effective for the fireplaces, adding richness to the plain stone slabs. The Allangate Library ceiling is a fine essay in the Jonesian manner, and Dresser is on record as believing this to have been his masterpiece. Dresser particularly admired Jones's interiors for St James's Hall

(1857–8), a concert hall in London's Piccadilly that was a 'mixture of Greek, Egyptian and other historical elements in perfect blending.'[18]

The 37 design rules proposed by Jones in the *Grammar* were Dresser's guiding light, notably Proposition 8 ('all ornament should be based upon geometric construction') and Proposition 13 ('Flowers or other natural objects should not be used as ornaments, but conventional representations founded upon them sufficiently suggestive to convey the intended image upon the mind, without destroying the unity of the object they are employed to decorate.')[19] Jones's publishing triumph was his *Plans, Details, Elevations and Sections of the Alhambra* (1842–5), with its superb

19. Stained glass window, Allangate, Halifax, built for Thomas Shaw, *c*.1869–70.

20. Fireplace surround, Allangate, Halifax, built for Thomas Shaw, *c*.1869–70.

chromolithographic plates enriched with gold. In 1867 he published *Examples of Chinese Ornament*. These books sparked off wide interest in exotic ornament.

South Kensington and the Cole circle

The supreme effectiveness of Cole can be judged from his most tangible legacy, the Museum of Ornamental Art (later the South Kensington Museum and now the V&A). The museum's mission, to provide inspiration to designers and manufacturers and to improve public taste, has a direct relevance for the development of 'artistic' taste in home design and decoration.[20] The debates that raged back and forward at South Kensington around the sensitive topic of the moment – 'art for all' and issues around elitism and populism, access and exclusivity – reveal a paternalistic streak in Cole and his cohorts, but the trend was inevitably towards the edification and encouragement of the working classes.[21] The ideal of bringing culture – and its perceived consequence, good domestic

design – within reach of the working man and his family was simply unrealizable, however cheaply the goods were produced. Dresser kept faith with the ideal, stating in *Principles of Decorative Design* (1873) that art should be accessible to all, regardless of social class. He also repeatedly reminds the reader of *Principles* about the usefulness and accessibility of the collections and library at South Kensington.

Cole and his colleagues refused to accept the gulf that had opened up since the mid-eighteenth century between fine and decorative art, and vigorously promoted the latter. A theme running through Cole's writings, and many subsequent analyses of the state of design and manufactures, was the willingness of artists in earlier times to turn their attention to the arts of decoration; emphasis was placed on the need for contemporary painters and sculptors to involve themselves in ornamental and commercial art in the same way. John Ruskin made this point in his 1859 essay *The Two Paths, Being Lectures on Art and Its Application to Decoration and Manufacture.* He wanted to 'get rid, then, at once of any idea of Decorative art being a degraded or a separate kind of art'.[22] He also decried as 'absurd' the notion that 'room decoration should be by flat patterns – by dead colours – by conventional monotonies, and I know not what.' This insistence on the superiority of the artist as designer – an article of faith to which Morris was also committed – was not helpful to trained professionals in industrial design; it was an implied attack on the rules of ornament and pattern formulated for the Schools of Design by Owen Jones for the *Grammar of Ornament*, and a full-frontal dismissal of Jones's wallpapers and fabrics.

In 1861 Dresser defended the principles of abstract ornament in a series of lectures delivered to the Society of Arts on decorative art (issued in book form in 1862 as *The Art of Decorative Design*). As 'the leader of the Natural School' he found that Ruskin had 'little knowledge of ornament'. Dresser continued to speak and publish in favour of abstract ornamentation as a separate intellectual concept, superior to the purely pictorial. In fact, Dresser admired much of what Ruskin said. When he later used the columns of the *Furniture Gazette* to restate some of his most cherished precepts, Ruskin was among those quoted.

The Egyptian Revival

A significant source for Dresser in his early design career was Ancient Egypt. Pugin's furnishing and decorating in the Gothic style had been remarkable, given how few examples of domestic artefacts from the medieval period survived into the nineteenth century. The situation regarding the more or less contemporary Egyptian Revival was completely different. Since the publication in 1837 of Sir John Gardner Wilkinson's *Manners and Customs of the Ancient Egyptians*, a large repertoire of models had been accessible in clear linear illustrations (opposite). Wilkinson was regarded as the founder of British Egyptology and his book remained the standard work on everyday life in ancient Egypt for more than a century.[23] He was 12 years in Egypt, much of the time at Thebes (modern-day Luxor), and his collection of Egyptian artifacts entered the British Museum in 1838. However, the timing of this mid-nineteenth-century Egyptian mania suggests it was inspired by the second (1854) abridged edition of Gardner Wilkinson's book.[24]

According to his own recollection, in about 1855–6 William Holman-Hunt designed a chair 'based on the character of an Egyptian stool in the British Museum'.[25] The chair, inlaid with ivory and ebony, was made by J.G. Crace, Pugin's furniture supplier for the Palace of Westminster and the 1851 Mediaeval Court. Hunt goes on to say 'When I showed my small group of household joys to my PRB [Pre-Raphaelite Brotherhood] friends the contagion spread and Brown [Ford Madox Brown], who idolised the Egyptian chairs, set a carpenter to work to make some of similar proportions'. Madox Brown's version was stocked by the Morris firm. Gottfried Semper, who taught metalwork and furniture design at the School of Design from 1852, illustrated the so-called Thebes stool in *Der Stil* (1860–63), his important treatise on the origins of style in art. The descent from Holman-Hunt and Morris, through *Der Stil*, to Liberty's in Regent Street, who retailed the best known of the 'Thebes' models over a long period, can be traced through Dresser and Edward William Godwin in the 1870s. It is probably no coincidence that the Egyptian influence surfaced again in Dresser's work at exactly the moment when the final, revised (1878), edition of Gardner Wilkinson's *Manners and Customs* was published posthumously.

also used, the seat being only from 8 to 14 inches high, and of

63.

64. Chairs. *British Museum.*

Fig. 27.

The furniture of the ancient Egyptians conformed to the 'principles' enunciated by design reformers from Pugin onwards: sound construction and subservient ornament.

Egypt and the Crystal Palace at Sydenham

After the closure of the Great Exhibition, Sir Joseph Paxton formed a private company to remove the Crystal Palace to Sydenham, where it re-opened in 1854. Jones was sent with Sir Matthew Digby Wyatt on a world tour to obtain plaster casts from the great art collections and monuments of antiquity. Among the courts illustrating earlier civilizations was one devoted to ancient Egypt, planned and arranged by Jones (along with the Alhambra, Greek, Roman and modern sculpture courts). The illustrated guides

to Crystal Palace were Jones's work too. He acknowledged Gardner Wilkinson, with whom he had worked on illustrations of the antiquities for the *Manners and Customs* with the architect Joseph Bonomi – who was himself deeply involved with the Egyptian Court at Sydenham.[26] Gardner Wilkinson also contributed a publication himself, *The Egyptians in the Time of the Pharaohs; Being a Companion to the Crystal Palace Egyptian Collections.* A feature of the Egyptian Court was the brilliant colour, which Jones had observed for himself when he travelled in Egypt with Jules Goury, his collaborator on the *Alhambra* volume. The works

of Gardner Wilkinson and the Egyptian Court at Sydenham (overleaf) were both key influences on Dresser's Egyptian Revival designs, facts that he emphasized in *Principles of Decorative Design.*[27]

In the 1860s Dresser was 'Professor of Ornamental Art and Botany' at the Crystal Palace. He was a great admirer of this ambitious enterprise, which he promoted in his 1862 publication, *The Art of Decorative Design.* One of the attractions was the collection of palms and other rare plants (plate 24) formed by the famous Hackney nurserymen Loddiges over 100 years, and purchased for the interior of the Crystal Palace by Paxton.[28] This is where the student of Egyptian design will be able to find the lotus or blue waterlily, according to Dresser.[29] In addition, the full-size dinosaur reconstructions in the park, supervised by Prof. Owen and modelled by the leading zoological illustrator

Benjamin Waterhouse Hawkins, should not be forgotten. There are a number of lizard-like creatures and winged skeletal grotesques in Dresser's early frieze motifs for Minton ceramics.

Dresser's early career as a botanist, 1854–68

On completing his training in 1854, Dresser was found some teaching engagements including an appointment as lecturer on botany at the female School of Design (then known as the Metropolitan School, Gower Street).[30] The teaching posts were probably engineered by Redgrave or Playfair.

Dresser had already married Thirza Perry, his senior by four years, on 24 May in Islington. There is no mystery about this premature move on the part of a 19-year-old whose education was barely over: the couple's first child was born on 6 August, only 10 weeks after the wedding. Thirza's father, William Perry, was a Methodist churchman, described as a City Missionary. They eventually had 13 children, of whom one died in childhood. At various times the offspring assisted in Dresser's design studio, but only one, Louis Leo, actually followed in his footsteps when he went to work at Liberty's in 1882. The couple embarked on married

23. Philip Delamotte. *The Crystal Palace, Sydenham: Egyptian Court*, interior photograph, 1854. V&A: 39.306.

life at 4, Swiss Cottages, Black Lion Lane, Hammersmith, moving in about 1860 to St Peter's Square, Hammersmith – a more substantial address, where Dresser established his design studio.

Under their talented headmistress, Mrs Fanny McIan, the female schools had achieved successes

24. Philip Delamotte. *The Crystal Palace, Sydenham:* building filled with palms, photograph, 1854. V&A: 39.292.

against the odds, and by 1850 the girl students were winning a great number of prizes. Manufacturers purchased some of the award-winning designs to be produced for the Great Exhibition in the following year. In 1853 many of the girl pupils were found to have snatched first prizes from the men, among them Dresser himself. He was to prove an inspiring teacher; in the 1856 'Department of Science and Art Third Annual Report' Mrs McIan wrote of his 24 'Artistic Botany' lectures, 'these lectures are extremely interesting, and of the utmost importance in the study of ornamental art'.[31] He lectured on 'the best mode of investigating the

form and structure of plants with a view to the treatment in ornament'. Dresser's large-scale botanical drawings made for teaching survive, combining scientific observation with abstraction, the basis for all his designing (plate 42).

At this time Dresser was concentrating on botany, delivering and publishing papers and books (*The Rudiments of Botany* and *Unity in Variety* both appeared in 1859 and *The Popular Manual of Botany* – described by Dresser as 'a Ladies' book' – in 1860) and, also in 1859, receiving his doctorate from the University of Jena, a distinguished centre for the natural sciences. Given the non-academic character of his education, this was a significant achievement and one that Dresser plainly cherished. He thereafter styled himself Christopher Dresser, Ph.D., and later used a facsimile signature for his designs: 'Dr C. Dresser'. In January 1860 Dresser was elected a Fellow of the Edinburgh Botanical Society, and at much the same time was appointed to teach botany at St Mary's Hospital, Paddington. In July the support of William and Joseph Hooker, Thomas Bell (president of the Linnean Society) and others gained him another teaching job at the London Hospital Medical College, but in the same year he failed to gain the chair of botany at London University.[32] The system of patronage in Victorian professional circles was a complex web of lobbying and influence, and Dresser's network failed him in this instance. The chair went to botanist Daniel Oliver, senior curator at Kew and another Hooker protégé; he was also, as a close confederate of Charles Darwin, in the very innermost workings of the scientific establishment and probably the better-qualified candidate. In 1861, this time with the support of the Hookers, Dresser was elected a Fellow of the Linnean Society, the absolute epicentre of botanical innovation and debate. Neither of the medical appointments lasted long. He was also teaching at the School of Design at South Kensington, where he stayed until 1868. With a growing family he needed something more profitable than lectureships, and he turned his teeming imagination to designing and writing on design.

A career in design

By his own account Dresser was formulating his earliest design ideas in about 1859, and, with this career gathering momentum, botany was abandoned. Dresser was pressed by 'manufacturers of the greatest eminence' to supply designs in the run-up to the 1862 International Exhibition in London.[33] Evidence suggests that these eminent manufacturers were Jackson & Graham (a carpet design), Scott, Cuthbertson & Co. (a matching wallpaper), Minton's, and Chubbs, the locksmiths and safemakers. Dresser was finalizing *The Art of Decorative Design* (1862), his first book to focus mainly on design. Clearly indebted to Semper, as well as Dyce's 1842 *Drawing Book* and Pugin's *Floriated Ornament* of 1849, it was presented, in his 1861 lectures to the Society of Arts, as a guide to 'the manufacturers and art workmen in view of the coming contest' – in other words, the 1862 International Exhibition in London. International exhibitions had indeed become contests between the industrial nations, the fiercest rivalry at this date being between the French and the British.

Although Dresser acknowledged his debt to Dyce, Jones and Redgrave, he never lost sight of his viewpoint as an industrial designer for a commercial and urban population. His design commitments – and the directing of a busy design studio – must have been very demanding, but he kept up an unceasing programme of writing and lecturing. His first important series, 11 articles on the relationship between botany and design for the *Art Journal* in 1857 and 1858, was followed by the botanical papers that led to his doctorate. In 1862, as well as bringing out *The Art of Decorative Design*, he was reporting at length on the International Exhibition. Articles in the *Technical Educator* (1870–73) were collected into *Principles of Decorative Design*, written, as he claimed, 'for the working man'. *Studies in Design* (1874–6) was published in monthly parts, containing the most inventive and original of his demonstrations of ornamental design. In 1870 he had been elected a member of the Society of Arts, and during the 10 years of his membership he delivered a number of important papers.[34] The last two of his major publications, *Japan: Its Architecture, Art and Art-Manufactures* and *Modern Ornamentation*, appeared respectively in 1882 and 1886. This relentless programme of publishing was designed – effectively – to keep his name before the public, but he was also a born instructor and his urgent need to communicate his ideas is implicit in every

line. Much of what he was promoting was new and untried and he was delighted by evidence that the ideas were put into effect.[35]

It is all too easy to lose sight of the web of influences criss-crossing the design profession in the second half of the nineteenth century. Among Dresser's near contemporaries were Edward William Godwin (1833–86; architect-designer), Daniel Cottier (1838–91; architect-decorator), Bruce James Talbert (1838–81; architect-designer), George Ashdown Audsley (1838–1925; architect, Japanist and author), Thomas Edward Collcutt (1840–1924; architect-designer) and Charles Locke Eastlake (1836–1906; architect and writer on decoration). William Burges and Thomas Jeckyll were a little older; both were born in 1827 and both died in 1881. These were the leading members of the art movement. They had many traits in common, and shared many aims for the progress of design. Dresser's life and career would touch them tangentially, as a design theorist, as a connoisseur and collector of Japanese art, as an industrial designer, and as the proprietor of a firm of art-furnishers, but he had a very different professional training, and although he described himself as an architect, he arrived at architecture through design. Trained architects such as Godwin and Collcutt took on design from the opposite position, and it is noticeable that their focus remained on the architectural elements in decoration and furnishing rather than on the equipment of the household.

Morris's decorating 'Firm' was an important – perhaps the most important – link between the initiatives of Pugin and Cole, with his Summerly scheme, and the 'art-furniture' ventures of the 1870s and 1880s. In keeping with the trend, a number of firms called themselves 'Art-furnishers' (notably Cottier & Co. and Collinson & Lock, for whom Collcutt, Godwin and Talbert designed) or 'decorators'. Cox & Sons, the ecclesiastical warehouse in Southampton Street, described itself as 'artistic furniture manufacturer', marketing the work of Talbert as well as designs by John Moyr Smith (1839–1912; architectural assistant, designer and illustrator), Dresser's one-time studio assistant. Dresser's various schemes for selling his own designs and imported goods through Charles Reynolds & Co. (later Londos & Co.), Dresser & Holme and the Art Furnishers' Alliance span the years 1873–83. The network of firms and designers at this point is so complex that attributing designs becomes a matter of inspired guesswork, in the absence of documentary evidence.

Instruction manuals and pattern books, notably Eastlake's *Hints on Household Taste,* written for *The Queen* (1865–6) and published as a book in 1868, and Talbert's *Gothic Forms Applied to Furniture Metalwork and Decoration for Domestic Purposes* (1867), provided a new impetus for manufacturers, who began to value the contribution of a named designer. The importance of these publications in Dresser's eyes can be gauged from the fact that he singles them out for comment – with illustrations – in his *Principles of Decorative Design.*[36] Dresser was a generous promoter of his contemporaries, often commending schemes that rivalled or superseded his own. His writings suggest strongly that he subscribed to an idea of the fraternity of artists and designers. Talbert's career has many similarities with Dresser's, as a busy commercial designer working for many of the same manufacturers.[37] All Scottish-born, Talbert, Cottier and Moyr Smith were known as 'the London Brethren', members the Glasgow circle of Alexander 'Greek' Thomson who had moved south, and it is worth noting that it is their work that is closest to Dresser's, although the fact that he too was born in Glasgow is simply coincidence, since his childhood was spent elsewhere.

Eastlake was involved with the short-lived Art Furniture Company in Covent Garden (1867), which seems to have made up furniture designs from *Hints,* among other things. In 1877 William Watt issued a catalogue of 'Anglo-Japanese' and 'Old English' furniture, and wallpaper and stained-glass designs by Godwin for his Artistic Furniture Warehouse. Dresser's abstraction of ornament and construction can be compared with Godwin's; the two men shared an austere aesthetic, using black freely and paring down forms to the barest minimum.

Dresser's designing activities during the 1860s have been pieced together from various sources, including an early sketchbook backed up by *The Art of Decorative Design* and the identifiable products from his earliest employers, Minton, Wedgwood and Coalbrookdale. They show some of his most distinctive ideas already emerging, and confirm his reputation as a daring innovator using a great variety of exotic source references. Egyptian, Persian and Chinese motifs predominate in Dresser's ceramic designs from the 1860s and '70s, some recognizably from publications known to him, such as Jones's *Examples of Chinese Ornament,* and from the British Museum collections (see chapter 4). However, there is an energy in the abstraction that is entirely his own. His 'Ipswich' sketchbook, dated from internal evidence 1861–5, contains radical

shapes that were only put into production at a later date. An album put together in the 1880s, in which he collected some of his most striking and outlandish designs from across the whole of his career, has proved a useful source for identifying his unattributed work.[38] The drawings for Minton span the period from 1860 to the mid-1880s (above); the collaboration with the Coalbrookdale foundry dates from 1867–72 (plate 31); the art-work in the Wedgwood archive is dated 1866–8. Wedgwood was going through a difficult transition, moving on from the legacy of the great Josiah Wedgwood in the eighteenth century to the design-driven exhibition products of the mid-nineteenth century.

Dresser was a man of his age, there is no other way to explain his success; Victorians loved the grotesque, and Dresser's monsters and insects should be seen in the context of Darwinism and palaeontology. The Neo-Gothic gargoyles and drag-

25. Christopher Dresser. Watercolour design, 'Band of Brothers'. Minton Museum and Archives. Originally for a Minton flowerpot, *c.*1867, this motif was included in the *Album of Designs,* now in the Metropolitan Museum of Art, New York.

ons in the frieze patterns of birds and crouching beasts contain intimations of Burges. His shapes and patterns drawn from a diverse range of exotic ethnic sources are probably best comprehended in connection with the Victorian passion for 'curios' and novelties of all kinds. The works that have surfaced are his most extreme and distinctive; only a modest percentage of the hundreds of flat patterns for textiles, wallpapers, carpets and linoleums that formed the day-to-day business of his design studio has been identified (see chapter 3). With these in context, his precise place in the mainstream of Victorian domestic design would be easier to estimate. However, there is one aspect of his practice that stands far in advance of his time: he was a pioneer in the branding of products. From 1874, his signature acted as a guarantee of originality and design quality. In *Studies in Design* he remarked, 'Messrs Jeffrey and Co., of Essex Road, Islington, have published a series of my decorations expressly to meet the requirements set forth in this work, each having my name printed on the margin of the strip.'[39] Here is

evidence that Dresser was increasingly taking the initiative in the design process.

The 1862 International Exhibition

The 1862 exhibition was a great improvement on the Great Exhibition. It was important for Dresser. He was now a professional designer and a participant; in an article reporting on the exhibition he singled out many categories for praise: for example

ABOVE LEFT
26. Hukin & Heath. Detail of an electroplated cruet-set, with maker's mark, design registration marks and 'DESIGNED BY Dr C. DRESSER', 1874. Harry Lyons.

'we now show wall enrichments of a high order'; in glass 'rapid progress'; in metalwork, 'works of great excellence'.[40] He picked out a radical chair design in the Morris display:

> While we cannot commend them as works of beauty,
> that with the low back is worthy of special notice,
> owing to one constructive peculiarity, which consists
> in the side portions of the seat-frame being
> continued backwards beyond the general body of the

27. Philip Webb.
Ebonized and gilded
chair, 1862. Society of
Antiquaries, Kelmscott
Manor.

RIGHT

28. Christopher Dresser.
'Egyptian Chair',
ebonized wood, *c*.1880.
V&A: W.35–1992.
This chair was retailed
through the Art
Furnishers' Alliance.

chair, in order to support the rods which act as strengtheners to the back ... if the hint given were attended to, and the principle modified and incorporated with elegance, an advance would be achieved. (plate 27)

It was left to Dresser himself to develop the idea and supply the 'elegance' (above). In praising Minton's offering, he was, it seems, giving himself a pat on the back.

Dresser was later to claim that it was at this exhibition that he encountered the arts of Japan.[41] The Japanese Court was furnished with a collection of Japanese decorative art made by Sir Rutherford Alcock during his stay in that country as Britain's first consul-general and then minister plenipotentiary. It is obvious, however, that Dresser had already made contact with Alcock and that he also knew Cole's collection of contemporary Japanese

ABOVE 30. Pottery tea-bowl, Japanese. V&A: 608–1877. Bought for the South Kensington Museum from the Londos warehouse, 1877.

RIGHT 31. Coalbrookdale. Cast iron hall table (detail), marked 'Coalbrookdale' with the cipher for October 25, 1869. The Birkenhead Collection.

OPPOSITE
29. Japanese blue-and-white ceramic flowerpot, c.1860. V&A. Acquired for the South Kensington Museum from the 1862 International Exhibition. Illustrated in *The Ceramic Art of Japan* (1875) by G.A. and W.J. Audsley.

objects, bought for the Schools of Design in the early 1850s.[42] Until 1854, Japan had been isolated, culturally and commercially, from the West for two centuries, and this constituted one of its main artistic attractions. Burges was an early collector of Japanese prints, and Japanese motifs spice the Gothic forms of his furniture and decoration. Artists and amateurs were already collecting Japanese woodblock prints and ceramics – mainly blue-and-white porcelain – by the mid-1850s, and it was the larger public who were introduced to Japan at the 1862 exhibition, through Alcock's collection. Dresser obtained permission to make drawings of some 80 of Alcock's pieces and after the exhibition he bought a 'fair selection' of them'.[43]

By 1867 Dresser had an impressive output of designs on show at the Paris Exposition, among them a massive cast-iron hallstand by the Coalbrookdale company (below) and a large-scale ceramic vase with intricate polychrome and gold 'Egyptian' decoration, for Minton's (overleaf). Designs for Wedgwood of this date are among his most uncompromising, drawing on Egyptian models and an organic abstraction that is quite without parallel in Victorian design (plate 136). He was striving to invent a truly modern style from his observations of scientific botany and his explorations of Oriental and ancient Egyptian art with Owen Jones. He wrote a series of illustrated articles on the exhibition for *The Chromolithograph*, which, *inter alia*, demonstrate his admiration for the

French cloisonné enamel exhibits in the Japanese manner.[44] It may be that it was on Dresser's advice that Elkington & Co. had begun to experiment with Oriental techniques around 1865; they showed a group of cloisonné pieces in Philadelphia in 1876.

In 1868 Dresser was sufficiently established and prosperous to move his family into the impressive Tower Cressy, Aubrey Road, a six-storey Italianate house built in 1852–3 for Thomas Page, the engineer who designed Westminster Bridge (plate 33). Dresser was an admirer of Page, commenting on his bridges – 'more artistic than those of any other engineer' – in a paper given to the Society of Arts.[45] The remarkable edifice high up on Campden Hill in Kensington towered, literally, over its more modest picturesque and 'Gothic' neighbours. It was damaged during the Second World War and demolished shortly afterwards. Dresser lived there until 1882. From its eminence, Tower Cressy overlooked Aubrey House, home of Whistler's patron, William Alexander, a connoisseur and collector of Japanese art. Many artists' houses were built in the 1860s and '70s nearby and on the adjoining Holland estate. The whole area was a haunt for the artistic- and literary-minded, with fancy-dress parties and musical evenings throughout the Season. It is hard to measure Dresser's place in this social milieu, since his name never features in connection with any of these events. As early as 1862 he was writing, in *The Art of Decorative Design*, about the lowly status of designers, almost pleading with his readers to remember the effort and its small reward that went into producing a successful textile or wallpaper.[46] His surviving work has surfaced almost entirely unprovenanced and it is a puzzle to work out who were the owners of his vast output of domestic artifacts and patterned goods. His known patrons were – with the exception of his solicitor – from among his manufacturing contacts.

Dresser maintained his ties with South Kensington after his lecturing commitments ceased in 1868. He was entrusted with missions in connection with a succession of international exhibitions, which required delicacy and a diplomatic touch. His closest contact was Cole's successor as director of the South Kensington Museum, Sir Philip Cunliffe Owen, a genial cosmopolitan figure from an affluent background – a great contrast to the off-hand and abrasive Cole – which suggests that

32. Minton's China Works. Large porcelain vase, designed by Christopher Dresser for the Paris Exposition Universelle, 1867. The Birkenhead Collection.

Dresser had early exhibited considerable social aplomb. He was a personable and good-looking young man, well read and, as one of his pupils described him, a genial man who maintained happy relations with his workers.[47] In lectures in the 1870s he had got away with some stringent criticisms of the South Kensington teaching methods and the organization of the museum, and even had some effect on both. The most important – and most sensitive – undertaking on behalf of the museum was his trip to Japan in 1876–7 to deliver a gift of European decorative arts to the newly built Imperial Museum in Tokyo (see chapter 6). His official status as an emissary of the director emboldened him to describe himself as 'of the South Kensington Museum'. He retained a number of his colleagues in the art and educational establishment as friends, and the lists of guests he submitted to the Society of Arts for his lectures include figures in the world of Japanese scholarship, such as Rutherford Alcock. He was intensely gratified to be invited to Marlborough House to explain the arts of Japan to the Prince and Princess of Wales, and was not shy of drawing attention to the occasion in a lecture.[48]

Inexplicably, in an age of cheap and widely available portrait photography, when friends and colleagues eagerly exchanged the popular 'carte-de-visite' images, only two photographs of Dresser have come to light, one as a young man (plate 2) and one near to the end of his life. His intimacy with the museum establishment seems not to have survived the illness that dogged him in the 1880s, and the failure of the Art Furnishers' Alliance in 1883.

His design career was forging ahead in the 1860s; in the *Building News* in 1865 he was already emerging as a leading designer for carpets and wallpapers. He was running a commercial design studio supplying patterns to manufacturers across the country and its activities must have been absolutely frenetic. He was to claim in 1871 that he had 'much the largest practice in the kingdom' (see chapter 3). It is hard to say exactly how the studio was constituted and it probably operated on a somewhat ad hoc basis, responding to the demands of the moment. A number of his assistants may have been with him for quite a short time. It is on record that he took articled pupils.[49] Certainly Dresser's children worked with him as soon as they were old enough. His intervention in the products credited to him seems to have varied considerably, from total control of the design to acting in a purely advisory capacity.

His influence spread through his assistants and pupils as they established independent careers, and also through blatant plagiarism of his published designs. The huge popularity of Eastlake's *Hints* in the United States inspired the 'Eastlake' style in furniture – repudiated by the author – which bears unmistakeable marks of Dresser's influence. Moyr Smith claimed that while he was with Dresser he 'made some thousands of designs for ironwork, furniture, pottery, wallpapers, lace curtains, carpets, decorations and kindred works'.[50] He dedicated his book, *Studies for Pictures* (1868), to Dresser, but his time in the studio was brief, and he was soon working with Collinson & Lock, on *Sketches for Artistic Furniture* (1871), alongside Collcutt. He was already working for Cox & Co. by 1872, and possibly for Talbert as well. Because of the similarity of their designs, Dresser was forced to disclaim any connection with the Cox firm, but the fact remains that Cox made the stained glass for Dresser's Bushloe House. Both Moyr Smith and another of Dresser's assistants, R.A. Boyd, published their own designs after departing from Dresser's employ. Given the way in which the studio system worked, the very individual look imposed by Dresser is a remarkable feature of his production. His daughter, when she was interviewed in old age, said that no designs were ever issued without her father's approval.[51]

Dresser also contributed designs to Cole's series of small-scale international exhibitions at South Kensington in 1871–4. He exhibited porcelain, items from the Coalbrookdale Co. and carpets by Crossley's for the first time under his own name in 1871, his opening bid for personal visibility as an artist. The year 1873 was particularly pressurized: as well as participating in the Vienna International Exhibition he was appointed art advisor to the Alexandra Palace Co., set up to import Japanese art. Alexandra Palace at Muswell Hill, North London's equivalent to the Crystal Palace at Sydenham, utilized the reconstructed building from the 1862 International Exhibition. The idea was to install examples of national building styles in the form of a Japanese village, a Moorish house and an Egyptian house. The 'entire Japanese colony' from the Vienna exhibition was brought over, as well as several other ethnic exhibits. After a disastrous fire, the palace reopened in 1875. The guidebook drew attention to the quality of the goods, in contrast to the 'goods of inferior workmanship, manufactured expressly for the England market', which were available elsewhere. 'From the Alexandra Palace such trash will be banished' it claimed.[52] Contributions came from leading suppliers, including Minton, Chubb, Benham & Froud, Elkington and Liberty's. Dresser used the model village for selling imported Japanese, Egyptian and Moroccan objects collected for him in 1875, and Jackson & Graham carried displays of his wallpapers for Jeffrey & Co. At the same time he was transforming the wholesale warehouse of Charles Reynolds & Co. into a beguiling display of imported Oriental decorative art in furnished room settings. Of this installation, a *Furniture Gazette* critic remarked,

> It is by bringing to the homes of the people, objects of Art and beauty at a low price that more good is done in refining the middle and lower classes than by all the museums in existence. The effect of the latter is transitory, while the former is to a certain extent, permanent.[53]

Hardly a point of view to find favour with Cole, who believed implicitly in the power of museums to sway public allegiances in taste, and to improve manufactures.

Philadelphia, San Francisco, Japan, 1876–7

Given the scope and impact of Japonism, it is surprising how few of the participants travelled to Japan. Dresser was among those few, and it lent authority to both his writing and his designing. Many expressed the wish. Friendship with Whistler and Godwin ensured Oscar Wilde's interest in Japan; he was anxious to study what he referred to as 'the artistic side of Japanese life' and in a letter of 1882 speaks of his 'irresistible desire to wander, to go to Japan, where I will pass my youth, sitting under an almond tree in white blossom, drinking amber tea out of a blue cup, and looking at a landscape without perspective.'[54] Designs using Japanese motifs and forms made up an important element in the artistic interior. At their best they explore abstraction and asymmetry in the distribution of mass and void; the use of surface effects and flat colour instead of costly materials and finish, and black ebonizing with reeded borders and stylized motifs picked out with gilding. Ceramics were decorated with subjects from Hokusai's prints, the ornamental crests, or 'mons', which were known from woodblock-printed books, and novel glaze effects; shapes were borrowed from ancient wares and bronze temple vessels. Some were little better than novelties, with much play made of the comical aspect of Japanese applied art. The 'drab coloured, rough and unglazed earthenware', seen for the first time at the 1871 South Kensington exhibition, made little headway with ceramic manufacturers. Dresser, of course, already knew of this aspect of Japanese ceramic art and had drawn attention to it in the *Technical Educator* in 1870.[55]

Rutherford Alcock, who retired from his diplomatic career in 1872, showed examples that year from his collection in the London International Exhibition, and several pieces were acquired for the South Kensington Museum. At the same time, in consultation with Cunliffe Owen, now the museum's director, a mission headed by two of Japan's most modernizing officials was planning a comprehensive display of Japanese art for the 1873 International Exhibition in London. Dresser assisted Cunliffe Owen with its organization. These contacts inspired Dresser to propel Charles Reynolds & Co. into this area of trading. Two of his associates, William Churcher, who became his secretary, and Caspar Purdon Clarke, who in fact seems to have been in Persia already, were in 1875 searching for products in Spain, Morocco, Egypt, Italy, Greece, Turkey, Persia, Thailand and China, to be sold through the Alexandra Palace Co. Purdon Clarke went on in 1883 to a distinguished career at the South Kensington Museum, eventually becoming director.

Meanwhile the Japanese themselves, who had modernized their culture and systems of government under the more enlightened and outward-looking Meiji Dynasty (1868–1912), sought to exercise greater control over the supply of modern Japanese manufactures to the West. From 1873 they participated directly at international exhibitions, instead of relying on haphazard representation through European collectors. After the 1873 Vienna exhibition the Kiritsu Kosho Kaisha company, set up to promote traditional craft industries, represented the government at several international exhibitions; branches opened in New York (1876) and Paris (1878). Goods for the Japanese village at Alexandra Palace came from the com-

pany, although Dresser reported to the Japanese after his 1876–7 trip that they were too expensive to be successful exports.[56] The Western fixation with popular woodblock prints was baffling to the Japanese, and the products submitted to the public through various government initiatives were in the 'exhibition' style familiar all over the world; in other words, high technical sophistication at the expense of traditional artistic values. Inevitably this damaged the image of Japan, conveyed through its first enthusiasts, as a quasi-medieval culture.

In 1875 Cunliffe Owen, who was English commissioner for the Philadelphia Centennial Exposition of 1876, collaborated with the Japanese commission under Sano Tsunetami, who had been in charge of the Japanese exhibit at Vienna in 1873, to select a collection of ceramics to be exhibited there before going into the South Kensington Museum. Cunliffe Owen's British contact in Japan was his kinsman Fritz Cunliffe Owen, of the Japanese service in Tokyo. The collection, consisting of

RIGHT

34. Linthorpe Art Pottery. Earthenware 'double-gourd' vase, c.1880, inspired by the Japanese bronze vase, plate 35. The Birkenhead Collection.

FAR RIGHT

35. 'Double-gourd' bronze vase, Japanese, acquired for the South Kensington Museum from Samuel Bing in 1875. V&A: 148–1876.

216 pieces, cost £600. The most highly valued were the decorative contemporary articles, the cheapest were the rough pottery tea-bowls, which are now highly regarded (plate 30). Dresser was in daily contact with Cunliffe Owen over the choice of objects to take to Japan as a gift to the Japanese Government, and he must have shared in the deliberations over the Philadelphia collection. He would also have seen the pieces acquired at the 1875 auction in Paris of Siegfried Bing's collection of Japanese art, pieces that later served him as models for his own designs. Cunliffe Owen and Dresser shared a cultured and academic interest in Japan that had little in common with the aesthetic approach of artist-collectors such as Whistler and Dante Gabriel Rossetti – the very people now identified as having the greatest impact on the European taste for Japan. Whistler and Rossetti and their friends were obsessed with blue-and-white porcelain, much of which was Chinese. The Philadelphia selection includes few blue-and-white pieces.

Dresser's mission to Japan encompassed many strands – official, educational, commercial – with a number of different bodies involved. This epic trip, whose implications in terms of Dresser's art are only now being fully appreciated, is described in detail in chapter 6. In part he was on a fact-finding mission, in part an official government emissary to the Imperial Museum in Tokyo, with the gift of European decorative arts chosen by Cunliffe Owen. He was also retained to collect Japanese art works and decorative pieces for Londos & Co., (formerly Charles Reynolds' City Art Warehouse, plate 168) and for Tiffany & Co. of New York. He left Liverpool in October for Philadelphia where he visited the exhibition, and delivered a series of lectures on art museums and art industries at the newly founded Pennsylvania Museum and School of Industrial Art. He made useful contacts, including American wallpaper manufacturers. Some 13 of his designs for the firm of Wilson & Fenimores were registered with the US Patent Office in 1877. Dresser went to San Francisco from Philadelphia, and there embarked, in company with General Saigô Tsugumichi and the entire Japanese staff from the Philadelphia exhibition, on the *City of Tokio*, arriving in Yokohama on 26 December.

Dresser was treated as an honoured guest, received by the Mikado and given access to places from which Westerners were still excluded. In fact he was the first professional designer to have virtually unrestricted access in Japan. He was able to experience the very final stages of traditional Japanese life; indeed the Satsuma rebellion, which removed the last vestiges of Samurai tradition, was actually raging during his stay. In four months he toured over 1,700 miles around the country, visiting 68 potteries, 100 temples and amassing more than 1,000 photographs. He departed on 3 April aboard the *Malacca*, returning via Marseilles to London. Some 8,000 items of lacquer, metalwork, enamels, ceramics and textiles for Tiffany & Co. were delivered to New York. These were exhibited as the 'Dresser Collection of Japanese Curios: Articles Selected for Tiffany & Co.', before being sold by Leavitt, Auctioneers, on 18 June 1877. Tiffany's made a name as the foremost *Japoniste* silversmiths, commended at the Paris 1878 International Exhibition. Dresser gives more than a hint of his critical role in their success: he believed himself responsible for the fact that 'Messrs Tiffany and Co. produced new works which secured to the firm the "grand prix" at the last Paris exhibition'.[57] In truth, although Tiffany had produced 'Japanese' patterns since 1871, their shapes and particularly their metal-working techniques became more authentic from 1877.

On his return from Japan Dresser was kept very busy. He immediately offered the Society of Arts a lecture on 'The Art Manufactures of Japan, from personal observation of the processes made during a journey of two thousand miles in the interior when the nation's guest'. This was duly delivered, with a very much shorter title, on 30 January 1878. He set up a new wholesale company, Dresser & Holme of Farringdon Road, in partnership with Bradford businessman Charles Holme (who went on to become owner and editor of *The Studio* magazine in 1893) to import Japanese art. Sir Rutherford and Lady Alcock were present at the opening in June 1879.[58] The Japanese end of this enterprise was run from Kobe by his sons, Christopher and Louis. In 1877–8 Dresser had to arrange for exhibitions of carved wood panels, and casts of shrine ceilings (which were still in his reference collection at his death; one is now in the V&A) and slot-together rooms sent by the Japanese emperor.[59] The first display was set up in 1877 by Jackson & Graham. As well as the latticework panels there were some 2,800 art objects, described by Dresser as 'suggestive for the British manufacturers'. The following year he persuaded Edwin Streeter, diamond dealer, jeweller and silversmith, of 18 New Bond Street, to erect one of the rooms in his showroom. Streeter used the opportunity of the exhibit to show 'Japanese curiosities – plates of inlaid silver of marvellous perfection, *cloisonné* enamels, jewellery, ancient vessels, all remarkable for some peculiarity utterly unfamiliar to the Western world.'[60]

Meanwhile he was a juror for Class 22 (paper hangings) at the 1878 Paris Exposition, and he recalled providing designs for no less than 11 manufacturers exhibiting there.[61] He had contracts to design silver and plate for Hukin & Heath of Birmingham (1878) and for James Dixon & Sons of Sheffield (1879), while at the same time he was involved with the Linthorpe Pottery in Middlesbrough. In 1880 he opened the Art Furnishers' Alliance in London and agreed to become art-editor of the *Furniture Gazette.* Hardly surprisingly, he was unable to continue with his weekly articles after the final issue of that year.

Radical designs

The trip to Japan brought out the full maturity and individuality of Dresser's designs. His appreciation of the Japanese ceramic aesthetic underwent a quantum transformation, going far beyond a more decorative Japonism that appealed to the public and characterized a number of the items in the collection acquired by the South Kensington Museum in 1876. He unleashed an astonishing creative energy on his new projects: silver and electroplate for Hukin & Heath and Dixon, brass and copper for Benham & Froud, japanned metal as well as brass and copper for Richard Perry, Son & Co., of Wolverhampton. By any standards the pieces are exceptional, but they are even more so when compared with the popular historical pastiches that were the staple product of the silverware and metal trades of the time. Some of the teapots are like paper origami rather than metal. The chamber sticks for Perry are unlike anything ever seen in the Wolverhampton japanned ware trade, which was still stuck in a high Victorian rococo groove. Even in terms of Japonism all his metal wares are highly unusual.

The metalwork designs – not only for silver and electroplate, but also the brass and copper riveted kettles and teapots for Benham & Froud and the red-painted tin pieces for Perry's – could be regarded as Dresser's finest contribution to design reform in the nineteenth century. James Dixon, the firm for which he designed some of his most uncompromising pieces, had discovered early on how hazardous the involvement of inexperienced designers could be when it encountered Redgrave's designs for the Summerly scheme in 1847. Redgrave's charming ideas for silver were quite impractical, since he had no idea of controlling costs by standardizing components such as handles and lids. Dresser should have been an entirely different case since he was concerned about the economical use of costly materials. He was obsessed with function and the techniques of machine production, but his rush of inspiration after Japan betrayed him into some shapes that were far too expensive (see chapter 4).

Dresser was still heavily involved with ceramic design, his new work being characterized by shapes unprecedented in the Western tradition. The pots for the Linthorpe and Ault potteries seem even now to be innovative in their exploitation of the living clay. Japan had opened his eyes to the potential for form in decorative art, and to the potential for materials to create form. The straightforward 'ornamentist', as he had styled himself, was left behind – indeed it is significant that he describes himself as a 'designer' on the post-Japan works. He added to his non-Western repertoire with shapes from Peru and Mexico; the 1876 Philadelphia Exposition had an important display from Peru, but Dresser's attention at that time was so focused on Japan that it seems probable the Peruvian shapes were from another source.[62]

The Art Furnishers' Alliance

Dresser started the Art Furnishers' Alliance by taking out a 21-year lease on the premises on 14 June 1880. The firm was incorporated on 12 April 1881 and the showrooms opened at 157 New Bond Street in May 1881. The directors were George Hayter Chubb (of the safemakers), John Harrison (owner of the Linthorpe Pottery), Edward Cope (lacemaker) and Sir Edward Lee (managing director of the Alexandra Palace Co.); the shareholders included a number of the suppliers, among them Arthur Liberty, James Dixon, William Cooke (the wallpaper manufacturer, who had the largest shareholding of £300), Harrison and Chubb, and note. Bond-street rejoices in two, one of which is the new Gallery of the Art Furnishers' Alliance, and the other the Exhibition of Decorative Art under the management of Mr. T. J. Gullick. The Albert Hall also contains a capital collection of art furniture.

The inauguration of the "Alliance" has been watched with considerable interest by the trade, for Dr. Dresser is "art director," and "no objects, whether important works or mere adjuncts of house furnishing, are offered for sale unless their art qualities have been duly tested and approved." I must confess to have had a great desire to see such happy "objects," and consequently took an early opportunity to allay a morbid curiosity. What was my delight on strolling into 157, New Bond-street, to see something like this!

and attired in æsthetic colours too : a sort of "greenery-yallery" dress, ruby sash, and mob cap "to harmonize." Accepting the Doctor's printed assurance that "the art qualities of every article, &c.," unstinted admiration at once possessed me.

There are a great many nice things in these galleries (in addition to the foregoing) selected for the most part from stocks of well-known manufacturers ; the rest made from Dr. Dresser's own designs. The style of the latter may be gathered from the seat indicated in the sketch above. A sort of heavy Greek, in "black and gold" or vermilion enrichment. The effect of some of these pseudo-classic combinations is certainly impressive, but by-and-bye the designer will use less timber in their construction and resort to recognised conditions of comfort.

As may be remembered, the presiding genius over this establishment went out of his way to issue a tirade against the "Queen Anne rage" some twelve months ago. Having a lively recollection of his views, I was puzzled to find the "Alliance" flourishing in a building of "Queen Anne" exterior, and inside ... belonging to the same "depraved" period.

Dresser's solicitor and patron Hiram B. Owston. The rent of the showrooms was set at £1,500 per annum and the turnover for the first year was £11,000 (March 1882). In the second year it rose to £14,000, with orders pending of a further £3,700. As usual, Dresser arranged for full control of the designs. According to the prospectus, it was:

for the purpose of supplying all kinds of house-furnishing material, including furniture, carpets, wall-decorations, hangings, pottery, table-glass, silversmiths' wares, hardware, and whatever is necessary to our household requirements. The art direction of the new warehouse will be left in the hands of Dr Christopher Dresser, FLS etc., who will be the art authority of the company, and no object, whether an important work or a mere adjunct of furnishing, will be offered for sale in the Company's warehouse unless he testifies of its art qualities.

The artistically decorated showroom had goods displayed against walls lined with plain brown paper and 'pleasing young ladies aesthetically attired' to serve. According to a report in the *Cabinet Maker and Art Furnisher*, they wore 'greenery-yallery' dresses with ruby sashes and mob caps (left), a reference to Gilbert and Sullivan's *Patience*, which had opened at the Opéra Comique in London about a week earlier (23 April 1881).[63] The 'notes' on the Alliance from the magazine's editor open as follows:

Talking of the West [End], there is quite a deluge of art furniture exhibitions this summer in that district more or less worthy of note. Bond-street rejoices in two, one of which is the new Gallery of the Art Furnishers' Alliance ... The inauguration of the 'Alliance' has been watched with considerable interest by the trade, for Dr Dresser is 'art director,' and 'no objects, whether important works or mere adjuncts of house furnishing, are offered for sale unless their art qualities have been duly tested and approved.' I must confess to have had a great desire to see such happy 'objects,' and consequently took an early opportunity to allay a morbid curiosity.

The ensuing commentary was really far from favourable; the sarcastic and deflating tone of the article suggests that Dresser's often paranoid sense of the lowly position of commercial designers may have been justified. The criticism lasted for several paragraphs, but seemingly against his will the writer finally conceded some original and attractive qualities in the merchandise:

My recollections of Doctor Dresser's declaration, that the furniture of the day was a 'disgrace to England' has led me, I fear, to be a little hypercritical over the efforts of this distinguished censor of our trade. On the other hand, there are some excellent features in the galleries under his control. Here is a pretty little chair [the attached illustration shows Dresser's 'Egyptian' chair, plate 28] constructed by him, with the rails carried from top of chair right down to the back rail of the legs, thus securing great additional strength. The enrichments are incised into the ebonised wood, and filled with vermilion, certainly a charming mode of decoration.

There may also have been an element of rivalry, since the magazine was a committed supporter of Bruce Talbert, and by melancholy chance Talbert's long obituary followed the Alliance report almost on the next page. However, it is from this source that we have visual evidence of the type of designs stocked by the firm.

36. Art Furnishers' Alliance. Illustration from *The Cabinet Maker and Art Furnisher*, 1 July 1881. Michael Whiteway.

Bond Street was a vital centre of the London art trade, famous for its great variety of luxury suppliers, among them Hunt & Roskell, Edwin Streeter and the expensive cabinet makers, Wright & Mansfield and Johnstone & Jeanes – the last one carried out Alma-Tadema's designs for furniture for his millionaire American patron, J.P. Marquand. In 1875 Liberty had opened his exciting Japanese warehouse a few minutes walk away in Regent Street; in 1876 the newly-founded Fine Art Society took over 148 New Bond Street. It seems more than happy coincidence that led the Fine Art Society to redesign its façade only months after the opening of the Alliance. Godwin was the chosen architect and his sketch for the alterations is dated 28 July 1881; essentially the scheme survives more or less unaltered today.[64] Sir Coutts Lindsay's Grosvenor Gallery, an Italianate palazzo at no. 135, opened with a great social fanfare in May 1877. From 1877 Morris & Co. was not far away, at 449 Oxford Street. In 1874 Norman Shaw had designed a shop front just along the road, at 395 Oxford Street, for Murray Marks, Liberty's principal rival and purveyor-in-chief of blue-and-white porcelain. In 1876 Ernest George & Peto's 'Queen Anne' shop for Thomas Goode & Co. opened in South Audley Street. Goode acted as the retail outlet for Minton, the Royal Worcester Porcelain Co., and Wedgwood, offering a range of exotic wares, including Japanese, Persian and Moorish in an 'Aesthetic' showroom. Although Dresser acted as designer for these firms, none of them were advertised suppliers of the Art Furnishers' Alliance, or its creditors.

As the editor of the *Cabinet Maker* pointed out, the Art Furnishers' Alliance could not have been better placed as an avant-garde emporium. Dresser had been designing furniture for some time. He had been thinking about the 'Egyptian' chair with its long back struts since seeing Philip Webb's chair in 1862. Both Bushloe House and Allangate had striking pieces, basically black with incised gold and Egyptian-inspired painted decoration. In 1870 Benham & Froud had registered designs for coal boxes, uncompromisingly geometric and plain. The cast-iron tables, chairs and hall stands for Coalbrookdale are from the same era. For his new venture Dresser drew on the severity of Egyptian and Ancient Greek forms, using some of the same designs that he had proposed in the *Technical Edu-*

cator nearly 10 years earlier. The furniture was made by Thomas Knight of Bath on Chubb's premises. Other stock came from Liberty and Dresser & Holme for imported Oriental objects; James Dixon and Hukin & Heath for silverware; wallpapers from leading manufacturers including his early employers Scott, Cuthbertson of Chelsea and Jeffrey's; Sowerby for glass; Benham & Froud for metalwork; and pottery from Linthorpe. In many respects the Alliance was a re-run of the Alexandra Palace Co.

In spite of the array of adventurous manufacturers rounded up by Dresser, the venture foundered almost at once. His health was under strain, he was already in financial trouble; he retired from Dresser & Holme in August 1882 and gave up his membership of the Society of Arts at this time. In the foreword to his account of the Japan trip, *Japan: Its Architecture, Art and Art Manufactures* (London, 1882 – one of the most thorough accounts of the subject to be published in the nineteenth century), he confessed that a long and painful illness had delayed publication. In the events that now unravelled, as he said himself, his ill health – probably the result of overwork and the burdens of responsibility – left him no longer in command of these many ventures. It is hardly coincidental that his involvement with all of them ceased in 1882–3, and that his furnishing company folded with massive financial burdens in 1883.

By September 1882 he had surrendered his large house on Campden Hill and was leasing Wellesley Lodge at Sutton in Surrey.[65] Dresser was not the only casualty in the design world in the 1880s and early 1890s; Burges, Thomas Jeckyll and Talbert all died in 1881, Godwin in 1886, Daniel Cottier in 1891. None of them were old men. The country was in the grip of a disastrous economic recession that saw many luxury shops and manufacturers go under, among them Jackson & Graham. The Alliance went the way of almost all its predecessors except for Morris & Co.; Morris was the great survivor. Dresser's financial arrangements with the Art Furnishers' Alliance participants may have been imprudent; he was probably undercapitalized at £50,000, although, with a business set up as a co-operative, the need for working capital was less, since goods offered for sale did not have to be paid for 'up-front'. The list of creditors is of daunting length, but it provides a picture of the scale of the operation and the many firms involved. If Dresser kept to the letter of his prospectus and retained artistic control, then the list opens up new possibilities of identifying designs by him. Among the creditors are Sanderson (wallpapers), Craven, Dunnill of Ironbridge (tiles), Sir Arthur Elton of Somerset, Salviati and James Powell (glassworks) and Templeton's (woven hangings). Among the largest creditors are wholesale cabinet makers and house painters, which could suggest that the fitting up of the premises had not been fully paid.

The 'Alliance' legacy

The Alliance should have been the pinnacle of Dresser's achievement, the forum where he could demonstrate the full range and originality of his ideas. But it was also a place where he could affirm their relevance and practicality to the modern middle-class home. The failure of the company was the final blow to his ambition to supply everything for the artistic house. Writing in *The Studio* some years later, Holme suggested that it was 'perhaps partly owing to the fact that it was before its time. For it was alone in its mission in addressing a popular audience'.[66] The list of creditors enables a picture to emerge of the succession; Dresser's mantle, and, it seems likely, much of his stock was taken over by Liberty's.

Liberty's was the Mecca for Orientalist and artistic decorators, but what it lacked was furniture. Godwin lamented 'If it only had a little decent furniture, an artist might almost decorate and furnish his rooms from this one shop. There are matting and mats, carpets and rugs for the floor; Japanese papers for the walls; curtain stuffs for the windows and doors; folding screens, chairs, stools.'[67] It can hardly be a coincidence that the 'Art' furniture department opened in 1883, immediately after the collapse of Dresser's Alliance. Arthur Lazenby Liberty was a shrewd businessman and, like Morris, he was a survivor, not one to let the failure of a venture drag him down. He started his career as manager of the Oriental department of the well-established department store, Farmer and Rogers Great Cloak and Shawl Emporium. After the closure of the 1862 exhibition this firm took over items from the Japanese display; Liberty joined the firm shortly afterwards and remained there for 12

years. Then in 1875 he acquired premises in Regent Street and set up his own business, initially as a dealer in Oriental and Indian merchandise. The soft printed Oriental-style silks became synonymous with the Liberty name. Both Liberty himself and Charles Holme visited Japan in 1889–90, having first applied to Dresser for advice and introductions.

The collapse of the Alliance had disastrous implications for Dresser professionally. He had let down all his most valuable employers and supporters. Getting work in the wake of this debacle must have been hard, and it seems likely that it was at this point that he made up the 'Metropolitan Album' (pages 200–201) to act as an advertisement in his quest for commissions. Nothing underscores the side-lining of Dresser more cruelly than his absence from the *Loan Exhibition of Japanese Art* put on by Marcus Huish of the Fine Art Society. This important, and very large, show of Japanese art early in 1888 prompted Huish's best-known book, *Japan and Its Art* (1889), and the similarity with Dresser's title is hard to ignore. The exhibits were confined to art objects – ceramics, metalwork, lacquer and carvings – because an exhibition of Japanese drawings and prints was put on at the same time by the Burlington Fine Arts Club.[68] Huish, who was a respected authority in this field although he had never visited Japan, lectured during the run of the exhibition and wrote a series of articles, 'Notes on Japan and its Art Wares', for the *Art Journal.* From these he developed his book. The involvement of Cunliffe Owen in this enterprise makes the absence of Dresser all the more conspicuous. Cunliffe Owen was a significant lender to the exhibition.

Experiments in ceramics and glass

From 1884 to 1886 Dresser was associated with the Old Hall potters at Hanley in Staffordshire. The designs are striking but the manufacture in cheap pottery with transfer-printed decoration is more frankly commercial than any other example of his work so far identified. It seems possible that he went below his usual standards because he needed the cash. In 1886 he published *Modern Ornamentation*, his last book. For such a relentless writer and proselytizer, suspending this activity 18 years before his death speaks volumes for the disarray of his affairs. But the ceramic designs for

RIGHT

37. Japanese copper 'Hiroshima' candlestick acquired from the sale of Dresser's estate, 1905. V&A: 384–1905. The candlestick is illustrated by Dresser in *Japan, its architecture, art and art manufactures* (1882), fig. 180.

FAR RIGHT

38. Minton's China Works. Watercolour drawing for a vase inspired by the Japanese copper candlestick, plate 37. Minton Museum and Archives.

Ault & Co. (1890–1900) and the 'Clutha' glass venture (1888–1900) for John Couper & Sons of Glasgow demonstrate all his old energy and inventiveness. The Ault Pottery at Swadlicote was founded in 1887, and in 1890 William Ault bought a number of Dresser's moulds from the liquidation sale of the Linthorpe Pottery. In 1893 Dresser contracted to supply Ault with designs, and some of his most outlandish shapes – for example, the 'goat's head' vase and the 'tongue' – were the result. The 'Clutha' venture was a forerunner of Tiffany's 'Favrile' glass and many European 'Art' glass experiments in the Art Nouveau style. The glass was marketed through Liberty's. Dresser had managed to reinvent himself as an Art Nouveau designer.

In spite of all the catastrophes, Dresser's studio must have been turning out patterns as usual. The Alliance fiasco had forced him to return to his roots as an 'ornamentist'; Dresser's imagination was as fertile as ever (see chapter 7), but witnesses of his later years remember him mainly as a pertinacious and persuasive salesman. In 1889 he had moved from Sutton to Barnes, to a house with a large garden and stables overlooking the Thames. When he was not travelling on the Continent looking for clients, he preferred to tend his garden and conservatory. He died of a heart attack at the Hôtel Centrale in Mulhouse in November 1904, while on a trip to consult with Jean Zuber, head of the famous wallpaper manufacturers, and was buried in that French town. His effects, including a vast reference collection of non-Western artifacts, were sold in 1905, and the catalogue is a testament to his unrivalled knowledge of sources (above).

THE ART OF DECORATIVE DESIGN.

BY C. DRESSER, Ph.D.   LONDON, DAY & SON.

40. Band of decoration, presumably for a frieze,
from Dresser's *Studies in Design* (1874–6).
Although this design is in the 'new style'
that Dresser was publicizing in the 1870s,
Egyptian elements are clearly present. See Dresser,
Principles of Decorative Design, pp. 48–9.

39. Publisher's binding for *The Art of Decorative
Design* (1862), embossed and blocked in gold,
designed by Christopher Dresser. The design is
an ingenious paraphrase of Owen Jones' design
for the cover of his *Grammar of Ornament* (1856).
Michael Whiteway.

Dresser's Education and Writings

STUART DURANT

'The dawn of a glorious day-time has long since commenced and we live in the early morning ... the rays of the glorious sun of knowledge are shooting forth with power', wrote Christopher Dresser in 1860. He was 26 and at the beginning of his career.[1]

Christopher Dresser's creative life began when the Industrial Revolution was at its apogee. He died when modernism was in its infancy. In his era, scientific materialism and rampant commercialism had undermined tradition. Many people had been unnerved by the realization that the civilization of the future would be determined by technology. Dresser had no such misgivings.

In 1870 John Ruskin (1819–1900), the pre-eminent authority on art in the English-speaking world, wrote to his American friend Charles Eliot Norton on the death of Charles Dickens: 'Dickens was a pure modernist – a leader of the steam-whistle party'.[2] While Ruskin's 'steam-whistle party' is no more than an amusing construct, one cannot help harbouring the idea that this might be a terse way of describing Dresser's cultural allegiance. The modernizers in Britain were in the ascendancy when Dresser was in his youth. When he died their influence was in eclipse.[3]

Dresser was an outsider – a self-made man. His ideas appealed to the new class created by the Industrial Revolution. He belonged to that class himself. Aesthetes could not weave romantic tales about him. This is the reason for his posthumous admission to the British pantheon. Had Dresser succeeded in passing himself off as an 'artist' – and Nature, he claimed, had always intended him to be one – matters might have been different.[4]

In 1847 Dresser's parents sent him to the Government School of Design in London, set up a decade earlier, at Somerset House in the Strand. The Dressers, with their six children, would never have had enough money to apprentice him to an architect. He was 13 and a prodigy. He was allowed to begin his studies two years before the regulation minimum age of 15.[5]

The textile industry was a major source of Britain's wealth. By the 1830s Britain was losing her ascendancy in manufacturing. France and Germany were swiftly catching up. In 1834 Paris actually mounted the first large industrial exhibition.[6] The School of Design curriculum was devised to meet the challenges of Continental competition – British industry was greedy for new designs. Dresser would become the school's most illustrious alumnus.

William Dyce (1806–64), a fine painter, was the first substantial figure to be associated with the Somerset House school. During a government-funded visit to study Continental methods of teaching design for industry in Prussia, Saxony and France, Dyce closely observed the Prussian method at the Gewerbeschule in Berlin.[7] Under the influence of Karl Friedrich Schinkel (1780–1840), the great neo-classical architect, a sophisticated system for educating designers for the industrial age had been devised.[8] The technical grounding given to Prussian students of design impressed Dyce, who had studied science in Scotland before he took up painting.

Dresser would have been exposed to the idea that design has a technical dimension from the very moment that he entered Somerset House. In 1842 Dyce produced a manual for design students: *The Drawing Book of the Government School of Design.*[9] This was the first British manual to deal with designing for industry. Dyce's method of teaching was simplicity itself. Students began by learning rudimentary geometry. Next they learned how to draw flowers and foliage and organize them according to the elegant symmetrical skeleton-like arrangements that Dyce had devised. Nicknamed 'Dyce's outlines', these had a stylistic affinity with the structures of motifs in fifteenth- or sixteenth-century Italian fabric design. Dyce's outlines were unashamedly employed, unacknowledged, by Pugin in his *Floriated Ornament* of 1849.[10] Dresser used endless variations of the outlines throughout his career – they appear in his last book, *Modern Ornamentation* (1886). Hermann Muthesius, who studied the teaching of art in London schools in the late 1890s, showed that the outlines were still being taught to young children at that time.[11] Just as nature was inexhaustible so, too, were the permutations made possible by this simple means of generating designs.

Designing was widely considered at the time to be inferior to painting. The painter dealt with complex literary imagery and iconography, while a designer was merely expected to rearrange and juxtapose motifs in a manner that accorded with the prevailing canons of taste. Dresser once ruefully observed that while clerks in the offices of factories entered through front entrances, designers entered factories by the same entrances as the

machine operatives.[12] Dyce did not encourage his students to become autonomous artists. Intelligent, even cultivated, artisans, yes. But not artists.

Dresser joined the School of Design when the Dyce era was passing. Dyce had resigned in 1848 after 10 years of wrangling with the school council. Change was in the air. In 1849 there was a large industrial exhibition in Birmingham – a rehearsal for the Great Exhibition of 1851.[13] In the same year Henry Cole (1808–82) began publishing the *Journal of Design and Manufactures*, which ran until 1851.[14] Cole had the energy of a dozen men. He was a civil servant, a prime mover in postal reform, a watercolourist and publisher of children's books (to say nothing of the first Christmas card). He was also one of the earliest campaigners in the cause of good design. In 1846 he won a prize from the Society of

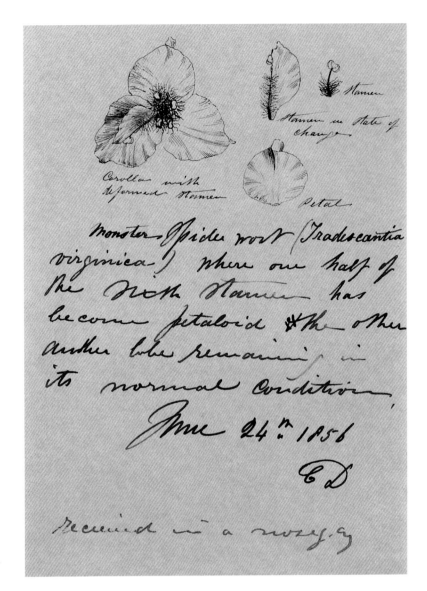

41. A botanical drawing in pen and ink, dated 1856, submitted by Dresser with his first botanical paper 'Contributions to Organographic Botany' which was read before the Linnean Society on 1 April 1858. Reproduced with the permission of the Linnean Society, London.

Arts for the design of a tea set. It was manufactured by Minton – in the 1860s the first major manufacturer to commission Dresser.

The painter Richard Redgrave (1804–88), who became headmaster of the School of Design in 1848, edited Cole's *Journal of Design*. He was inclined to the mawkish sentimentality of the times and was, in truth, a much lesser artist than Dyce.[15] Dresser must have attended two lectures given by Redgrave to School of Design students on the 'Importance of Botany to the Ornamentist' in 1849, which appeared in an early issue of the *Journal of Design*. Redgrave had been appointed botany master in 1847. While he was no scientific botanist, it is likely that it was Redgrave who first aroused Dresser's interest in the subject through these early lectures.

Dresser's education was punctuated by the Great Exhibition of 1851 – the first international celebration of consumerist culture. More than six million people visited Joseph Paxton's prefabricated glass and iron Crystal Palace. The dazzling displays from the Eastern nations were a particular feature of the exhibition. Dresser – an impressionable 17-year-old – was able to study there the finest collection of Indian fabrics that had ever been assembled. The Indian textiles, which used colour combinations

that were inconceivable in the West, played a part in Dresser's artistic awakening. Duranty, an early champion of the Impressionists, was to describe India as 'the motherland of fabrics'.[16]

Scientific botany was to become of the greatest consequence in Dresser's intellectual development. Each week the Royal Botanic Gardens at Kew sent flowers for the School of Design students to draw. Dresser must have been introduced to the Hookers, who presided at Kew, as an exceptionally promising student. Sir William Jackson Hooker (1785–1865) was director and his son, Dr Joseph Dalton Hooker (1817–1911), was assistant director.[17] Dresser collected plants for Dr Hooker – notably British orchids from the countryside around London.[18] Hooker was an early confidant of Charles Darwin and a lifelong friend.

Despite his apparent closeness to the Hookers, Dresser dedicated his first book, *The Rudiments of Botany* (1859), to Dr Lyon Playfair (1818–98). When he was 17, Dresser had attended Playfair's course of lectures on chemistry at the School of Mines.[19] He thanked Playfair 'for the aid which you have afforded me in every pursuit which had for its object the advancement of science ... and more than this, my love for the natural sciences was first

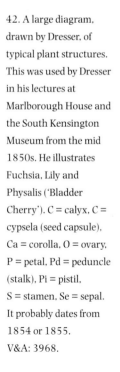

42. A large diagram, drawn by Dresser, of typical plant structures. This was used by Dresser in his lectures at Marlborough House and the South Kensington Museum from the mid 1850s. He illustrates Fuchsia, Lily and Physalis ('Bladder Cherry'). C = calyx, C = cypsela (seed capsule), Ca = corolla, O = ovary, P = petal, Pd = peduncle (stalk), Pi = pistil, S = stamen, Se = sepal. It probably dates from 1854 or 1855. V&A: 3968.

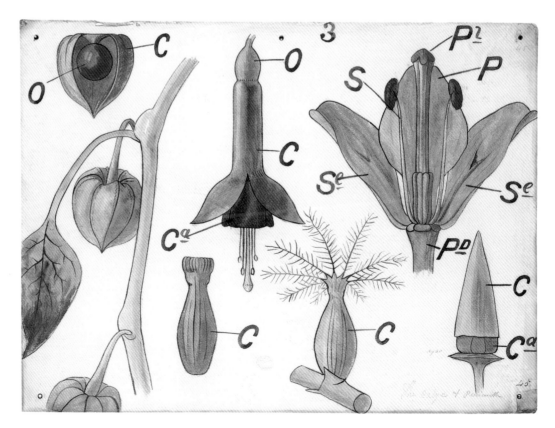

fully awakened by your ... lectures on Chemistry'. The association between Dresser and Playfair lasted for at least 20 years and in 1871, in the *Journal of the Society of Arts*, Dresser spoke of his former teacher as 'my respected friend'. One of the leading chemists of the era, Playfair played an important role in the organization of the Great Exhibition. As a Liberal parliamentarian, he was to do much for the advancement of scientific education.[20] Dresser's first teaching posts – lecturer in botany and master of the botanical drawing classes at the Department of Science and Art's art training institution at South Kensington – could well have been granted because of Playfair's influence.

After the Great Exhibition official attempts were made to link the arts and sciences. Playfair was a key figure in the setting up of the Department of Science and Art in 1853, and its first director of science. Scientists, for a brief period, actually lec-

tured to design students at the Department of Practical Art, Marlborough House – the re-named School of Design, newly installed after the move from Somerset House. Dresser would have heard, in November 1852, Dr John Lindley (1799–1865), one of the most distinguished botanists of the era, lecturing on 'The Symmetry of Vegetation ... the principles to be observed in the delineation of plants'.[21] At the beginning of his first lecture Lindley quoted from a lecture on design at the Great Exhibition by Owen Jones, 'An Attempt to Define the Principles which should Regulate the Employment of Colour in the Decorative Arts', which was to be published shortly afterwards in 1853. This contains the injunction – to become Proposition 13 in Jones's *Grammar of Ornament*, of 1856 – 'Flowers or other natural objects should not be used as ornaments, but conventional representations founded upon them sufficiently suggestive to

43. Diagrams showing typical arrangements of inflorescences. Derived initially from *Linnaeus' Philosophica Botanica* (1751). Dr John Lindley who lectured at the Department of Practical Art, Marlborough House, in 1852 – when Dresser was a student – adapted Linnaeus' diagrams. Dresser in turn treats the plant almost as a mechanism. It probably dates from 1854 or 1855. V&A: 3981.

303. The Endogen, then, has no separable bark, for the latter is held to, or united with, the central portion of the stem by means of the woody threads which pass into it.

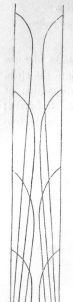

    a. 1. The exterior of the stem is, however, enveloped in a kind of skin, or thin rind, which is termed *false bark*.

    304. The new woody matter deposited in the interior of the endogenous stem, forces outwards that which is already formed;

    305. And the cellular matter increases simultaneously.

Fig. 82.   *Fig.* 81.

306. There is therefore no determinate limit to the life of an Endogen.

307. Nevertheless, the exterior of the endogenous stem frequently becomes obdured, in which case it is incapable of further extension;

Fig. 81.—Transverse section of the stem of a Palm, illustrating Endogenous growth. The central mass is entirely cellular; in this cellular mass, near its circumference, woody bundles are copiously deposited, which, by their development, thrust the cellular matter closer together, and cause it to become more condensed, as is shown in the figure. The whole is covered with a false bark.

Fig. 82.—Diagram showing the route of the bundles of wood in the endogenous stem.

was based to a considerable extent on extrapolating the principles – the aesthetic *modus operandi* – demonstrated in the collection of Indian fabrics and objects that had been purchased at the Great Exhibition as exemplars for the education of students. Dresser's earliest surviving drawings – a dagger and a turban – were of objects from this collection. Despite their sophistication, argued Ruskin, Indian principles did not demonstrate a proper reverence for nature. Indian art was 'wilfully and resolutely' opposed to 'all the facts and forms of nature'. Had

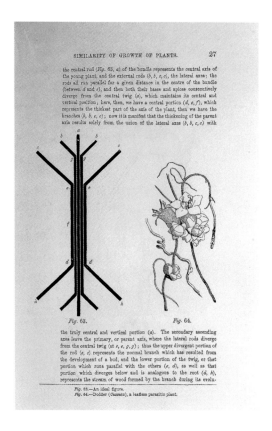

convey the intended image to the mind'. All the authorities on taste had condemned the proliferation of clumsy naturalistic decoration in the Great Exhibition. Stylization – conventionalization – was to be the leitmotiv of Dresser's decorative oeuvre.

    The intention of Lindley's lectures was to impress upon students the need to depict plants scientifically, but not naturalistically. Ruskin railed against such anti-naturalism in his collection of lectures, *The Two Paths* (1859). The first of these lectures, given on 13 January 1858 at South Kensington, was called 'The Deteriorative Power of Conventional Art over Nations'. Ruskin attacked the very foundation of the South Kensington method, which

44. Diagram of plant structure, from *Unity in Variety* by Christopher Dresser (1859). The clarity of Dresser's illustrations was praised in *Botanische Zeitung* (Leipzig, 10 August 1860), which strongly recommended the work to artists. Michael Whiteway.

45. Diagrammatic representation from Dresser, *Rudiments of Botany* (1859), of the growth pattern of a palm tree (after Hugo von Mohl, 1805–72). Lindley used the same diagram in his *Elements of Botany* (1861). Ruskin possessed a copy, but satirized Dresser's botanical diagrams with an illustration that he attributed to 'a clerk of the works' in *Modern Painters*, vol. V, chapter VII, part vi, pl. 56. Michael Whiteway.

not India been guilty of great barbarity during the Mutiny of 1857–8? There was a connection, insisted Ruskin, between morality and artistic expression – the 'ethical fallacy' according to Geoffrey Scott.[22] The ethical fallacy was in turn upheld by proponents of the Arts and Crafts.

Another famous naturalist who lectured at Marlborough House was the zoologist, botanist and palaeontologist Edward Forbes (1815–54). Forbes was the first authority to investigate marine organisms at various depths. He lectured on 'The Variety and Symmetry of Animal Forms' and on 'The Symmetry of Radiated Animals'. The illustrations to the lectures survive in the Print Room of the V&A. Dresser would have attended Forbes's lectures, which must have been among the earliest to proffer sea creatures as artistic models.[23]

Conventional ornament was for the most part symmetrical – bilateral and multilateral. Machine production favoured regularity and its concomitant symmetry. It is not by chance that the theme of both Lindley's and Forbes's lectures was symmetry. There is an arcane reason for their focus upon symmetry: order and conscious design are implied by symmetry. Here we confront one of the preoccupations of the *zeitgeist*. Was the world an emanation of the perfect mind of a divinity? Or could it be the result of random chance? Such questions were debated even before Darwin's description of the mechanism of evolution in *The Origin of Species* (1859). Dresser grew up at a time when the 'argument by design' held sway – when William Paley (1743–1805), with his 'natural theology', insisted that the sheer ingenuity of the design of the animal and vegetable kingdoms was positive proof of the existence of God.[24] The argument by design seems never far beneath the surface in Dresser's three botany books: *The Rudiments of Botany* (1859), *Unity in Variety* (1859) and *The Popular Manual of Botany* (1860).

Throughout his career Dresser found inspiration in the infinitely varied forms of plants. At the time of his death in November 1904 he was employing a full-time gardener to cultivate his large garden at Elm Bank, his house and studio by the Thames at Barnes.[25] When Dresser talks about design his language is refreshingly simple. He tells us more about his method of invention than any other designer does. In *The Art of Decorative Design* (1862), he declared:

The designer's mind must be like the vital force of the

zontally, but stands vertically; nevertheless, the parts of the exceptions being those cases which consist of a series of similar members (*Figs.* 48, 49, 50, 51).

Fig. 48.

Fig. 49.

Fig. 48.—*Astrophyton*, a species of Star Fish.
Fig. 49.—*Cidaris Blumenbachii*, found in the Jura. This is a fossil belonging to the class Radiata, and illustrates the radiate form of animal structure. This cut is from a paper published in the *Art-Journal* by Professor Hunt.
Fig. 50.—*Encrinites moniliformis*, or Lily Encrinites, a fossil belonging to the Radiate class. This cut is also from Professor Hunt's paper in the *Art-Journal* on fossil plants and animals.

Fig. 50.

plant ever developing itself into forms of beauty, yet while thus free to produce, still in all cases governed by unalterable laws; and in the action of the mind being controlled by rules we rejoice, and not mourn.

Not, perhaps – with its overtones of Goethe – the words of the modernist visionary who some have wanted Dresser to be. For Dresser, designing was analogous to the process by which nature produces variations. This is both in accord with the precepts of mid-nineteenth-century science and the Romantic ideals of the preceding generation. The 'vital force' functions as a convenient metaphor for creative energy. The idea of such an ineluctable force gave temporary solace in the face of the dethronement of the benign God of hallowed tradition by science.

Scientific botany brought Dresser a status that

46. Illustrations of undersea organisms from *Unity in Variety* (1859). Dresser seeks to convey the idea of the underlying unity of all living organisms. The illustrations are borrowed from an article by Robert Hunt (1807–87) in *The Art-Journal*. Hunt, an eminent geologist, was closely associated with Dr Lyon Playfair – Dresser's first scientific mentor. Michael Whiteway.

compensated for his modest social origins. At the age of 23, on 4 April 1858, he read a paper before the prestigious Linnaean Society of London – 'Contributions to Organographic Botany' – just two months before Darwin and Alfred Russel Wallace delivered their momentous joint paper on natural selection at the same institution. Dresser had not studied botany at any university, but it was perfectly possibly to be a self-taught scientist in the 1850s.

Dresser's botanical specialization was morphology – the study of the external form and structure of plants, animals and organisms. This was a characteristically mid-nineteenth-century preoccupation. In botany, this had been inspired by Goethe's writings. In particular, his assertion in *Die Metamorphose* (1790) that the leaf is the fundamental organ of the plant: *Alles ist Blatt* ('all is leaf').[26] Such ideas were to be promulgated by John Lindley in his *Introduction to Botany* (1832). It is also clear that Dresser imbibed Goethean ideas from other authorities, including Mathias Jakob Schleiden (1804–81), whose *The Plant; a Biography* – with its chapter epigraphs by Goethe – had appeared in translation in 1848, followed, in 1849, by his radical *Principles of Scientific Botany*. With Theodor Schwann (1810–82), Schleiden was co-originator of the postulate that living organisms were composed of separate cells – a theory almost as revolutionary as Darwin's natural selection itself. Schleiden was one of the giants of nineteenth-century science and the pre-eminent scientist at the University of Jena, which had the foremost botanical faculty in Europe. The University of Jena awarded Dresser a doctorate, *in absentia*, on 14 September 1859, for his two books of 1859 and a short paper on plant morphology. This was an exceptional honour for a foreigner of no more than 25.

Morphology, of the kind that Dresser researched, with its holistic assumptions, is no longer in fashion with scientists – now their preoccupation is with DNA.[27] Yet, in its day, morphology galvanized the thinking of naturalists. Darwin speculated upon the fact that vertebrate skeletal structures – the hand of a human and the wing of a bat, for example – invariably possessed morphological affinities.[28] Dresser himself proposed that the 'leaf was a modified branch': a vestigial branch that had transformed – metamorphosed – into a leaf.[29] Enshrined in such thinking is the idea of the archetype – a conceptual matrix, from which infinite variations could be generated. In other words, an updated version of the archetype of Plato's *Timaeus*.[30] Darwin's opponent, Richard Owen (1804–92), palaeontologist and the leading comparative anatomist, devised an ingenious 'archetypal vertebrate skeleton', a fish-like creature, from which the skeletons of all other vertebrates derived.[31] Earlier, there had been Goethe's 'primal plant', his *Urpflanze*.[32] There was a body of information to establish that profound morphological resemblances existed across the boundaries of species. Thus there existed the possibility of separate species being related and simply modified versions of an archetype – 'type' was the term preferred by contemporary authorities.[33] If there had been no morphology there would have been no evolutionary theory.

Where did Dresser stand in the evolutionary debate? The prefaces of his first two botanical books (March and April 1859) were dated just a few months after Darwin's and Alfred Russel Wallace's joint epoch-making Linnean Society paper on evolution, but before the publication of *The Origin of Species* on 24 November 1859. Dresser does, however, in *The Art of Decorative Design* (1862), employ a distinctly Darwinian argument to support the case of 'fitness for purpose' – 'functionalism' is a term that only came into its own in the 1930s. Plants were suited to the circumstances in which they grew. Plants with 'narrow rigid leaves' occupied exposed, windy, conditions. Plants with membranous leaves – if they grew in hostile environments – were never very tall and their leaves were tightly compressed together. Dresser recorded Sir William Hooker's observation that the stems of the Egyptian papyrus were of a triangular form 'well adapted for withstanding pressure ... one angle always meets the current, and thus separates the water as does the bow of a modern iron steam ship'.[34]

In 1860 Dresser applied for the chair of botany at University College London. (Lindley had held the chair since 1828, the year in which it had been created.) Dresser already held lectureships at leading London medical schools. Doctors were required to know the therapeutic properties of different plants. Medical botany formed an essential part of medical education – although, by the 1860s, the subject was seen as a relic from the era of the apothecary.[35] Dresser assembled an impressive portfolio of testimonials from leading scientists and his fellow teachers. Despite his influential supporters, the chair went to Daniel Oliver (1830–1910). Had Dresser continued to pursue botany, he would have attained distinction – certainly as an educator. It was, no doubt, this balking of an ambition, perhaps too exalted for someone so young, that prompted Dresser to take up designing to the exclusion of botany. His botanical career was virtually over by the time he was 28. But implanted in his mind was an understanding of the symbiotic relationship between science and design that industrialization predicated.

Dresser made some mark as a scientist – although, perhaps, his true importance was as a scientific popularizer. *The Rudiments of Botany* and *Unity in Variety* are essentially student manuals and modelled, to an extent, on Lindley's *Elements of Botany*, which ran into many editions. However, Dresser's illustrations are more lucid and pleasing to the eye. *The Popular Manual of Botany* (1860) is unashamedly populist.[36] It is an admirable example of a scientific work intended for the middle classes, who were avid for education: precisely the people who spent their weekends at the Crystal Palace in Sydenham, meandering through the painstakingly researched plaster replicas of historic architectural styles. Dresser lectured at Sydenham, incidentally, on ornamental art in the 1860s.

The London International Exhibition of 1862 played a major part in Dresser's transformation from botanist to designer. Although the exhibition was larger than the Great Exhibition of 1851, it never became part of national folklore. But it is important in the history of design. Morris, Marshall, Faulkner – later Morris & Company – exhibited here for the first time. With the rise of the Arts and Crafts movement a couple of decades later, the Morris influence was to be paramount in British design circles. The public had their first opportunity in 1862 of seeing the Japanese goods shown by Sir Rutherford Alcock (1809–97), Britain's first consul-general and then minister plenipotentiary in Japan. Dresser purchased many of Alcock's exhibits and his interest in Japanese design can be traced to this very occasion.

Dresser claimed in an article, 'The Art of Decorative Design' in *The Builder* of March 1862, that he had supplied many designs to manufacturers specifically for the coming exhibition – 'perhaps as many as any individual'. His work as a commercial designer must have begun a little earlier. Even by

1858, while his botanical career was in the ascendant, Dresser is known to have designed carpets for an important and expensive London furnishing company – Jackson & Graham.

Dresser published a critical guide to the 1862 exhibition – *Development of Ornamental Art in the International Exhibition* – an ephemeral paper-bound booklet that visitors could consult while standing in front of exhibits in order to learn what was to be approved. Dresser's guide, the precursor, perhaps, of the taped exhibition commentary, was the first publication of its kind. *The Athenaeum*, the leading London literary and artistic review, described Dresser's booklet as adapting 'it may be a little conceitedly, the propositions of Mr Owen Jones and others'. This is largely true. Dresser's

47. Minton's China Works. Porcelain vase, date cypher for 1867. The Birkenhead Collection. Dresser talks of this strange skeletal creature in his chapter on the Grotesque in *The Principles of Decorative Design* (1873), p. 28. He was particularly impressed with the Chinese, Japanese and Thai grotesque masks that he had seen at the Paris Exposition Universelle in 1867.

48. Drawing for a ceramic vase with skeletal figures, the design was called by Dresser 'Old Bogey'. Designed by Dresser for the Paris 1867 Exposition Universelle. Minton Museum and Archives.

views were entirely typical of the British authorities that sought to reform design.

Dresser published, to capitalize yet further on the 1862 exhibition, a delightful octavo chromolithographic book: *The Art of Decorative Design*. It attracted considerable critical notice. It is the earliest book in which a designer was to suggest methods of inventing designs. Earlier books on design – even Owen Jones's noble *Grammar of Ornament* (1856) – are invariably compilations of approved historic examples. Historicism, though generally less sophisticated than Jones's, characterized most nineteenth-century design. E.E. Viollet-le-Duc's *Entretiens sur l'Architecture* (1863–72), though it relies upon history for its rationale, is a notable exception.

'In ornament, as in science', said Dresser, 'it is necessary to have recourse to an analytical method.' He exploited popular science – of the kind purveyed by John Tyndall (1820–93). An eminent physicist and German-educated, Tyndall was the great scientific popularizer of the age.[37] In 1859 or 1860 Dresser attended a demonstration by Tyndall at the Royal Institution on glaciers, which made a great impression on him. In *The Art of Decorative Design*, he declared: 'by observing the aspects of matter when acted upon by various influences, and diligently inquiring into the nature of the mental conception of facts and occurrences, it will be found possible to express feelings and ideas by ornaments without the aid of symbolic forms'. By 'symbolic forms' Dresser meant

the language of the Gothic Revival, which had been publicized by Pugin in his *Glossary of Ecclesiastical Ornament* (1844) – still circulating in the 1860s. Here, without the slightest equivocation, Dresser was calling for a new kind of ornament based upon the discoveries of his own age.

Novelty was a desideratum. Dresser advocated generating new ornamental motifs by measuring the lengths of piano strings needed to play the notes of 'God Save the Queen', and then arranging them into a Greek anthemion pattern. Or, extraordinarily, copying the pattern of the eddies produced by resting a teaspoon on the surface of a cup of tea. He was particularly impressed by the experiments of the eighteenth-century German scientist Ernst Chladni (1756–1827), who had produced an infinite variety of radiating symmetrical patterns by drawing a violin bow across the edge of a square brass plate covered with fine sand.[38] Producing a mirror image of a word – such as, say, 'mathematics' – in copperplate handwriting would create a strange plant-like ornamental figure. Symmetrical images, as Hermann Rorschach was to demonstrate in 1921 with his diagnostic inkblots, suggest innumerable interpretations.[39] Dresser showed in *The Art of Decorative Design* that he understood the phenomenon of 'figure and ground' – the silhouettes of two faces confronting each other that can also be interpreted as an elegant vase is the best known example of 'figure and ground'. Accidental resemblances of ornamental configurations to the human face, particularly the grotesque, also fascinated Dresser. It is quite evident that he understood at an empirical level many of the phenomena that we have come to associate with twentieth-century Gestalt theory.[40] He must surely have been the earliest designer to have explored such a territory in any depth, although Owen Jones had begun to touch upon the subject in his little guide *The Alhambra Court in the Crystal Palace*, which had been published in 1854.[41]

Dresser's analysis of tessellation – the fitting together of geometric shapes – may well be the earliest to have been published.[42] Here he demonstrated how decoration could be constructed out of simple repeated units. The analogy with the processes of machine production is obvious. *The Art of Decorative Design* demystified design. Design was treated as if it was an intellectual game. No one had done this before. Dresser's suggestions, on occasion, seem to

antedate the creative exercises that Paul Klee advocated in his Bauhaus *Pädagogisches Skizzenbuch* of 1922, in which he 'takes a line for a walk'.

The *Athenaeum* praised Dresser's book. The *Art Journal* was far less enthusiastic: 'Dr Dresser's theories … startle us; they are so opposed to everything we have been accustomed to regard as beautiful in ornament'. Dresser's innovations seldom pleased critics. Undaunted, he continued to pursue his experiments in design.

Owen Jones (1809–74) had been the greatest single artistic influence upon Dresser. He was an architect, theorist, designer and publisher, as well as the most enthusiastic champion of Eastern design of his generation. We know him principally for his *Grammar of Ornament*, an artistic and intellectual *tour de force*. It still seems one of the loveliest books ever published. In a lecture that he gave at the Owen Jones Memorial Exhibition in 1874, Dresser told of how Jones had taught him how to 'think'. He was 'the greatest ornamentist of modern times'.

Another important influence upon Dresser was A.W.N. Pugin (1812–52), the most persuasive propagandist of medieval architectural practice.[43] This was accompanied by a call for a return to the Catholic faith – a response, no doubt, to the irreligion of industrialized society. Dresser, a convinced modernizer, rejected Pugin's ideals, but he was perfectly happy to emulate his simple formal treatment of plants in *The Art of Decorative Design*. Even 12 years later, in *Studies in Design* (1874–6) – a defiant attempt to create a modern ornamental style – there are distinct Puginian echoes.

Dresser's Ipswich sketchbook, which was probably assembled between 1861 and 1865, explains the way in which he worked. The designs in the sketchbook are mostly rapidly executed and, while energetic, are without elegance. This is not the kind of document that Dresser would have chosen to bequeath to us. It is far too intimate – but the more interesting for that. His last surviving daughter burned his studio record books in the mid-1950s. She was quite unaware that posterity would become interested in her father. Remarkably, this flimsy, battered, book survived[44].

Rather in the way in which Beethoven wrote down themes when he was out walking, Dresser swiftly noted down his ideas before they evaporated into the ether. Some of the hastily executed Ipswich designs are even sketched on the backs of used envelopes pasted into the book. Dresser must often have handed such sketches to his studio assistants, who would have turned them into the kind of immaculate drawings that survive in the Minton archive. There are many examples of ornament in the Ipswich sketchbook, some of which appear later as complete compositions in *Studies in Design*. There are eight designs for cut glass chandeliers, for an unknown client, which show how Dresser assembled fragments of glass into miniature architecture (like the shimmering glass fantasies of Paul Scheerbart, or Bruno Taut – architects from the years of Expressionism).

There are 16 sketches for ornamental compositions in the sketchbook. None of them could have taken much more than a minute to execute. Dresser tries to epitomize in visual terms salient lines from famous poems by Shelley, Herrick and Joanna Baillie. His possible motive, later to become fully explicit, was to raise ornamental design to a level where it could claim to be equal to the painting of pictures. Dresser knew that contemporary ornament had little intellectual content. Medieval Christian symbolism – of the kind advocated by Pugin – was not appropriate for the second age of enlightenment. Decoration 'must embody the mind of its producer', said Dresser in *The Builder* in 1862 – a mind informed by the scientific knowledge of the century. 'Knowledge is Power' was the motto on his studio door.

In 1870 Dresser began a series of 31 articles on design for the *Technical Educator*. This came out in parts every fortnight, and could later be bound together to form a four-volume compendium of useful knowledge. To judge from the number of copies that survive it must have been a singularly successful publishing venture. The readership was evidently the aspiring class of skilled workers and artisans. Dresser wrote on many subjects: history, colour, wall decoration, ceilings, carpets, woven fabrics, pottery, glass, silversmiths' work, wrought and cast iron and stained glass. It can safely be assumed that Dresser's Tower Cressy studio had supplied designs for all the products about which he wrote. The articles were well received and were published as the *Principles of Decorative Design* (1873). It went into several editions. The anonymous writer of 'The Work of Christopher Dresser', which appeared in *The Studio* in November 1899,[45] found the book contained 'not a line ... that would not be endorsed by

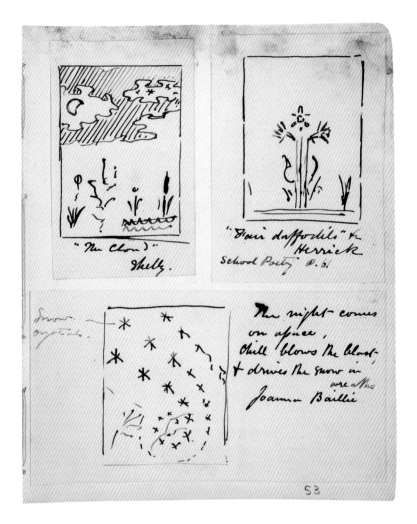

the most critical member of the Arts and Crafts Association'. A new generation of Arts and Crafts writers on design had by then arrived, and Walter Crane (1845–1915) and Lewis F. Day (1845–1910) were the leaders. It was Dresser, all the same, who had first attempted to explain design to the general public. If he had accomplished nothing else, this alone would have been a notable achievement.

In 1871, in 'Ornamentation considered as High Art', a paper read at the Society of Arts, Dresser argued that ornament should be accorded a higher status than pictorial art. Pictorial artists merely copied nature. Ornamentists drew upon the imagination. The faculty of imagination, reasoned Dresser, was higher than the imitative faculty. The semi-pictorial sketches in the Ipswich sketchbook of the 1860s suggest that the idea had been fermenting in Dresser's mind for some time. There are even two unprecedented semi-pictorial ornamental compositions in *The Art of Decorative Design*.[46] Critics ridiculed him. The idea was too revolutionary for

50. A sketch from Dresser's only surviving sketchbook, which appears to date from the mid-1860s. The sketch is for a semi-abstract ornamental composition taking its inspiration from lines from Percy Bysshe Shelley (1792–1822), the pastoral poet Robert Herrick (1591–1674) and a popular poet and dramatist Joanna Baillie (1762–1851). There are a number of other similar sketches based on lines of poetry in the sketchbook – all exhibit a similarly energetic approach to design. The Ipswich Museum.

an era in which the Pre-Raphaelite representation of nature was preferred. Might Dresser, in championing an art that shunned the literal portrayal of nature, have been a very early prophet of abstractionism? There are undeniable affinities between some of Dresser's ornamental compositions and the work, for example, of Wassily Kandinsky.[47] It is, of course, all too easy to attribute – retrospectively – such a primacy of invention to a figure from a more distant past, who lived in an entirely different cultural climate.

Dresser's *Studies in Design* is among the most remarkable among the great nineteenth-century chromolithographic pattern books. He tells us that the book had been prepared 'during the last fifteen years'. This takes us back to 1859, when he was 25, and still principally engaged in botany. He claimed that he had 'striven to attain newness', a claim that no one else would have risked making. Newness, in an era that sought comfort in an imagined past, was not what was expected of designers. The *Athenaeum* of 19 December 1874 described the few designs that had so far been issued as 'scientific rather than artistic ... mechanical ... however ingenious and self-consistent'. The *Art Journal* declared: 'Dr Dresser has some peculiar notions on the subject'. A quarter of a century later, *The Studio* noted:

> Looking at some of these designs again, a certain spiky uncomfortability impresses one as their least admirable feature; yet even now they may be justly credited with vigour, originality, and perfect regard for the materials for which they were designed ... in the case of some of the designs for ceiling papers, it is doubtful if any patterns of more recent years are so appropriate and admirable ...[48]

Some of the startling colour combinations in *Studies in Design* derive from Dresser's colour experiments. He gives some clues as to what these might have been in the *Technical Educator*, in which he wrote extensively about colour. He recommended studying the colours produced by 'gas tubes illuminated by electricity' – such tubes were the prototypes of neon lighting and their influence can be seen in *Studies in Design*. One should also study, wrote Dresser, the colours of the spectrum with the aid of a prism. 'Soap bubbles may also be blown and the beautiful colours ... carefully noted. These and any other means of cultivating the eye should constantly be resorted to, as by such means only can we become

51. *The Evening Star* (1862), a semi-abstract ornamental composition from *The Art of Decorative Design*, 1862, by Christopher Dresser. Michael Whiteway. Dresser has taken great pains to reproduce the muted colours of vegetation seen in the twilight. He was evidently attached to this design and used it on the cover of the short-lived literary magazine *The Planet*.

great colourists.' Dresser was among the most daring of colourists. As he once said, 'the sweetest harmonies' in colour are often closest to discord.[49]

His age gave birth to our own. And this is why we find much of what Dresser did – though perhaps less of what he said – familiar. One of Dresser's abilities, perhaps his greatest, was to orchestrate prevailing ideas – 'judicious plagiarism' was how Voltaire described originality. Dresser was caught, like us all, in the mesh of his time

When he died in 1904 his studio, with its dozen or so assistants and pupils, was flourishing. He was still selling designs to leading manufacturers. These were mainly modish designs for fabrics and wallpapers (the few that survive have the cloying charm of the period). His audacity, his wonderful books and his incomparable essays in colour belonged to another era. A century after his death we have begun to recognize Dresser's genius and the manifold nature of the age that formed him.

ENGLISH SILK AND WOOLLEN BROCADES.

VERY beautiful and not extremely costly fabrics for upholstering purposes, manufactured by Messrs. J. W. and C. Ward, of Halifax, from designs by Dr. Cornelius Dresser, who has done much excellent work not only in Art-decoration but also in the inculcation of the principles on which it rests. Dr. Dresser has given great attention to botany and the application of natural elements in ornament, and consequently has acquired remarkable skill in floral design, but he has also studied thoroughly the best examples of all the Oriental styles, and especially the Japanese, of which he is master. The results of these studies, and of a most skilful pencil and good eye for harmony of colour, have been an immense number of beautiful patterns for wall papers, china and other ceramic wares, silks and other decorative fabrics. The four specimens here given are fair specimens of Dr. Dresser's taste and skill.

CHAPTER

3

Furnishings: Textiles, Wallpapers and Carpets

HARRY LYONS

52. 'English Silk and Woollen Brocades',
page from the *Art Journal Illustrated
Catalogue* for the London International
Exhibition, 1871, held at South Kensington.
Michael Whiteway.

W riting to the *Journal of the Society of Arts* in 1871, Dr Christopher
Dresser stated: 'as an ornamentist, I have much the largest practice
in the kingdom; so far as I know, there is not one branch of art-
manufacture that I do not regularly design patterns for, and I hold regular
appointments as "art adviser" and "chief designer" to several of our largest art-
manufacturing firms.'[1]

A popular view of Christopher Dresser is as a designer of metalwork who also
worked with ceramics. This view is largely sustained by the fact that metal and
ceramics endure whereas textiles, carpets and wallpapers tend to be ephemeral;
they are used, replaced and discarded. This is particularly frustrating in Dresser's
case, since his position in the pantheon of Victorian designers will never be defini-
tively fixed while so much of his output in pattern-design – the most crucial and
prolific area of his activity – remains unidentified. It is not generally appreciated
that Dresser rose to fame through interior decoration. As early as 1865 he was
quoted in trade journals as being 'well-known for his carpets and wallpapers'.[2]
The impetus to realize Dresser's radical concepts in metal and ceramics came
about because he had an established reputation in interior design. This gave manufacturers such as Hukin & Heath, James Dixon and Sons and Linthorpe the
courage to run his innovative designs as serious commercial ventures. Moreover,
Dresser returned to his roots in interior design when his efforts to mould public
taste in other areas ran into difficulties in the early 1880s.[3]

Dresser's innovative approach to textiles, carpets and wallpapers was to sub-
ordinate them to the general decorative scheme of the room. The focus of any
room, he believed, should be the people and the furniture.[4] The role of wallpaper, carpets and textile hangings should therefore be a supporting one. This is
not to say that the design is less important. On the contrary, it presents a more
complex problem; the decorative design must first deliver simply colour-aware-
ness. Only later, once the visitor has adjusted to the room and has had time to
observe it in its entirety, should it reveal interesting patterns. Dresser achieved
this through fine gradations of scale and repeat and by overlaying an all-over
pattern with a bolder design.

53. Cotton cambric, printed by Hargreaves for Liddiard & Co., April, 1853, Christopher Dresser's prize-winning design, sample for registration with the patent office. Public Record Office.

Textiles

Textiles were undoubtedly Dresser's largest area of design work. He studied textile design under Oliver Hudson at the School of Design, and the first record of his talent in this field was as a prize-winner in 1851 at the School of Design for three geometrically based designs suitable for a silk dress,[5] and again in 1853, for a design, which was printed on cambric (above).[6] Dresser's success in textiles was due not only to an innate feel for design, but also through his thorough understanding of the machines that produced them.[7] It was this comprehensive grasp of his subject and knowledge of working practices that won Dresser the respect of the Manchester, Glasgow and Mulhouse cotton manufacturers, and it was this same respect for Dresser that led manufacturers to 'add another guinea' for his ex-pupil Frederick Burrows when he later sold them designs in his own name.[8]

To understand Dresser's textile designing, it must be seen in the context of the British textile trade nationally in the nineteenth century. Surviving records of the period show gorgeous rich silks, damasks and tapestries at the expensive end of the market. Such items were far beyond the means of the mass of the populace, who used plain woollens or cotton prints, and it was to this popular market that many of Dresser's client companies sold the bulk of their wares. Additionally, the United Kingdom, which then included all Ireland, manufactured textiles for the world – its exports were 10 times those of its nearest competitor, France. In 1865, for example, the UK manufactured cotton goods to a value 'in excess of £80 million', of which £52 million were exported.[9] One quarter of British cotton exports went to India, and further sizeable quantities were exported to Africa, China and South America.[10] The companies that supplied this market included many of the textile firms for which Dresser designed. This massive and far-flung market explains, therefore, the diverse range of Dresser's textile patterns (which is later hinted at in his last publication, *Modern Ornamentation*, 1886).

Textile companies designing for and selling to international markets found themselves absorbing the indigenous designs of a very varied client base, an influence that spilled over into textile design generally, from dress fabrics to furnishings, thereby prefiguring many twentieth-century art movements from Cubism to Op Art. One glance at the comprehensive collection of nineteenth-century textile designs preserved by the Patent Office

54. William Fry, Dublin. Sample of Bullrush design, woven wool, registered 1876. Public Record Office. One of the many manufacturers that Dresser probably designed for, William Fry of Dublin produced damask patterns based on designs by Dresser for Ward (plate 261c) and Cooke (plate 68).

RIGHT

55. William Fry, Dublin. Sample of Peacock design, silk, registered 1876. Public Record Office. This design was later taken up by Liberty of Regent Street and has become one of their best-known patterns.

FAR RIGHT

56. Steinbach, Koechlin, Mulhouse, Alsace. Sample of Chinese-style cotton, registered 1868. Public Record Office.

a formidable position for a designer to hold and one that he was to retain for over 40 years.

It is understood that Dresser designed textiles for companies exhibiting at the 1862 International Exhibition, but documentary evidence is lacking. In a guide to the exhibition, *Development of Ornamental Art in the International Exhibition* (1862), Dresser certainly saw himself as qualified to comment on the various textiles on display, including the first offerings of William Morris. In his preface to *Development*, Dresser referred to the many important manufacturers approaching him for designs, and on this basis it is possible to make an educated guess as to which these might be. Textiles exhibited in 1862 were largely at the expensive end of the market. Many textile companies were reluctant to exhibit, believing that they would expose their secrets to international competition.[11] In 1862 Dresser was very much under the influence

Design Registry in the National Archive in London makes one appreciate the maxim that there is 'little that is new'.

Dresser's mastery of the textile process – his knowledge of the weaves, textures and prints of expensive silks, linens, cottons and woollens or affordable serge and cotton prints – enabled him to fulfil the demands of fashion in any area. This was

of Owen Jones – this can be seen clearly in Dresser's early wallpaper designs, and it seems likely that the same applied to his textiles of this time. It was still too early for Dresser to have developed an identifiable, coherent style of his own, since his design career only began in 1859, and this may explain the lack of reference to him at the exhibition. However, study of designs registered with the Patent Office in the 1860s and '70s reveals a group of designs for manufacturers who specialized in the fashionable end of the market, such as William Fry of Dublin and Steinbach-Koechlin of Mulhouse,[12] as well as J.W. & C. Ward of Halifax, all of which bear Dresser's unmistakeable stamp. A similarly recognizable approach emerges among the registrations of affordable cotton prints.[13] Prints are a more difficult category for identifying Dresser's patterns, because print manufacturers were serving an international market as well as the home market, and the design boundaries were ever more blurred.

Dresser's experience in interior design, bolstered by commissions from rich Halifax families, had a positive effect on his confidence in developing his own style. The first identified commission came in 1865 from J.W. & C. Ward, the Halifax textile manufacturer, and shows Dresser creating composite decorative schemes.[14] One imagines that Ward, who was one of Dresser's design clients, would

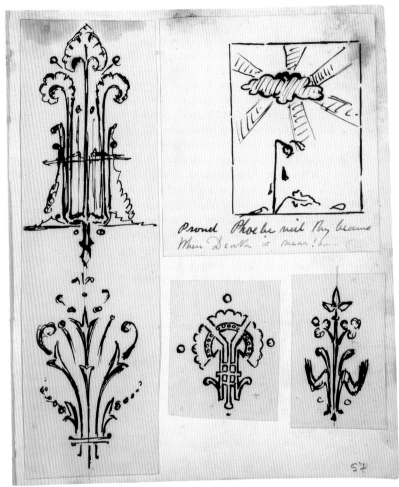

have used specially commissioned designs, as would Thomas Shaw for his new extensions at Allangate (plates 57–9). John Lister and John Lewis, like Shaw and Ward, both of them Halifax manufacturers, would have demanded the same exclusivity. Commissions such as these were from 'new money' – John Lister apart – and Dresser could have expected a degree of freedom to advise and choose the style employed. This was a time of expansion in the 'one stop' interior design house, and it is hardly surprising that Dresser's contacts with such businesses grew, the London firm of Jackson & Graham being the first of many such to have documented links with Dresser. Newcomers such as Newman, Smith, Newman and H. Scott Richmond were also serving this abundance of new money, and both these companies were to be connected to Dresser through the Art Furnishers' Alliance in the 1880s.[15] Dresser would have been pleased by the development of specialist interior design retailers as he had often complained about

OPPOSITE ABOVE LEFT
57. James W. & C. Ward.
Sample of woven wool
and silk fabric, registered
4 February 1868.
Public Record Office.

OPPOSITE ABOVE RIGHT
58. Page from the
'Ipswich' sketchbook
showing designs related
to the Ward textile sample.
Ipswich Museum.

OPPOSITE BELOW
59. James W. & C. Ward.
Patent registry record
book, 13 July 1871,
showing shadow where
damask sample was
removed (see plate 60).
Public Record Office.

60. James W. & C. Ward.
Woven damask designed
by Christopher Dresser
(see plate 59), 1871.
Shown at the London
International Exhibition,
1871. Harry Lyons.

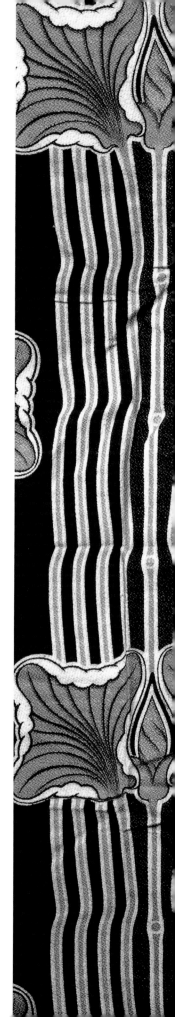

RIGHT
62. F. Steiner,
Accrington, Lancashire.
Sample of cretonne,
1896. Public Record
Office. This design was
illustrated in *The Studio*,
vol. XV, 1899, p. 109.

OPPOSITE TOP
63. F. Steiner,
Accrington, Lancashire.
Sample of printed fabric,
book BT50/285, 1898.
Public Record Office.
This design was
illustrated in *The Studio*,
vol. XV, 1899, p. 109.

OPPOSITE MIDDLE
64. F. Steiner,
Accrington, Lancashire.
Sample of fabric, 1902.
Public Record Office.

OPPOSITE BOTTOM
65. F. Steiner,
Accrington, Lancashire.
Sample of fabric, 1902.
Public Record Office.

61. Thomas Clarkson. Sample of printed fabric for Liberty, Regent Street, London, 1881. Public Record Office. Clarkson's were creditors of the Art Furnishers' Alliance.

the damage to the status of good design through poorly trained buyers in the big city stores.[16]

In 1882, after a damaging period of ill health, Dresser announced that he would henceforth focus on his work as an architect (which could be interpreted to mean as an interior designer) and ornamentist,[17] thereby concentrating his design work on textiles, wallpapers and carpets. Whatever the precise relationship Dresser enjoyed with A.L. Liberty, it seems to have coincided with the time when Liberty widened its interests to include Indian-, Moorish-, Egyptian- and British-made textiles and furniture. Dresser is credited with designing the Liberty fabric 'Mooltan'[18] and a further Liberty

fabric (above), manufactured by Thomas Clarkson, a company with which Dresser had links.[19] This expansion of Liberty's operation led to the creation of yet another sort of 'one stop' furnishing emporium, and by the mid-1890s those of moderate means, in effect, the British middle classes, could furnish their houses entirely at either this one retailer or other similar department stores. Liberty was destined to be a leader in the fashion for Art Nouveau, and nowhere more so than in textiles, particularly chintz. Dresser and his studio reacted to the new fashion as would any commercial studio and provided innovative, competent, well worked-out designs in the latest style (right). Art Nouveau, with its flowing plant forms, was hardly a great challenge to a trained botanist.

Although Dresser was spending more time travelling to solicit work, it is clear that he still retained a

LEFT

66. Engraving of a tablecloth, 'Stork and Peony', designed by Dresser for Messrs John Wilson & Son, London. *The Art Journal* (1891), p. 182. Photo courtesy of Harry Lyons.

67. Engraving showing Barlow & Jones's 'Empire Quilt', made for Queen Victoria's Golden Jubilee in 1887. *The Warehouseman & Drapers' Trade Journal* (11 June 1887), p. 7. Photo courtesy of Harry Lyons.

raised in relief. The border includes circles within a diamond showing stitched lines across, which gives the illusion of a spinning effect to the circles.

Barlow & Jones provides a good example of how Dresser operated as art advisor. He would furnish designs certainly, and attempt to improve the general standard of the company's design profile, but he seems to have extended his influence further by bringing in expertise from other companies for which he worked. When Barlow & Jones lacked expertise or

firm grip on the production of designs by his studio.[20] In lace, we know Dresser was active with Edward Cope of Nottingham in the 1870s and '80s. However, the fact that he illustrated lace patterns in *Modern Ornamentation* shows that he kept an interest in the whole concept from beginning to end and was not merely advising. In linens, Dresser was active with John Wilson of London (above); with textured materials, Dresser is known to have worked for Tootal Broadhurst Lee, and Barlow & Jones.[21] In the Tootal records there is a working drawing, which carries the initials 'CD',[22] but the best examples are to be seen among the registered designs at the National Archive, examples that truly merit the high praise that Tootal won at the International Exhibition in Paris in 1878. The US Commissioners reported that Tootal's expertise put the company a generation ahead of the competition.[23] Woven effects can also be seen in the designs for Barlow & Jones, whose display won a silver medal at the 1878 exhibition, and for whom Dresser was art advisor. The 'Empire Quilt' exhibited at the 1887 Jubilee Exhibition in Manchester by Barlow & Jones (right) shows the company's technical expertise – and by extension, Dresser's skill in understanding the industrial process – to supreme advantage. The quilt is patterned all over with designs that are

plant, work was contracted out; for instance, Stead McAlpin of Carlisle provided 'centres' for quilts, which were then sent to Barlow & Jones to be worked in.[24] An example from the 1878 Paris exhibition shows how a new material, a cotton weave with a 'terry' finish, which would hang like heavier woollen fabrics, was sent to Carlisle for printing, before being displayed in Paris. Local press reports remarked on the affordability of the new material.[25]

Wallpapers

Wallpapers to Dresser's design were exhibited at the 1862 London International Exhibition,[26] probably by Scott Cuthbertson, Jeffrey & Co., and William Woollams, all of London, and William Cooke of Leeds. Dresser designed wallpapers all his working life – indeed, it was on a visit to Jean Zuber, Mulhouse, that he died. In fact, Dresser preferred painted walls with stencilled decorations to wallpaper,[27] but he diplomatically conceded that wallpa-

68. William Cooke & Sons. Sample of wallpaper, 166031, registered 12 September 1863. Public Record Office. This design was used for a damask by William Fry of Dublin.

pers would be around for a long time as they were an affordable means of decoration.

Dresser cautioned against paper being used as so much material to cover over a space. He designed his wallpapers to take account of the prevailing fashion for dividing a wall into three sections, the dado, filling and cornice, using complementary, but contrasting, papers. The proportions of each part of the wall were subtle – that is to say ratios of 4 : 8 were to be avoided in favour of the less obvious 3 : 5, dado : filling. The Design Registry records for the period from the 1850s show the remarkable change in British wallpaper designs between the Great Exhibition in London in 1851 and the 1870s. Owen Jones is owed much of the credit for this, particularly at the expensive end of the market, but undoubtedly it was the consistent availability of well-designed papers at moderate prices from Dresser's pencil that was responsible for the sea change in national taste. At a time when French

design was assumed to be superior, it was with delight that *Building News* reported: 'Dr Dresser ... one of the most active revolutionisers in decorative art of the day is also largely engaged designing carpets and paper hangings for the principal manufacturers of England, and even for some French houses. The latter fact is significant, as reversing the tables which have so long been against us.'[28] William Cooke & Sons was to prove the most prolific of Dresser's wallpaper collaborations. Established in 1856,[29] Cooke had a short manufacturing life, closing in 1893, but throughout was highly regarded both for block and machine printing. According to a standard work on the history of wallpaper,

At their zenith, William Cooke & Sons were among the most notable houses in the trade. They were appointed 'Makers to Queen Victoria' [following a commission for green flock paper with gold fleur-de-lis for Prince Albert's bedroom at Balmoral]. They were pioneers in lustre paper and brought out

a special line in block about 1879, called 'gold lustre silks', a feature of which was the powdering of the mica ground with gold dust.[30]

Dresser's reputation in wallpaper design was such that he was nominated vice-chairman of the wallpaper jury at the International Exhibition in Paris in 1878. Many of his richest designs come at this period (plate 70) for Jules Defossé of Paris. Novel ideas were always of interest, and Dresser was amongst the first to take advantage of new manufacturing processes, which would enable advances in design and affordability. As early as 1860,[31] he was promoting a new process for Scott Cuthbertson giving raised ornamentation, similar to medieval embossed leather. We see the same aspirations coming out with his work for Cooke, and later with the launch of Anaglypta, where Dresser was among the first to supply designs, many of which were still being run well after his death.[32]

Carpets

Dresser quoted eight principles governing the design of carpets.[33] These principles might be further summarized to remind us first, that a carpet covers a flat surface, and decoration should not suggest otherwise. Carpets should have a firm border and the general appearance should either be 'bloomy', resembling a bank, richly covered in flowers, or they should be geometrical and radiate from a centre. Dresser's first commission for a carpet was from Jackson & Graham in 1859. Evidence suggests that he produced several carpets for the International Exhibition in London in 1862, but the documentary evidence for this has yet to surface. Certainly, as with textiles and wallpapers, Dresser felt himself competent to comment on the carpets displayed there, both in his guide to the exhibition and as a critic for the *Illustrated London News*.[34] The illustrations accompanying reviews in

69. William Cooke & Sons. Sample of wallpaper, 133144, bk. BT/43/99, 1 September 1860. Public Record Office.

the *Art Journal* and *Illustrated London News* are not textbook examples of Dresser's design style, but 1862 is still early for a coherent style to have emerged and his commissions may not have allowed him free rein.

70. Photograph submitted to the design registry by Jules Defossé, showing wallpaper as part of a decorative scheme. Public Record Office.

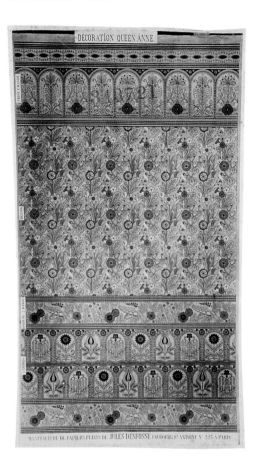

Although singled out by the *Building News* in 1865 as being well known for his carpets, the first important accolades for Dresser's carpets came in 1867 at the International Exhibition in Paris. George Augustus Sala, Dresser's friend and advocate, dwelt at some length in his account of the exhibition on the Brinton & Lewis exhibit.[35] He quotes Dresser as a designer and art advisor to the firm, which was awarded a gold medal. Sir Matthew Digby Wyatt also referred to the exhibit in his official report of the exhibition. Dresser's champion at Brinton & Lewis was John Lewis, and when Lewis left the partnership in 1870, to join his uncles at John Crossley of Halifax, Dresser followed as art advisor and designer to Crossley.[36] Dresser, in his role of art advisor, undertook refurbishment of the Crossley design offices, and inspired the display of carpets at the London International Exhibitions

of 1871 and 1872, for which Crossley won praise. In 1871 there were seven carpets and the display drew fulsome words from *The Graphic*: 'The real competition [in carpets] is between ... Sir Matthew Digby Wyatt, Mr Owen Jones, and Dr Dresser. To the last named must be awarded the palm. Seven large carpets[are displayed]. In two of these especially, Dr Dresser has made an advance for English artwork. Owen Jones' carpets ... good as they are do not manifest the same indigenous originality as the two ... by Dr Dresser'.[37] In 1872 there were 12 carpets, all by Dresser, of which six were designed to show the rich 'bloom' of Indian carpets that Dresser particularly admired.[38] The remainder were described as 'novel'. However, John Lewis decided in 1871 to move once more, opening his own manufactory in Halifax. In 1873, Lewis exhibited on his own account at Vienna. There are no identifications of designers, but it is likely that Dresser's designs featured in the display along with those of Owen Jones. In 1878 Dresser returned to John Brinton (Lewis's former partner) as art advisor, and the Brinton display at the Paris exhibition in 1878 won acclaim and a gold medal.

Dresser was now, however, occupied with his ambitions to improve British taste, and this period would appear to be the zenith of his reputation in carpet design. After his retrenchment in 1882 there is less mention of carpets. True, he provides two pages of carpet designs in *Modern Ornamentation* (1886), and he may have continued to sell carpet designs, but his daughter Nellie, who helped in the studio, expressed surprise when interviewed in 1951 about carpet designs.[39] The best testimonial to Dresser as a carpet designer is a quote from F.J. Mayers, an acknowledged authority, in 1934: 'Some three quarters of a century back, Dr Christopher Dresser, a designer of much initiative and ability, lectured on sanity and fitness in design ... Many manufacturers bought his designs freely and produced them, and although many of them were really excellent designs, they were mostly failures commercially. They were probably above the heads of the purchasing public ... But Dresser's principles of design hold good today and need but the most trifling revisions to make them adoptable as guides for the development of design in the present and future. There is nothing whatever that our art teachers are now preaching that he did not say sixty or seventy years ago.'[40]

The following represents a list of manufacturers for whom Dresser is known to have supplied designs (the information comes from various documented sources, including the registered designs at the Public Record Office, publications by Dresser himself and contemporary periodicals). Manufacturers for whom Dresser may have worked, selected on the basis of design attribution, are also given.

71. William Cooke & Sons. Three wallpaper samples, 160324/5/6, 1862. Public Record Office.

TEXTILES

DOCUMENTED SOURCES

Barlow & Jones, Manchester and Bolton

Thomas Clarkson, Preston and London

Edward Cope, Nottingham

Stead McAlpin, Carlisle

Swaisland Printing Co., Crayford, Kent

Tootal Broadhurst Lee, Manchester

Turnbull & Stockdale, Manchester

J.W. & C. Ward, Halifax

Wardle, Leek

Warner, London

John Wilson, London

ATTRIBUTED SOURCES

William Fry, Dublin

Steinbach Koechlin, Mulhouse, France

Jas Templeton, Glasgow

Dresser supplied designs to the following interior design companies:
Newman, Smith, Newman, London (documented); H Scott Richmond, London and New York (attributed).

WALLPAPERS

DOCUMENTED SOURCES

Allan, Cockshut, London

Anaglypta, London

William Cooke & Sons, Leeds

Scott Cuthbertson, London

Jules Defossé, Paris

Jeffrey & Co., London

Knowles & Essex, London

Lightbown, Aspinall & Co., Manchester

Lincrusta Walton, Sunbury

John Line, Reading

Potters, Darwen

Arthur Sanderson, London

Wilson & Fennimores, Philadelphia, USA

Wylie & Lockhead, Glasgow

Jean Zuber, Mulhouse, France

ATTRIBUTED SOURCES

(Attribution on the basis of similarity in handling, as well as on the network of professional links in Victorian manufacturing.)

Turquetil, Paris

William Woollams, London

CARPETS

DOCUMENTED SOURCES

Brinton & Lewis, Kidderminster

John Crossley, Halifax

Jackson & Graham, London

John Lewis, Halifax

ATTRIBUTED SOURCES

James Templeton, Glasgow

Dresser's Wallpaper and Textile Designs
1860–1880

72. William Cooke & Sons. Wallpaper sample, 155129, bk. BT/43/99, September 1862. Public Record Office.

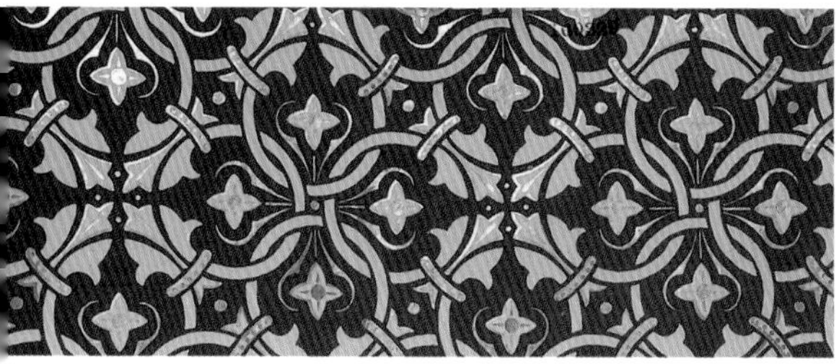

73. William Woollams & Co. Wallpaper sample, registered 6 March 1863. Public Record Office.

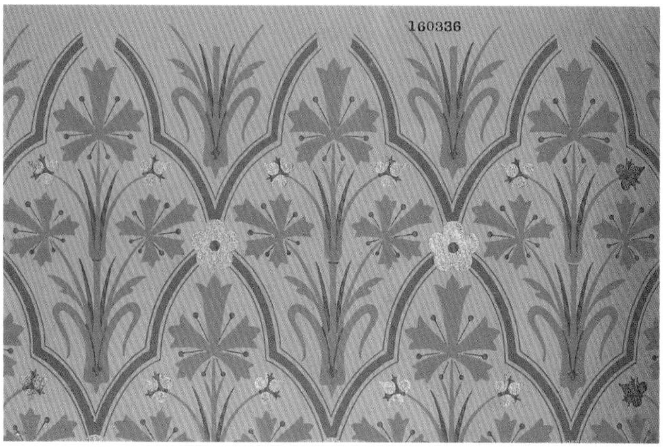

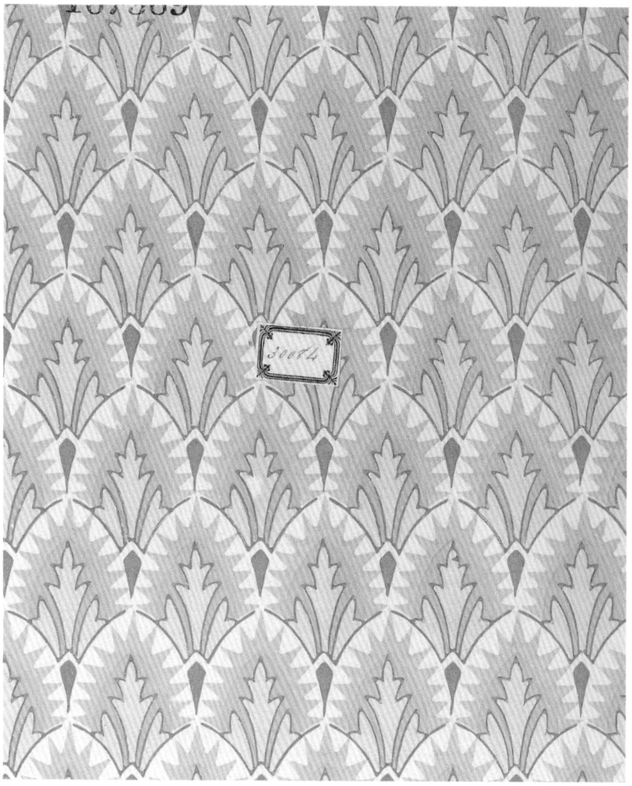

ABOVE 75. Jeffrey & Co. Wallpaper sample, 167369, bk. BT/43/99, 1864. Public Record Office.

BELOW 77. William Cooke & Sons. Wallpaper sample, 166037, 12 September 1863. Public Record Office.

ABOVE 74. William Woollams &Co. Wallpaper sample, registered 6 March 1863. Public Record Office.

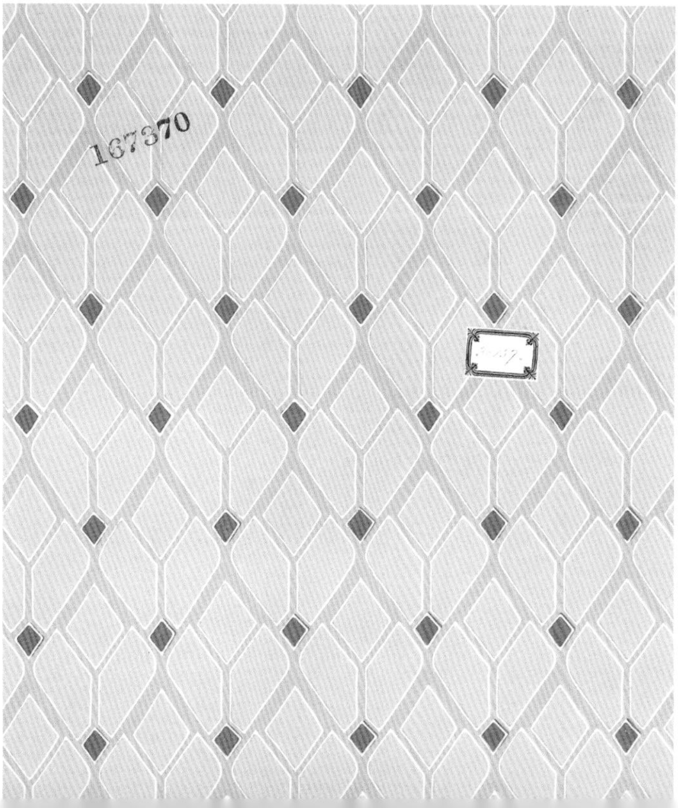

76. Jeffrey & Co. Wallpaper sample, 167370, bk. BT/43/99 1864. Public Record Office.

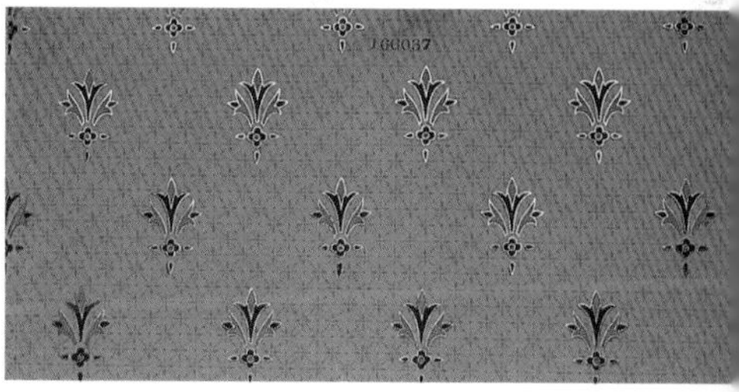

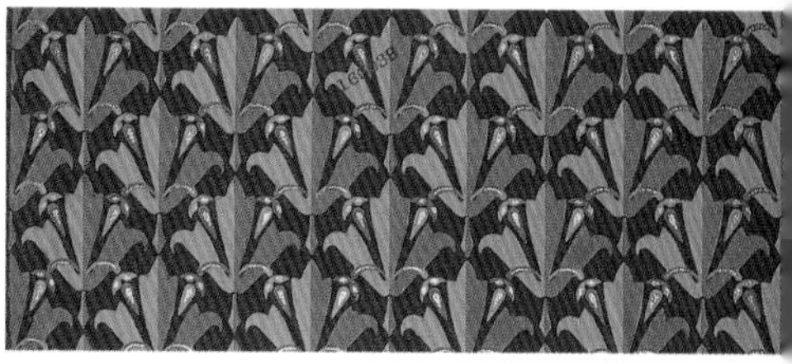

78. William Cooke & Sons. Wallpaper sample, 166038, 12 September 1863. Public Record Office.

79. James W. & C. Ward. Samples of woven silk on wool, 264315/6, 20 July 1872. Public Record Office.

80. James W. & C. Ward. Sample of woven silk on wool, February 1868. Public Record Office.

RIGHT 81. James W. & C. Ward. Sample of woven silk on wool, 264325, 7 February 1872. Public Record Office.

83. James W. & C. Ward. Sample of woven silk on wool, 260425, 20 July 1872. Public Record Office.

82. James W. & C. Ward. Samples of woven silk on wool, 260426, 260427, 7 February 1872. Public Record Office.

LEFT 84. James W. & C. Ward. Sample of woven silk on wool, 272193, 18 March 1873. Public Record Office.

RIGHT 85. James W. & C. Ward. Sample of woven silk damask showing different colourways, 268062, 21 November 1872. Public Record Office.

86. William Cooke & Sons. Wallpaper sample, no. 313419, bk. BT/43/101, 30 August 1877. Public Record Office.

LEFT 87. William Cooke & Sons. Wallpaper sample, no. 313428, bk. BT/43/101, 8 September 1877. Public Record Office.

89. William Cooke & Sons. Wallpaper sample, no. 313435, bk. BK/43/101, 8 September 1877. Public Record Office.

BELOW 88. William Cooke & Sons. Wallpaper sample, no. 313426, bk. BT/43/101, 8 September 1877. Public Record Office.

RIGHT 90. William Cooke & Sons. Wallpaper sample, no. 313426, bk. BT/43/101, 8 September 1877. Public Record Office.

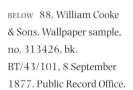

91.

91–95. William Cooke & Sons. Wallpaper samples.
(91) no. 338142, bk BT/43/103, 1 August 1879. (92) no. 338143,
bk BT/43/103, 1 August 1879. (93) 'bird and butterfly', no. 313425,
bk. BT/43/101, 8 September 1877. (94) no. 338144, bk BT/43/101,
1 August 1879. (95) no. 338141, bk BT/43/101, 1 August 1879.
All Public Record Office.

92.

93.

94.

RIGHT 95.

CHAPTER

4

Dresser and his Sources of Inspiration

JUDY RUDOE

In order that you acquire the power of perceiving art-merit as quickly as possible, you must study those works in which examples of bad taste are rarely met with, you must at first consider art-objects from India, Persia, China, and Japan, as well as examples of ancient art from Egypt and Greece.[1]

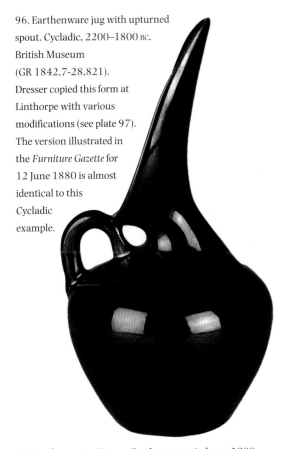

96. Earthenware jug with upturned spout. Cycladic, 2200–1800 BC. British Museum (GR 1842,7-28,821). Dresser copied this form at Linthorpe with various modifications (see plate 97). The version illustrated in the *Furniture Gazette* for 12 June 1880 is almost identical to this Cycladic example.

97. Linthorpe Art Pottery. Earthenware pitcher, *c*.1880, impressed signature, mark 'HT'. Private Collection.

These words, from the conclusion of Dresser's *Principles of Decorative Design* (1873), reveal in a nutshell his debt to the art of ancient and contemporary civilizations alike. If this is how the eager student is to cultivate good taste, he learns from a master who is steeped in the entire vocabulary of historic ornament. But lest the student should be misled Dresser adds a further proviso: in selecting modern (as opposed to ancient) works from the East, choose those that have not been produced under European influence. This means that they must pre-date contact with Western commerce. The art-works of Japan, he notes, have in the last 10 years deteriorated to a lamentable extent, precisely because they have been supplied to meet European demand. But such instances apart, the student may rely on the beauty of all works from China, Japan, Persia and India, nations where inharmonious colouring does not appear to be produced at all.

Dresser's emphasis on the necessity for knowledge of historic ornament runs through all his writing. The reader of *Studies in Design* (1876) is urged to 'study whatever has gone before; not with the view of becoming a copyist, but with the object of gaining knowledge, and of seeking out general truths and broad principles ... our works should be superior to those of our ancestors, inasmuch as we can look back upon a longer experience than they could.'[2] Dresser freely admits that when he sits down to design a pattern he draws on his scholarship of the past. He might decide that the pattern is to be Arabian, Chinese, Indian or Moresque in style. But, he continues, 'my success in the production of such a pattern depends largely on the extent to which I become, in feeling, for the time a Chinaman, or Arabian, or such as the case requires ... for it is only by understanding their faith and usages that I can comprehend the spirit of their ornament.' He goes on to say that one of the plates that follows, with Arabian border patterns, was produced under such feelings and circumstances (*Studies*, pl. XXIX).

Many other plates are described as Indian, Chinese, Moresque, Medieval or Gothic style.

This is not to say that all of Dresser's work has its origins in historic ornament. It does not, and he is careful to describe some of his designs either as 'new' or in a style 'peculiarly that of the author'. These have been included, he argues, to demonstrate how new ornament may have the dignity of the Egyptian, the grace of the Greek, the richness of the Arabian or the intricacy of plot of the Moorish, without succumbing to extremes and eccentricities.[3] To a modern eye, some of his designs are nothing if not eccentric, but others, such as Plate XXII of *Studies*, are remarkable for their vigour and originality.[4]

Principles of Decorative Design is the crucial text for understanding Dresser and his sources. The introductory chapter runs through the entire gamut of historic ornament, with directions where the best examples may be studied. So for Egyptian ornament, the student is directed to the British Museum, for Greek to the Greek Court at the Crystal Palace, for Celtic to Westwood's great work on illuminated manuscripts.[5] Later in the book, he singles out the Indian carpets and textiles at the Indian Museum in Whitehall, ancient ceramics and glass in the British Museum, Chinese cloisonné enamel at the South Kensington Museum, and so on. But there are some periods with which he has no sympathy at all:

> I enjoy the power and vigour of Egyptian ornament,
> the refinement of the Greek, the gorgeousness of the
> Alhambraic, the richness of the Persian and Indian,
> the quaintness of the Chinese and Japanese, the
> simple honesty and boldness of the Gothic; but with
> the coarse Assyrian, the haughty Roman, and the
> cold Renaissance, I have no kindred feeling – no
> sympathy. They strike notes which have no chords
> in my nature: hence from them I instinctively fly.[6]

The absence of Renaissance ornament in Dresser's work is rarely remarked upon and to say as frankly as this that he detests it goes right against contemporary taste. In speaking of Roman decoration, revived in the Renaissance, he writes: 'What can be worse than festoons of leafage, like so many sausages, painted upon a ceiling, with griffins, small framed pictures, impossible flowers ... all with fictitious light and shade'.[7] Raphael's frescoes in the Vatican, even the ceiling of the Sistine chapel, are criticized as false, because a room so decorated cannot attain the realization of repose. This leads us into another significant fact to emerge from a detailed reading of *Principles*. In the various categories of ornament that Dresser discusses – furniture, ceilings and walls, carpets, fabrics, hollow vessels, hardware and stained glass – the illustrations combine source material with designs of his own. Out of a total of 184 plates, 23 are described as 'original sketch', 'prepared by me', or 'my views', with a further 40 unattributed illustrations included as examples of good design, so the assumption here is that they are his or from his studio. But in the section on ceilings and walls, all the illustrations are his original designs. In contrast to the wild perspective and relief ornament of the Italians, he writes, the ideal ceiling decoration was a flat painted or stencilled pattern that repeated equally in all directions, in blue and white or cream. At this time, prior to his visit to Japan, he had found no models in historic ornament.[8] This was not the case with carpets, textiles, ceramics, glass and silverware.

Floors, like ceilings, are flat; they should not be made to look otherwise, Dresser tells us. His preference was for all-over patterns: these were the most common in India and Persia. For Dresser Indian and Persian carpets were the models of what carpets should be, as marvels of colour harmony and radiant bloom combined with a neutral general effect. He gave special praise to Indian silk rugs shown at the International Exhibition of 1862 and carpets from the Paris Exhibition of 1867. As for fabrics, the Indian Museum at Whitehall was once again the student's Mecca, while those students outside London had access to 'a large series of specimens of these cloths, deposited with the Chamber of Commerce in most of our manufacturing towns.'[9]

The next section discusses hollow vessels, divided into pottery, glass and silversmiths' work. Here Dresser gathers a panoply of historic shapes and decoration to illustrate his views on fitness for purpose. Egyptian lotus cups demonstrate the correct use of natural form, that is, drawn conventionally instead of imitatively. Greek water vessels stand pre-eminent in Dresser's eyes for grace of form. A Mexican vase, by contrast, represents 'quaintness', while painted jugs from Morocco are included as examples of decoration on tall vessels that 'will not suffer by perspective, for there is

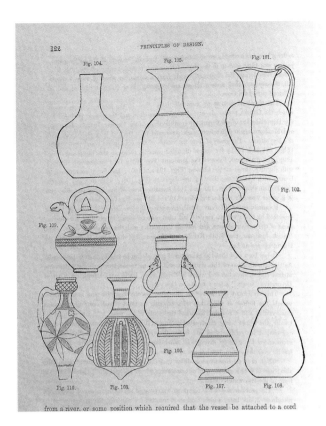

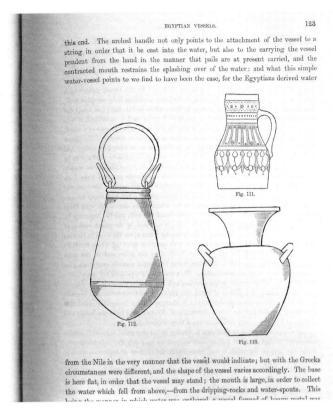

98. Historic shapes and decoration used by Dresser to demonstrate fitness for purpose in *Principles of Decorative Design* (1873). Top row: Chinese (left and centre) and Greek (right); centre: Chinese and Greek (left and right) and Japanese (centre, with two handles); bottom: Moroccan (left), Mexican (2nd left), Indian (right)

99. Clutha. Glass vase, *c*.1890. The curved spout is inspired by Persian glass rose-water sprinklers of the 17th and 18th centuries. Private Collection.

scarcely any portion of the ornament that can be seen otherwise than foreshortened' (above).[10] When it comes to glass, he favours plain simple shapes, despising the over-ornamentation of much contemporary Venetian glass. Roman glass is noted particularly for its soft and delicate tints, far more suitable for red wine than the strongly coloured glasses then fashionable.

Significantly, his own designs for ceramics and glass are absent. *Principles* was written long before his work for Clutha glass in the late 1880s, in which he combined soft tints with exotic shapes inspired by Persian seventeenth- and eighteenth-century rose-water sprinklers (right).[11] Nor was the Linthorpe Pottery yet in existence. But Dresser had been acting as art adviser to Minton since the early 1860s. Why did he not include any of his Minton designs? Perhaps he did not regard them as the way he wanted his ceramics to be. His role at Minton has always been surrounded with uncertainty. Minton, like any big firm at the time, tended to conceal their designers: none of the Minton pieces bears his signature on the base and most of the original artwork in the Minton archive is unsigned. This makes it difficult to know exactly what shapes or what patterns are his, and suggests

100. Minton's China Works. Blue and white glazed earthenware tile with flying cranes. *c.*1875, 20 × 20 cm (8 × 8 in). Cooper-Hewitt National Design Museum, New York.

that the factory exercised considerable control. This was unquestionably true for Dresser's Japanese-style frieze of flying cranes and waves. Two different designs survive in the Minton archive, both carefully drawn to show the foreshortened angles that fascinated Dresser. There is no doubt that they are by the same hand and since one of them, exceptionally, is signed, we can be sure that we are dealing here with Dresser's original artwork. The signed design has not been recorded on any Minton work. The unsigned design was used virtually unchanged on tiles, the ideal shape for a frieze (above).[12] In Japan, the crane is an emblem of longevity and occurs throughout Japanese art in landscape settings, whether in architectural ornament, textiles, lacquer or porcelain.[13] When Minton registered their own version of a design with flying cranes and waves, they re-arranged it in circular form as the border of a plate, which made nonsense of the subject.[14] Even when applied to a more suitable shape such as a cylindrical jardinière, the design bears little relation to Dresser's hand: the foreshortening of the cranes has been misunderstood and they seem to have been plucked from some other pattern book and placed in a random repetitive sequence.[15] Perhaps such mis-uses of his designs influenced his later insistence on the appearance of his signature.

Dresser's final category of hollow vessels deals with silversmiths' work.[16] Here the student should study the beautiful 'Arabian' vessels in the South Kensington Museum, hand-raised with the hammer and chased with intricate detail. He illustrates a group of these Islamic brass vessels, noting that

101. Detail of the end papers from *The Preacher* by Owen Jones (1849). These dense fan-shaped scrolls are echoed in Dresser's frontispiece design, 'Knowledge is Power' for *The Art of Decorative Design* (see frontispiece).

'facsimiles of these lovely works, in the form of electrotype copies, have been prepared by Messrs. Elkington & Co. ... and these are procurable at small cost. For purposes of study these copies are of almost equal value with the originals.' So much so that he recommends the copies as far more suitable for the adornment of a sideboard than 'the meretricious electroplate which we often see in our shop-windows'.[17] According to Dresser the problem with modern European silversmiths was that they made pictorial works, an error that the Arabians, Indian and Japanese never perpetrated. He greatly admired Japanese inlay work, as well as Indian *bidri* ware, a black metal alloy inlaid with silver.[18] The inlaid copper tray by Benham & Froud with coloured overlays echoes work of this kind (plate 237).

Of all the ways of applying colour to metal,

Dresser saw enamelling as the most beautiful, above all, the opaque Chinese and Japanese cloisonné enamels, 'now so skilfully produced by Barbedien and Christophle'. Barbédienne's imitations were in fact not cloisonné at all, but champlevé (a type of enamel in which the enamel is laid into troughs engraved into metal; in cloisonné, the enamel is laid into a cell-work of applied metal strips). Dresser's passion for Chinese cloisonné had a huge impact in a general sense on his own bold colour palette, and, more specifically, on the number and range of imitation cloisonné pieces produced by Minton. These are frequently attributed to Dresser and while some of them may be, his own writing questions such an assumption. In his paper on the influence of Eastern art, which is entirely based on objects at the Vienna Exhibition of 1873, he writes: 'Minton's vases are copies of the cloisonné enamels of China, or of old Persian works'. He then compares them with those by Worcester: 'because the productions in ivory porcelain by the Worcester Works are further removed in character from the examples studied, while they yet produce a like amount of beauty with them, I think them better than those of Minton's works which are derived from the cloisonné examples.'[19] Would he have written like this of works that he had designed? Often the patterns were taken straight from Owen Jones's *Chinese Ornament*, published in 1867.[20] This is one of many instances where Dresser must have told the factory artists what to look at.

Indeed Owen Jones's earlier publication, the *Grammar of Ornament* (1856), is cited throughout *Principles* as an important source for historic ornament. It is well known that Dresser contributed the final botanical plate to this seminal work. But there was another work by Owen Jones that is completely forgotten today: much of Dresser's 'medieval' or 'Gothic' ornament was inspired not by medieval models but by *The Preacher* (1849). Dresser refers to it in *The Art of Decorative Design* (1862) and reproduces one of the vignettes, but it is a rare book and Dresser's use of it has been overlooked. Inside carved wood covers the Book of Ecclesiastes is reproduced in the manner of a Gothic illuminated manuscript with delicate penwork motifs, coloured and gilded initials, and a startling all-over design in red and blue for the end papers (plate 101). One only has to compare these with the plate most frequently reproduced from *The Art of Decorative Design*, a lozenge with the words 'Knowledge is Power', and the connection is evident (frontispiece).[21] The linear tendrils, fleshy leaves and dense fan-shaped scrolls of Jones's Gothic can be seen throughout Dresser's work, for example in his design for stained glass in *Principles*, fig. 184. For medieval ornament Dresser was also indebted to A.W.N. Pugin. Dresser's 'powderings', the name he gives to simple formalized motifs placed at regular intervals over a plain ground, owe much to Pugin's *Floriated Ornament* of 1849.[22]

One aspect of Dresser's approach to historic ornament that tends to be overshadowed by the lack of information about his career and the problems of attribution is his classification of ornament 'by affinities resulting from equality in respect to the embodiment of mental power'. In *The Art of Decorative Design* he explains this as follows: natural treatment embodies the smallest amount of mental power, as it is purely imitative, while ideal ornament is the highest branch of decorative art. Conventionalized plants form a middle stage as nature in its purest or typical form, or a mental idea of the perfect plant. So in ascending order he has naturalistic ornament, then conventionalized nature and finally ideal form. By such a canon he places the Alhambra much higher than the Vatican as a decorative scheme.[23] Greek, Moorish, much of Indian, medieval and Japanese come in the most exalted grade; much of Egyptian and Chinese in the second class, later Gothic in the third, with Pompeiian and 'our own modern floral patterns' last. No wonder then that his work of the 1860s and up to the mid-1870s is dominated by flat pattern, demonstrated by his concentration on carpet and wallpaper design at this time, or that *Studies in Design* contains so many plates in the Arabian, Moresque and Gothic styles.

Only from the late 1870s, after his visit to Japan in 1877 and under the influence of archaeological discoveries and changing tastes in collecting material from different cultures, does the full range of his creative genius become apparent. The Dresser of the 1860s is much more a product of his time than the Dresser of the 1880s. His Egyptian-style terracotta flask for Wedgwood of around 1867 (plate 102) fits into the Egyptomania following the opening of the Suez Canal in that year. It is based

on an Egyptian blue faience flask in the British Museum to which Dresser has added feet and a winged motif on the body (right).[24] He owned examples of Egyptian pottery himself: included in the sale of his collection held after his death were 'two water bottles of Egyptian red earth'.[25] His designs for carpets, textiles and wallpaper grow out of his theories of ornamental art and his admiration for oriental and North African textiles, as we have seen. His designs in cast iron for Coalbrookdale of the late 1860s, startling though they are, belong to a tradition of hardware in the medieval style, as Dresser himself notes in *Principles*, with his praise for the ecclesiastical work of Hardman and Skidmore at the 1862 Exhibition. Skidmore's Hereford Cathedral screen is described as 'one of the finest examples ... for the ease with which iron may be treated ... rolled into a volute or hammered

102. Wedgwood. Egyptian-style terracotta flask, *c*.1867. The Birkenhead Collection. Dresser was inspired by an Egyptian flask in the British Museum, see plate 103.

103. Egyptian blue faience New Year flask with incised decoration, *c.* 650–600 BC, from the 'Isis tomb' at Vulci, southern Italy. British Museum: GR 1850,2-27,58.

out into stems and leaves' (plate 263).[26] The Hereford screen was all hand-made. Dresser's real innovation here is in creating designs for cast ironwork for multiple production and for secular, not ecclesiastical use (see plate 31). The colossal Minton vase of the late 1860s, which may or may not be by Dresser, also belongs here, in its dense mixture of medieval and Byzantine fleshy leaf ornament (see plate 32).

But none of this prepares us for what follows from the late 1870s. Dresser's visit to Japan in 1876–7 is discussed elsewhere. Suffice it to say here that he knew a great deal about Japanese art before this date. In his paper on the art manufactures of Japan in 1878, he freely acknowledged that he owed his love of Japanese art to Sir Rutherford Alcock, and that he subsequently acquired many of the objects brought from Japan by Alcock

for the 1862 Exhibition. To these items he had added constantly, 'till my house is now rather a museum than a comfortable abode for civilised beings, at least, so says my wife.'[27] The catalogue of his collection sold after his death contains more works from Japan than from any other culture.[28] The Vienna Exhibition of 1873 had a huge influence on his appreciation of Japanese art; in his 1874 paper on 'Eastern art and its influence' he described the Japanese works of art in detail. Japanese kettles and fabrics are singled out for special attention; he must have purchased a number of pieces himself, for he had with him actual examples to show his audience at the Society of Arts. One of these was a Japanese dress, 'the finest piece of fabric at the exhibition', with flowers and butterflies treated as flat ornament.[29] At this time the South Kensington Museum had acquired little from Japan. The best group of Japanese ceramics then available in London went on show at the Bethnal Green Museum in 1872: this was the private collection of Far Eastern ceramics formed by A.W. Franks of the British Museum. But by the mid-1870s the South Kensington Museum's holdings in different media had increased significantly, with purchases from Siegfried Bing in Paris from 1875 onwards and a huge group from the Philadelphia Exhibition of 1876.[30]

Dresser saw the Philadelphia Exhibition en route to Japan. His tour of the entire country encompassed visits to manufactories, craftsmen and collections. He saw the respect with which Japanese art objects were treated and understood for the first time the different status of the artist in Japan; this must have affected his decision to sign much of his later work, whether metalwork by Elkingtons, the Birmingham and Sheffield firms and Perry & Son, or Linthorpe and Ault pottery, and Clutha glass. Pieces with Dresser's facsimile signature have become synonymous with his name, but it cannot be over-emphasized that such a practice was extremely unusual at the time.[31]

On his return from Japan, he created his famously 'modern' electroplated silver designs for Hukin & Heath and Dixon & Sons. There are few precise antecedents, though Dresser's picnic set for Hukin & Heath in its compact front-opening case must have been conceived with Japanese travelling tea sets in mind.[32] Recent writing on Dresser has tended to explain the simplicity and purity of the metalwork forms as a consequence of his visit to Japan, but this is only partly true. Firstly, the Japanese themselves were appealing to a very different taste for highly elaborate ornamentation.[33] Secondly, Dresser was also concerned to make his forms easy to produce, and in this he was not always successful. The series of prototype teapots for Dixon never went into production, not because the shapes were too avant-garde, but because they were too expensive to make (see plates 3–6). The spherical or conical forms could be spun, the handles and feet cast. But the unusually-shaped prototypes involved in many instances flat sheet metal, cut and assembled by hand. Dixon & Sons' recently re-discovered costing book reveals that the rectangular teapot now in the British Museum was the most expensive of all, in terms of the amount of sheet metal and the labour time required.[34] This is the only prototype that has a direct source of inspiration. It is based on Chinese models, the most likely being Yixing stoneware teapots, which occur in an extraordinary variety of shapes from the eighteenth century onwards.[35] Dresser may also have seen porcelain examples of the same rectangular shape. Other electroplate prototype teapots show Yixing elements: the hemispherical teapot (plate 200) has a tripartite handle, attached at the front with a double arm on each side of the body; there are close parallels in Yixing forms, set vertically.[36] A number of the production designs, by contrast, have clear antecedents, such as Greek amphorae (plate 180) or drinking vessels ('Rhytons').

By the early 1880s Dresser was creating designs in base metal, often painted to imitate Japanese lacquer, for Perry & Son. The most astonishing of these was a candlestick formed of two hemispheres with a central cylindrical stem (plate 245), an idea perhaps derived from Japanese lacquered wood drums, although the stems are much longer.[37] The Benham & Froud ovoid jardinière, formed of riveted horizontal copper, brass and white metal (right), has a clear relationship to the pair of Japanese bronze vases purchased by the South Kensington Museum from Londos & Co. in 1878 (plate 105). The body of each vase is formed of horizontal riveted bands of metal in red, yellow, green and white patinated bronze.[38] In his book on Japan, Dresser had written, 'No people but the Japanese have understood the value of colour in metal composi-

tions. We make steel fenders, coal scuttles, tin kettles, and iron grates; but we have never fully realised the fact that by producing metal alloys, and combining these with pure metals, a world of colour is open to us.'[39] A few pages earlier he had illustrated a bronze candlestick from Hiroshima, of tall conical shape with pierced floral decoration.[40] He owned two of them, both purchased by the V&A from the 1904 sale of his collection (see plate 37).[41] He must have obtained them long before his trip to Japan for an identical design, adapted to ceramics, is to be found in the Minton archive (see plate 38). Perhaps they came from the 1862 Exhibition. Metal versions made by Chubb for the Art Furnishers' Alliance have been recorded in contemporary photographs, but no examples have so far come to light.[42]

The Linthorpe pottery designs are altogether different for it is here that Dresser's sources of inspiration are at their most varied. Dresser was art director from 1879 until 1882 and had total control. Chinese and Japanese shapes include the

104. Benham & Froud. Jardinière made of riveted bands of different metals, c.1880. The Birkenhead Collection.

took a whole range of ideas, such as crumpled rims or incised decoration of parallel vertical wavy lines (plate 220).[45] The lobed vessels produced both at Linthorpe and Ault are loosely based on Chinese ceramics, while the Ault hemispherical vases are certainly inspired by Chinese Kangxi beehive water-pots (plate 283).[46]

In the 1860s Dresser looked at Classical Greek forms. He continued to do so in his pitchers with high square handles, cut-off spouts and narrow necks (plate 231), based on Greek wine vessels from southern Italy with reel-shaped bodies;

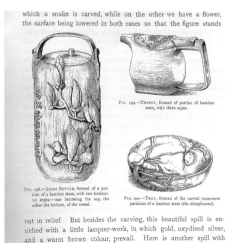

which a snake is carved, while on the other we have a flower, the surface being lowered in both cases so that the figure stands

FIG. 198.—SACHI BOTTLE, formed of a portion of a bamboo stem, with two horizontal septa—one becoming the top, the other the bottom, of the vessel.

FIG. 199.—TEAPOT, formed of portion of bamboo stem, with three septa.

FIG. 200.—TRAY, formed of the carved transverse partition of a bamboo stem (the *dissépiment*).

out in relief. But besides the carving, this beautiful spill is enriched with a little lacquer-work, in which gold, oxydised silver, and a warm brown colour prevail. Here is another spill with

105. Japanese bronze vase, the body with applied riveted bands of metal patinated in different colours, 19th century. V&A: 120–1878. Purchased from Londos & Co. for the South Kensington Museum in 1878.

double-gourd vases that he had praised in *Principles* but had not yet created himself (see plate 234), as well as shapes inspired by Japanese bronzes or lacquered bamboo carvings (right). The bamboo dish copied here was acquired by Dresser in Japan and illustrated in his account of his journey.[43] The tall Linthorpe vase in the form of an elongated double gourd (plate 34) is based either on the Japanese bronze vase acquired by the South Kensington Museum at the sale of Siegfried Bing's Japanese objects in Paris in 1875, or on a similar vase of this type (plate 35).[44] And from Japanese ceramics he

106. Linthorpe pottery dish, 1879–82. Private Collection. This dish is a direct copy of a carved and lacquered bamboo dish acquired by Dresser in Japan in 1877.

107. Illustration from Dresser's *Japan, its architecture, art and art manufactures* (1882). Michael Whiteway.

108. Bronze Age earthenware beaker vase excavated at Goodmanham, Yorkshire by Canon Greenwell and acquired by the British Museum in 1879. Illustration from Greenwell's *British Barrows* (1877).

LINTHORPE ART POTTERY Manufactured by — JOHN HARRISON.— SOLE AGENTS — Dresser & Holme, FARRINGDON ROAD, LONDON.

Dresser has cut away the body leaving just the upper part of the vessel. He was now looking also at Minoan and Cycladic pottery. The jug with upward-pointing spout (plate 97) is based on early Greek Cycladic jugs; one very close example entered the British Museum in 1842 (plate 96).[47] He surely saw them then but it was not until the establishment of Linthorpe that he was able to experiment with shapes such as this; he made several versions of it. The version shown in a group of Linthorpe pots illustrated in the *Furniture Gazette* for 12 June 1880 is identical to the Cycladic jug in plate 96. The jugs with slanting angled spouts are also based on Minoan pottery shapes (plate 191). Others take elements from Roman glass, such as the angled handles ending in undulating trails as they join the body (plate 222).[48] Dresser was not alone in copying early Mediterranean wares: Doulton, for example, copied Cypriot vases in 1879, soon after they had entered the British Museum.

But few if any manufacturers had at that time drawn inspiration from the early cultures of Britain. The middle years of the nineteenth century saw a dramatic increase in the systematic excavation of Prehistoric and Bronze Age barrows. Yorkshire, where Linthorpe was situated, yielded vast amounts of material and Dresser must have been

109. Detail from an illustration of Linthorpe pottery from the *Furniture Gazette* (5 June 1880). NAL. This vase with a pattern of incised triangles is inspired by Bronze Age pottery, see plate 108.

aware of the rich discoveries made by antiquarians active in this county such as John Mortimer and Canon William Greenwell, both of whom published reports of their finds. Excavations quickly became events of local interest and parties went off to see the diggers on Sunday afternoons. Greenwell's *British Barrows* came out in 1877, and his collection was purchased by the British Museum in 1879, just as Dresser was creating his Linthorpe pots. Bronze Age beaker pots, with their simple bands of horizontal incised decoration, conformed perfectly to Dresser's ideals. The rich glossy glazes of his Linthorpe pots, however, disguised the incised decoration and made them look very different from unglazed red earthenware beaker pots. Only when line drawings of Linthorpe pots in the *Furniture Gazette* are compared with Bronze Age pots is the derivation obvious. Among the few complete pots illustrated by Greenwell in 1877 is one from Goodmanham with a double row of zigzags; there is little doubt that Dresser copied this very pot at Linthorpe (plates 108–9).[49] Even more unusual were his copies of Anglo-Saxon cremation urns; no other nineteenth-century designer or manufacturer seems to have taken any interest in these dark-bodied bossed and incised vessels (below). Examples had entered the British Museum by the early nineteenth century, but as further excavations took place, the displays at the Museum were expanded and a number of publications followed. One of the finest books, published in 1852 with beautiful colour lithographs, illustrated several pots discovered by the antiquarian R.C. Neville, later Lord Braybrooke, in a Saxon cemetery in Cambridgeshire.[50]

If his Bronze Age and Anglo-Saxon shapes were unusual, Dresser's Pre-Columbian Peruvian bridge-spouted vessels broke totally new ground and went right against the prevailing Aesthetic movement taste for the sophisticated world of Islam and the Far East. No one at that time had made copies of what were then regarded as primitive wares. Dresser ignores the painted decoration on the Peruvian pots, covering his shapes instead with the mottled oriental-style glazes that were a speciality of Linthorpe and Ault. In this way they became 'Aesthetic movement' pots despite their extraordinary shapes. The most characteristic have a flat handle forming a bridge between two spouts, or an arched handle from which issues a single vertical spout (plate 233). Dresser sometimes gives the arched handle an angled form that is not found in Peruvian

110. Group of Anglo-Saxon cremation urns, 5th century AD. Line-drawing from J.M. Kemble. *Horae Ferales* (1863), pl. XXX.

111. Detail from an illustration of Linthorpe pottery from the *Furniture Gazette* (1 May 1880). NAL. The pot at the far right of the back row is based on Anglo-Saxon cremation urns, see plate 110.

112. Linthorpe pottery vessel with six onion-shaped chambers. Private Collection. The idea for this shape may have come from a Peruvian pot with onion-shaped chambers in the British Museum, see plate 113.

Even more astonishing than the Peruvian shapes was the ash-tray in the form of a spread-eagled male figure.[55] This is based on a Fiji priest's ritual drinking vessel of carved wood; an example was acquired by the British Museum in 1842, which Dresser would certainly have known (plate 114).[56] The head, however, bears no relation to the heads of Fiji dishes; its inspiration is oriental and relates closely to some of the Japanese earthenware figures illustrated by Audsley & Bowes.[57] The Linthorpe ash-tray shown in plate 114 is the only work by Dresser to have entered the British Museum in the nineteenth century; it was bequeathed in 1897 by A.W. Franks. Franks was a key figure at the British Museum: serving for nearly half a century from 1851 to 1896, he was responsible not only for the

pots; nevertheless the derivation is clear. Shapes such as these are immediately obvious as copies of Peruvian vessels; there are a number of other Linthorpe shapes, however, that have not previously been matched with Peruvian originals. One of these is a vase with scalloped ornament at each side and a central face mask and bands of horizontal incised decoration (plate 216). This is a direct copy of a pre-Columbian Peruvian form.[51] The second example is one of Dresser's most extraordinary shapes: a low vessel with six onion-shaped chambers surrounding a central spout (above); here Dresser has almost certainly looked at a Chimu vessel with multiple chambers and a spout in the form of a human figure (right). This vessel belonged to Sir Hans Sloane, whose collection became the foundation of the British Museum in 1753.[52] It will be evident by now that Dresser knew the British Museum collections intimately. Peruvian pots were displayed at the British Museum from at least the 1850s and he may have needed no other impetus.[53] That said, he would also have seen them at the Philadelphia Exhibition of 1876[54] and he probably knew contemporary publications in which they were illustrated, such as E. George Squier's *Peru: Incidents of Travel and Exploration in the Land of the Incas* (New York, 1877).

The Ethnographic collections at the British Museum were a rich hunting ground for Dresser.

113. Chimu pottery vessel from Peru with multiple chambers. British Museum (Sloane Collection, Sl.728). This vessel, with four onion-shaped chambers, may have inspired the Linthorpe vase shown in plate 112.

Early British, Post-Roman, medieval and later collections, which he assembled and displayed, but also for ceramics and Ethnography. Sadly, he is as elusive as Dresser; they must have known each other yet no records survive to prove that they did. With their omnivorous interests in the art and artefacts of ancient and modern societies, they had much in common. For all we know, Dresser may have been bidding alongside Franks at the sale in 1872 of the Belcher collection of Pacific artefacts. The Canadian naval officer and scientist, Sir Edward Belcher (1799–1877), acquired his collection during his command on the *Sulphur*, a Pacific surveying voyage of 1836–42; he presented a significant group of items to the British Museum on his return, among which was the Fiji oil dish. Franks bought extensively at the 1872 sale so there is no doubt that he had a strong interest in Pacific material.[58] Whether he purchased the Linthorpe ash-tray or whether it was a gift from Dresser is not recorded. Suffice it to say that few contemporary pieces of Western applied art entered the British Museum at this time; Franks no doubt included it in his bequest as an interesting study piece that copied an object in the British Museum, but it took the best part of a century for it to be appreciated once again.

This brief survey has been highly selective, but if it has succeeded in drawing together the different strands of Dresser's early thoughts on historic ornament and the way in which he put those thoughts into practice in later years, it will have served its purpose. Dresser, the master of surface ornament in his early career, developed a skill in re-interpreting the art of other cultures and adapting it to industrial manufactures that has perhaps never been bettered. In his own words:

> we must not be copyists, or merely servile imitators; on the contrary, from the fullness of our knowledge we must seek to produce what is new, and what is accordant with the spirit of the times in which we live; but what we do produce must reveal our knowledge of the ornament of past ages.[59]

114. Linthorpe pottery ash-tray together with the carved wood ritual drinking vessel from Fiji that inspired it. British Museum (Linthorpe dish: OA 10711; Fiji dish: Ethno 1842.12-10.147).

During this period, as Dresser embarked on his career of commercial designer, he was very active, employed by a wide range of leading manufacturers. His work was shown by them in international exhibitions from 1862, and in 1871 he exhibited for the first time under his own name, at the South Kensington International Exhibition in London. Apart from his long and prolific connection with the wallpaper and textile trades (see chapter 3), he was designing furniture, carpets (for Jackson & Graham of London, Brinton & Lewis of Kidderminster and John Crossley of Halifax), ceramics, cast ironwork and copper and brass wares. Otherwise, his principal employers seem to have been Minton's, the Coalbrookdale iron foundry and, probably, Elkington & Co. Drawings by Dresser are in the archive of the Worcester Porcelain factory (right), although pieces made from them have not yet come to light. Effectively at this stage he was selling his designs or expertise as an art advisor, and he had little control over the use of his work. This was particularly the case in firms with a talented and successful art director of their own, such as Minton (Léon Arnoux) and Wedgwood (Emile Lessore). Only later was he to assume control of the design and manufacturing process, which he had to relinquish after the failure of the Art Furnishers' Alliance, to return to his former practice of selling designs from his studio.

115–6. Designs by Dresser for Royal Worcester Porcelain Co. Photographs courtesy of the Royal Worcester Porcelain Co .

115.

116.

Dresser and Manufacturers
1860–1876

MINTON STOKE-ON-TRENT

Founded in 1793 and commenced production in 1796 of blue-and-white transfer-printed wares, notably the perennially successful 'Willow' pattern, Minton's was transformed under the inspired direction of Herbert Minton, the founder's son, who took over in 1836. He expanded the production into new ranges and techniques, including majolica wares, Parian 'statuary' ware, industrially produced encaustic tiles and plates, and printed pottery using a patent lithographic process. He employed professional artists and designers, including refugees from revolutionary Europe. He collaborated with Pugin at the Palace of Westminster and on the Mediaeval Court at the 1851 Great Exhibition, and with Henry Cole on his 'Felix Summerly' scheme. When he died in 1858 he was succeeded by Colin Minton Campbell, his nephew, and Michael Daintry Hollins. A dispute resulted in Campbell and Hollins going their separate ways in 1868, with Campbell assuming responsibility for the chinaware and decorative tile production (Minton & Co.), and Hollins for the commercial tile production (Minton Hollins & Co.). The Minton Art Pottery studio in Kensington was established in 1871, under the direction of W.S. Coleman, one of the firm's most successful decorators. Dresser's connection with the firm lasted from around 1860 until the 1880s. He designed intricately decorated ceramics with lavish use of gold for Minton's displays at the 1862 London International Exhibition and the 1867 Paris exhibition. The firm was represented at all major international exhibitions in the nineteenth century. Other designs were produced under Dresser's supervision by his studio. He also acted as an art advisor, directing their attention to motifs and shapes from Chinese and Japanese cloisonné, lacquer, bronzes and jades as well as Islamic metalwares and pottery. Both Minton and the Worcester Royal Porcelain Co., under R.W. Binns, established large study collections, particularly rich in Japanese wares, to inspire their in-house designers.

117. Drawing for the U-shaped vase no. 2695. Minton Museum and Archives.

118. U-shaped porcelain vase designed by Dresser. Joseph Holtzman Collection, New York.

119. Small porcelain vase decorated in gold and enamelled colours on mat brown body, date code for 1866. Carnegie Institute, Pittsburgh. Designed for the Paris Exposition Universelle, 1867.

ABOVE 120. Porcelain vase with stylized lotus decoration. The Birkenhead Collection. Dresser gives a diagram of lotus petals for the decoration of ceramics in his *Principles of Decorative Design* (1873), fig. 118.

LEFT 121. Porcelain spillvase and moonflask with a spread-winged bird motif, *c.*1867. The Birkenhead Collection. The design for the moonflask, no. 1303, is in the Minton archives, in sequence with the small vase, plate 119, above.

RIGHT 122. Porcelain vase with chinoiserie and Japanese cloisonné-style decoration. Joseph Holtzman Collection, New York.

123. Design by Dresser for the 'butterfly' jardinière, 1867. Minton Museum and Archives.

124. Porcelain jardinière with butterfly motifs, c.1870. Private Collection.

RIGHT 125. Cylindrical porcelain vase with abstract linear decoration on gold designed by Dresser, see *Studies in Design* (1874–6), pl. 19. Joseph Holtzman Collection, New York.

127. Long-necked porcelain vase with silvered decoration. Joseph Holtzman Collection, New York.

126. Two porcelain vases based on Japanese bronze shapes with motifs of Japanese badges or 'mons'. Joseph Holtzman Collection, New York.

128. Small porcelain vase, designed by Dresser, with a band of flowered diaper decoration in the Japanese style, related to a drawing in the Minton archive. Joseph Holtzman Collection, New York.

ABOVE 129. Blue and gold wide-necked porcelain vase, related to a drawing in the Minton archive. The Birkenhead Collection.

ABOVE RIGHT 130. Three-legged porcelain vase with bands of pink and diapered decoration, designed by Dresser. Joseph Holtzman Collection, New York. There is a drawing for this shape in the Minton archive. Dresser repeated the idea for a Linthorpe three-legged vase (plate 230).

131. Two circular porcelain vases with chinoiserie decoration. Joseph Holtzman Collection, New York.

OPPOSITE 132. Two square-necked porcelain
vases with cloisonné-style decoration.
Joseph Holtzman Collection, New York.

133. (a) Geometric pottery tile, designed
by Dresser and illustrated in *Studies in Design*,
(1874–6), marked Minton, *c.*1875. Harry
Lyons. (b) Butterfly pottery tile, registered
design, 1870. Stuart Durant. (c) Stylized flower
pottery tile, marked Minton Hollins, *c.*1870.
David Bonsall, Image Bank Ltd.

134. Two Japanese-style
porcelain 'insect' vases,
*c.*1870. Joseph Holtzman
Collection, New York.

135. Porcelain dish,
gold border with flying
cranes, single crane
centre. Joseph Holtzman
Collection, New York.

WEDGWOOD STOKE-ON-TRENT

Josiah Wedgwood, the famous potter, was one of the leading manufacturers of the Industrial Revolution. Like Minton, the firm was also involved with Cole's 'Summerly' venture. By the time of Dresser's brief connection (1866–8) with this famous and long-established firm (founded 1759), it was in the hands of Godfrey Wedgwood, the founder's great-grandson who was also a nephew by marriage of Charles Darwin. Recognizing the importance of the Art movement to the ceramic industry, he was determined to modernize the firm, and, like Minton, sought expertise and artistic inspiration from France. Emile Lessore, a painter who had already worked at Sèvres and Minton's, was the firm's art director from 1860. Wedgwood showed works at the

1851 exhibition and subsequent international exhibitions. Following Minton's, they were experimenting with Parian and majolica wares and employing professional designers – for example Walter Crane, at the same time as Dresser – in order to compete in the immensely popular and profitable Victorian market for painted decorative wares. Dresser's ideas for Wedgwood were highly innovative, introducing new shapes and abstract organic patterns. A surviving estimate book for 1866–8 shows the range of designs he made for the firm, which were used on tablewares, toilet wares, majolica and ground-laid wares, right up until the close of the century. Dresser's designs were included in Wedgwood's displays in Paris in 1867 and London in 1871.

136. Ceramic jardinière with dolphin handles
and Egyptian winged motif. Drawings for the vase and for
the winged motif are in the Wedgwood Archive, Barlaston,
Staffordshire. Nicholas Boston.

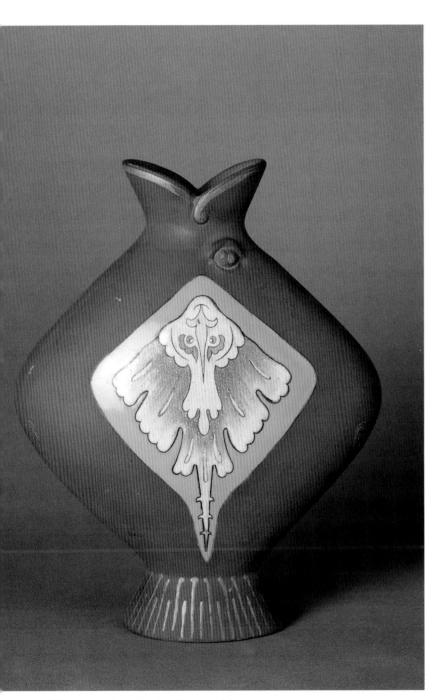

137. Cream-body unglazed earthenware fish vase,
c.1867. The drawing for the sting-ray motif
is in the Wedgwood Archive, Barlaston, Staffordshire .
Joseph Holtzman Collection, New York.

138. Fish-shaped unglazed earthenware vase,
mat brown body with an enamelled fish
on a gold ground, c.1867. The Birkenhead Collection.

WATCOMBE TORQUAY

G.J. Allen, the founder of the Watcombe Terra-Cotta Clay Co., discovered the local red clay unique to this part of south Devon when building Watcombe House and set up his art pottery venture there in 1867. The evidence for Dresser's connection with the pottery is entirely circumstantial, but overwhelming. Not only was terracotta one of his favourite materials at this point in his career, but the shapes are similar to those used in other media throughout his design practice. Plain terracotta and pieces decorated with gilding and a distinctive turquoise-blue enamel as well as glazed black-and-brown vessels with stylized flower and leaf ornament, in shapes bearing the unmistakeable stamp of his work were produced between 1869 and 1873.

140. Terracotta jug with turquoise enamel and gold rim. Private Collection.

139. Terracotta jug with silver lid and rim, marked Watcombe, registered 1872. Private Collection.

OPPOSITE 141. Copper pitcher with white metal bands, signed on the base with indelible pencil, maker unknown. Documentary piece to support the evidence for Dresser having designed for the Watcombe Pottery. The Birkenhead Collection.

142. Terracotta plate enamelled with
stylized flowers and leaves, *c.*1872.
The Birkenhead Collection.

143. Blue-glazed ceramic
vase with two necks and
a butterfly. The Andrew
McIntosh Patrick Collection.

COALBROOKDALE SHROPSHIRE

Ironbridge Gorge in Shropshire is regarded as the birthplace of the Industrial Revolution and the Coalbrookdale iron foundry was one of the most important of the pioneering initiatives, which resulted in Britain's leading position in the industrialized world. The firm was at a low ebb in the first quarter of the nineteenth century, and in 1830 the then owners, Abraham Darby IV and his brother Alfred, took the decision to move into ornamental domestic furnishings in cast iron. John Bell, the sculptor and one of the artists involved with Henry Cole's 'Summerly' venture, was acclaimed for his contribution to the Coalbrookdale display at the Great Exhibition in 1851. The Coalbrookdale Co. was represented at most of the major international exhibitions. Dresser believed that it was possible to bring some of the qualities of wrought-ironwork into the cheaper production of cast iron. He was designing for the firm from 1867, a series of distinctive hallstands as well as garden seats and umbrella stands, until the 1880s.

144. Hallstand, cast iron, *c.*1867. The Birkenhead Collection.

145. Hallstand, cast iron. Cooper-Hewitt
National Design Museum , New York.

146. Garden bench, cast iron and wood,
*c.*1870. The Birkenhead Collection.

147. Garden chair, 'Lily' pattern in cast iron
and wood, *c.*1870. The Birkenhead Collection.

148. Chair, cast iron with wooden seat, marked 'Coalbrookdale'
with the cypher for 8 March 1870. The Birkenhead Collection.

149–50. Hallstands, cast iron, *c.*1870. The Birkenhead Collection.

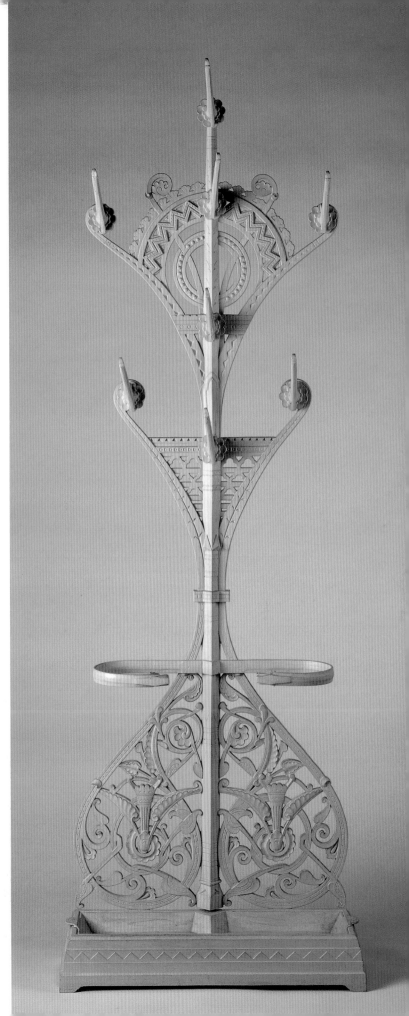

CHAPTER

5

152. Detail of label from tin candlestick
(plate 158).

151. Wallpaper, marked on the margin
'Dresser inv'. Cooper-Hewitt, National Design
Museum, 1941-17-1. Donated by Wilmer
Moore in 1941. This piece was one of a lot that
the Moore's purchased from an antique dealer
in Pennsylvania. The dealer said he purchased
them from a very old store. The frieze was used
in the office of William M. Singerley of the
Philadelphia Record (built 1880), see: *Artistic
Houses*, New York, 1883–4, vol. I, p. 173.
This wallpaper is shown in combination with
the Lincrusta filling made by Frank Walton,
(see p. 6) in an illustration to the *Journal of
Decorative Art*, March, 1884, p. 476. The filling
(Cooper-Hewitt, National Design Museum,
1937-57-3) was donated to the Cooper-Hewitt
in 1937 by John D. Rockefeller, Jr. The sample
was removed from his father's house at 4 West
54th Street in New York City.

Dresser in
the United States[1]

DAVID A. TAYLOR

In the autumn of 1876, the 42-year-old Christopher Dresser prepared to embark on the most important journey of his life. On 5 October he put his affairs in order by signing his last will and testament[2] and, on the next day, sailed out of Liverpool, bound for New York City aboard the Cunard steamship *Russia*.[3] The journey would take him around the world,[4] but his principal destination was Japan, the exotic land whose talented craftsmen produced the superb ceramics, metalwork, fabrics, furniture and other art manufactures he had deeply admired and avidly collected for many years. Visiting Japan would fulfil the 'greatest desire of my life',[5] Dresser remarked.

Dresser, characteristically energetic and enterprising, had several objectives for his trip. He would present a collection of British art manufactures to Japan's Imperial Museum, acquire representative collections of Japanese art objects for the British firm of Londos & Co. and the American firm of Tiffany & Co., and conduct an extensive field study of Japanese architecture and decorative art and write a report about it. These were Dresser's primary objectives, but he had others as well, including some he would pursue in the United States where, in his words, he 'tarried' for a 'short time'.[6] Although Dresser's stay in the United States was comparatively brief and his activities there were greatly overshadowed by what he accomplished in Japan, an examination of the nine weeks he spent in the country illuminates several aspects of his business practices, social connections, and personal character, as well as the impact he had on Americans during the period of his visit and later on.

Dresser arrived in New York aboard the *Russia* on 20 October 1876.[7] In an article about him published in the *New York Times* the following year, he is described as 'a full-grown Cockney—black of beard and bright of eye and who would talk a man into a state which American ingenuity illustrated some time ago by a skeleton in a deal box; but his chat is charming.'[8] In other words, Dresser, though charming, was so loquacious, the writer joked, he could talk a man to death. Although this is one of the few descriptions of Dresser's personality that has been found, in light of what is known of his remarkable productivity as a writer, facility as a public speaker, and prodigious energy, it is not difficult to conclude that the American reporter's quick take on 'the Doctor' has a ring of truth.

According to a brief item in the 9 December 1876 issue of the British trade publication the *Furniture Gazette*, Christopher Dresser came to the United States

> with a threefold purpose. First, a desire to visit the International Exhibition. Second, at the urgent request of the Pennsylvania Museum and School of Industrial Art, under whose auspices he [would deliver] a series of lectures ... and thirdly, to perfect and complete his contract with Messrs. Wilson & Fenimores, Philadelphia, manufacturers of

> paperhangings, who have secured his services to furnish to them exclusively in America with his latest designs in wall and ceiling decoration.[9]

The 'International Exhibition' mentioned in the *Furniture Gazette* was the Philadelphia Centennial Exhibition, a gargantuan, six-month-long event, held on the 100th anniversary of the birth of the nation, that publicly displayed the art and manufactured goods of many countries.[10] Like similar world exhibitions that preceded it in London (1851, 1862), Paris (1855, 1867) and Vienna (1873), it showcased, among other things, industrial ingenuity and manufacturing prowess, and allowed nations to gauge their progress vis-à-vis that of others. For an industrial designer of Dresser's stature, the attraction of the Philadelphia exhibition must have been irresistible, for there he could assess the latest developments in design and manufacturing, visit clients whose goods were on display (including some designed by Dresser himself), make contact with prospective clients and others who might advance his interests in one way or another, and write notes about the exhibition

153. *Main Exhibition Building, Philadelphia Centennial Exhibition*, illustrated in Gardner, Dorsey ed. *Grounds and Buildings of the Centennial Exhibition, Philadelphia, 1876* (Washington: Government Printing Office, 1880) at Plate D.

that he could use in articles and talks. While the precise nature of Dresser's activities at the exhibition is not known, it is reasonable to assume that he did all these things. It should be noted that Dresser had been invited to be a member of the pottery jury at the exhibition, but declined because of his 'many pressing engagements'.[11]

The date when Dresser arrived in Philadelphia has not been determined; it is possible that he spent a few days in New York, where, perhaps he conferred with senior staff at Tiffany & Co. about the collection he would acquire for the firm in Japan. Dresser may also have visited the Metropolitan Museum of Art.[12] In any event, it is known that he arrived in Philadelphia by 24 October, because, in a handbill addressed 'To the Trade' and dated 'Oct. 24, 1876,' the firm of Wilson & Fenimores announced that on that day it had 'consummated a contract with the celebrated CHRISTOPHER DRESSER ... to furnish us EXCLUSIVELY in America with his latest designs'. The firm goes on to state: 'Dr. Dresser is now in this City, and has already devoted the greater part of a day to us upon INTERIOR DECORATING. During his stay here, which is necessarily limited on account of engagements in Japan and elsewhere, he will

deliver three lectures on Art, under the auspices of the Pennsylvania Museum and School of Industrial Art, and the Pennsylvania Academy of the Fine Arts.' On the evening of 30 October Dresser gave the first of the three lectures he would deliver in the city. The *Philadelphia Inquirer*, in its issue of 30 October, reported:

> It is expected that Dr. Dresser's lectures on 'Art Museums,' at the Academy of Fine Arts, to begin this evening, will have the effect of creating an interest in the subject, and it is probable that other lectures will follow. Dr. Dresser, who is at the head of art matters, now that the celebrated Owen Jones, of the Crystal Palace, is deceased, is now on his way to the East, accompanied by Lieut. Reeve, R.N., who has been sent out by the English Government to aid the doctor in his study of Oriental decoration.[13] His lectures in this city are to be delivered at the express invitation of the managers of the museum, and, as they are to be free to the public, will, doubtless, be largely attended.[14]

The circumstances behind Dresser being invited to lecture in Philadelphia are worth noting. An article in *The Press*, another Philadelphia newspaper, reports that the invitation came from two officials of the Pennsylvania Museum and School of Industrial Art – Coleman Sellers, its president, and William Platt Pepper, its managing director.[15] The impetus for the invitation appears to have come from their desire to capitalize on the success of the Centennial Exhibition by establishing a combined museum and school that would further stimulate the improvement of artistic appreciation and industrial design. Edward Gallaudet, whose report 'Governmental Patronage of Art' was included in the *Reports of the Commissioners of the United States to the International Exhibition Held at Vienna, 1873*, pointed out that a major reason that British manufacturers had made rapid advances in the artistic quality of their products, that, in turn, had led to greater commercial success, stemmed from the government's support of the South Kensington Museum.[16] Thus, the South Kensington Museum (now the V&A) was identified as a model for the United States.[17] Philip Cunliffe Owen, the director of the South Kensington Museum who had been the secretary of the British Commission at the Vienna Exhibition, endorsed this view and did what he could to support the creation of a museum and school of industrial art in the United States.[18] In 1876, for example, he helped arrange loans of rare artefacts for the nascent museum and endorsed the selection of Dresser as a guest lecturer. Indeed, during his second lecture in Philadelphia, on the subject of art museums, Dresser acknowledged Owen's role:

> Knowing that I have been acquainted with the South Kensington Museum from its first formation to the present time, and also feeling that I had exceptional opportunities for judging of the influence which it has exerted upon English taste, my excellent friend, Mr. Philip F. Cunliffe Owen, the director of that institution, asked me to set before you its rise and progress, believing that you would be interested in its history at this particular time when you are founding a museum of your own.[19]

Londos & Co., the London firm that had engaged Dresser to acquire a collection of Japanese art objects on its behalf and also brokered an arrangement between Dresser and Tiffany & Co. for the acquisition of a similar collection,[20] may also have had a hand in arranging for him to lecture in Philadelphia. In a letter dated 18 November 1876, William Platt Pepper, the managing director of the Pennsylvania Museum and School of Industrial Art, wrote to 'Messrs. Londos & Co.' about the three lectures Dresser had by then delivered. He also noted that he had conferred with Dresser about a collection Londos would be loaning his museum. While Pepper does not make it clear that Londos arranged for Dresser's lectures, the grateful tone of his letter suggests that this is a possibility.[21]

Dresser delivered his Philadelphia lectures on 30 October, 2 November and 6 November, speaking on the topics of art industries, art museums and art schools, respectively. The texts of the lectures were later published in the *Penn Monthly*.[22] As Stuart Durant has pointed out, they closely resemble portions of his articles published in the *Technical Educator* and lectures he presented to the Society of Arts in 1872 and 1874.[23] In an article about the first lecture, published in *The Press*, it is reported that 'William Platt Pepper, Esq., James L. Claghorn, Esq., president of the Academy of Fine Arts, and several other gentlemen occupied seats upon the platform, and the hall was crowded with one of the most intelligent and cultivated audiences ever assembled in Philadelphia.'[24] William Platt Pepper, in his letter to Londos & Co., reported that Dresser's lectures 'attracted great attention and the room was filled to overflowing (many persons being obliged to stand up). We were all much pleased with him and he seemed pleased with his stay in Philadelphia.'[25]

An article about the second of Dresser's three lectures was published in the *Philadelphia Inquirer*. The reporter noted that the lecture was presented

THE PHILADELPHIA INQUIRER—TUESDAY, OCTOBER 31, 1876.

ARTISTIC ORNAMENTATION!

By special contract with Dr. CHRISTOPHER DRESSER, Ph. D., M. A., F. L. S., F. E. B. S., &c., of London, we have the exclusive privilege in America of producing his original designs for WALL and CEILING ADORNMENT. We have already six sets of these in process of manufacture, and will soon offer them to the consideration of the public.

WILSON & FENIMORES,

MANUFACTURERS OF

PAPER HANGINGS

915 MARKET STREET.

before a 'fine audience', and then made it clear that Dresser had successfully driven home the point that art museums can be a major asset to national industry:

> The subject [of art museums], the speaker said, was of utmost importance, and he congratulated the American people upon the fact that they were about to make so practical a use of their great Exhibition, as to found a Museum of Art similar to that at South Kensington, London. Prior to 1851 the English had no such institution, but owing to the South Kensington Museum, and schools of art which followed its foundation, enabled England to make such an advance in industrial art as had never been made by any nation in a similar period of time.[26]

Later on, the reporter wrote:

> In conclusion, Dr. Dresser earnestly appealed for a liberal support for the museum in the park. He knew of no more useful means of serving the public good. Merchants, particularly, should be liberal and generous in their aid of the institution through which the American name can be made equal to

that of any European nation for excellence in art manufactures.[27]

The site of Dresser's lectures is noteworthy. He presented all three at the Pennsylvania Academy of the Fine Arts,[28] an impressive building that had opened about six months before. Designed by Frank Furness and George W. Hewitt, it is a bold, eclectic structure that is a 'vigorous union of English and French sources'.[29] Of particular interest with regard to the present discussion is the building's interior decoration, which employs motifs that could have been inspired by Owen Jones's influential book the *Grammar of Ornament*, or even by Dresser's writings.[30] Michael J. Lewis, a biographer of Furness, suggests that Dresser and Furness met in Philadelphia.[31] Under the circumstances – one of the foremost authorities on design lecturing in the new building Furness had designed – such a meeting seems highly likely.

There is no doubt that Dresser met with representatives of the Philadelphia firm of Wilson & Fenimores, manufacturers of paper hangings. This

155. The *Philadelphia Inquirer* (31 October 1876), p. 5.

156. Three of Dresser's designs for Wilson & Fenimores. US Patent and Trademark Office, Examiner's Room files.

is clearly evidenced by the previously mentioned handbill 'To the Trade', and also by a large display advertisement the firm placed in the *Philadelphia Inquirer* and *The Press*, beginning on 31 October (plate 155).[32]

It seems likely that Dresser had been in contact with Wilson & Fenimores before he left England, since he consummated an exclusive contract with the firm only four days after his arrival in the United States and delivered six sets of wallpaper and ceiling paper designs. According to an item published in the 9 December 1876 issue of the *Furniture Gazette*, while he was in Philadelphia, Dresser 'spent considerable time at [the Wilson & Fenimores] factory, superintending the arrangement of colors for his designs, and otherwise completing the details for bringing them out in the most perfect manner possible.'[33] It was also reported that Dresser had delivered six sets of designs, with each set composed of individual designs for dado, dado-rail, sides, frieze and ceiling, for a total of 30 unique designs.[34]

Fortunately, 13 of the designs Dresser executed for Wilson & Fenimores have survived. They are in the files of the United States Patent and Trademark Office, where they have resided since they were submitted for patent protection in 1877.[35] According to official Patent Office reports, applications for the patenting of 13 wallpaper designs, numbered 9,975–9,987, by patentee Christopher Dresser, assignor to Wilson & Fenimores, were filed on 17 March 1877 and registered on 15 May 1877. The term of patent protection was three and a half years. Dresser's wallpaper designs were the only ones registered in the United States that year.[36]

Because the facsimiles of Dresser's designs at the Patent Office are not in colour, one is unable to appreciate the full effect of his work. However, the essential patterns of the designs are easy to see. Botanical motifs predominate, especially flowers, leaves, stems and vines. Some of the designs are 'diaper' patterns, in the Japanese style;[37] others, with bands on opposite sides, appear to be intended as bordering known as frieze or dado-rail ornaments; and others, which are not framed or bordered, feature stylized plant forms and were probably intended to cover large areas of walls. When the designs that Dresser created for Wilson & Fenimores are compared to the designs for wall and ceiling papers illustrated, in full colour, in his book *Studies in Design*,[38] certain similarities become evident, and one can better imagine how Dresser might have used colour – always a critical element for him – in his designs for the Philadelphia firm.

Dresser's relationship with Wilson & Fenimores would continue, at least into the next year, as we shall see presently.

On 6 November, at the close of his third and final lecture in Philadelphia, Dresser said he would have to say good-bye to the people of Philadelphia 'within the next few hours'.[39] Therefore, it is probably safe to conclude that he took his leave of the city later that day or on the morning of the next. The impression that Dresser made on those he met in Philadelphia was apparently a strong one. In an article published in the *Philadelphia Evening Bulletin* seven months after his departure, the writer notes: 'Dr. Dresser became well known to all our lovers of art, and of art furniture and decorations, during the Centennial Exhibition.'[40] In April 1877 a reporter for the *Daily Graphic*, a New York City newspaper, wrote of Dresser:

The name of Dr. Christopher Dresser, Ph.D., is well remembered in this country as that of one of the most intelligible and sympathetic of the many experts who swung over to our shores entangled in the fringes of the International Exhibition. Where the French experts were insulting and contemptuous, where Italian experts were boastful and vague, where Japanese experts where out of the question, Dr. Dresser was definite, communicative and understood by all.[41]

Dresser's whereabouts and activities from the time he left Philadelphia until 19 November have not been traced, but it is possible that he went to New York to visit Tiffany & Co. or travelled to other eastern cities to visit other clients or prospective clients. It is possible, too, that he went north to visit his son Henry, who was also in the United States. Documents at the Albany County Hall of Records, in Albany, New York, confirm that 22-year-old Henry Dresser, from England, petitioned to become a citizen of the United States on 26 October 1876.[42] Why he came to the United States is unknown, but one may speculate that he came, perhaps in response to his father's encouragement,[43] to seek his fortune in Albany, a bustling city with a population of over 70,000. Henry appears to have been in Albany as early as 1875, since the Albany city directory for that year lists a Henry Dresser who was employed as a salesman.[44] While no evidence has been found that verifies that Christopher Dresser and his son Henry met during the former's visit to the United States, it remains an intriguing possibility.

After his departure from Philadelphia, the next time Christopher Dresser's whereabouts can be confirmed is 19 November. On that day, according to the *Chicago Tribune*, he registered at a local hotel called Tremont House.[45] The fact that Dresser was in Chicago makes it clear that he was heading west on his way to Japan, but a short notice in the 22 November issue of the *Tribune* reveals another reason for his presence in Chicago:

Dr. Christopher Dresser, who is now en route for Japan, China, and India, under the protection of the British Government and at the instigation of the Kensington Art Schools and various merchants in Europe and America in search of art treasures, etc., has been spending two days in Chicago at the invitation of Mr. John J. McGrath.[46]

John J. McGrath was the proprietor of a large

Chicago retail establishment that specialized in wallpaper. According to Sharon Darling, between 1873 and 1885 McGrath's establishment was managed by Joseph Twyman, an Englishman who had settled in Chicago in 1870. Due to Twyman's efforts, McGarth's 'acquired a reputation as the place to buy trend-setting papers imported from England and France'.[47] It is likely, therefore, that Twyman introduced Dresser to McGrath, since he is known to have travelled to England on buying trips and may very well have met Dresser in this connection.[48] During the time Dresser and McGrath spent together in Chicago, it is likely that they discussed Dresser's latest designs for wall and ceiling papers and toured McGrath's store. It

became Marshall Field & Co., and went on to become one of the largest and most prominent department stores in the United States.

Dresser left Chicago, probably on 21 November, and undoubtedly travelled west on one of three principal railroad lines to Council Bluffs, Iowa, the transfer point for all passengers and the eastern terminus of the Union Pacific Railroad.[50] From Council Bluffs it is likely that he travelled further west on what was called the Pacific Railroad, a popular choice of travellers going to the West Coast, which was actually a combination of the Union Pacific Railroad and the Central Pacific Railroad into one line that ran all the way from Council Bluffs to San Francisco.

157. The steamship *City of Tokio*. 'The Century: Its Fruits and Its Festival', *Lippincott's Magazine* (January–June 1876), vol. 17.

is also possible that the bold idea of mounting a major exhibition of decorative papers designed by a raft of the top English, French and American designers resulted from their conversations. Such an exhibition, which McGrath sponsored in 1879, is described below.

According to the *Chicago Times*, while Dresser was in Chicago he also met with W.H. Judson, head of the carpet department at Field, Leiter & Co.[49] Presumably, he met with Judson in order to offer carpet designs to the firm or promote the idea of Field, Leiter & Co. buying carpets designed by Dresser that were manufactured in Great Britain. At the time, Field, Leiter & Co. was one of Chicago's leading dry-goods emporiums. In 1881 the firm

While Dresser may have been dreaming about the wonders of Japan that awaited him, it is difficult to imagine that he was not captivated by the vastness and the natural wonders of the American West that passed before him on his 1,900-mile journey to the Pacific across a transcontinental route that had been completed less than seven years before.[51] After leaving Iowa, his journey would have taken him through five states – Nebraska, Wyoming, Utah, Nevada and California – exposing him, at a leisurely average speed of 16 to 20 miles per hour,[52] to an ever-changing landscape that ranged from the flat prairies of the Great Plains to the lofty, majestic peaks of the Rocky Mountains.

Little is known of the impression this long rail journey made upon Dresser, but publications of the period, such as *The Pacific Tourist*, *Crofutt's Trans-Continental Tourist* and *Crofutt's New Overland Tourist and Pacific Coast Guide*, provide fascinating and extremely detailed descriptions of virtually everything he would have seen along the way.[53] Another publication – *Westward by Rail: The New Route to the East*, by William F. Rae – provides an Englishman's vivid observations on the scenes and people he encountered on this same route a few years before.[54]

The 25 November issue of the *Salt Lake Daily Tribune* reports that 'Dr. C. Dresser, London', had arrived in Salt Lake City and was staying at the Walker House,[55] a hotel described elsewhere as being 'first-class in every particular, with steam elevator and central location'.[56] The view from Salt Lake City, with the snow-capped Wasatch Mountains in the distance, is a memorable one, and we know it made an impression on Dresser because he commented on it briefly, in his book *Japan: Its Architecture, Art and Art Manufactures*, as a point of comparison with a beautiful view from his hotel balcony in Kyoto.[57]

It is unlikely that Dresser lingered long in Salt Lake City; perhaps he stayed only overnight. Reboarding the train, he would have travelled 36 miles further on to Ogden, Utah, then transferred to the Central Pacific Railroad for the final leg of the journey, an 882-mile run[58] through the remainder of Utah, across the entire state of Nevada, over the Sierra Nevada mountain range, across California's upper San Jaoquin Valley and quickly on to San Francisco. Dresser arrived in San Francisco on 27 November[59] and registered at the Palace Hotel,[60] an impressive new hotel located at the corner of Market and Montgomery Streets.[61]

On the next day, Japanese General Saigô Tsugu-michi and 10 associates arrived in San Francisco and also registered at the Palace Hotel.[62] All 11 men were returning to Japan after participating in the Philadelphia Centennial Exhibition as official representatives of their country; General Saigô, the highest ranking, had served as vice-president of the Japanese commission to the exhibition.[63] Saigô would later provide much assistance to Dresser in connection with his various activities in Japan.[64]

After a few days rest in San Francisco, Christopher Dresser and General Saigô and his associates left San Francisco, probably on 2 December,[65] on a voyage to Yokohama aboard the steamship *City of Tokio*. The fact that Dresser took his leave of the United States on this vessel is freighted with symbolic significance. He had attended the Philadelphia Centennial Exhibition, which proudly displayed American industry and culture to the world, and heralded the start of a remarkable period of invention and industrial productivity for the nation. He had travelled across the country on the new transcontinental railroad, a powerful symbol of American ingenuity, determination, and unification. And now, as he steamed away from the California coast, he was directly connected to a third powerful symbol of the United States' growing industrial progress since he was borne away by the *City of Tokio*, the largest American steamship at that time.[66]

Thus, Christopher Dresser left the United States and sailed away to Japan for a sojourn that would fulfil the greatest desire of his life, profoundly affect his subsequent designs and yield a sensitive, keenly observed study of Japanese artistry that was a significant contribution to the literature. In comparison, Dresser's visit to the United States, while packed with a great deal of activity, may not have seemed especially significant to him. Nevertheless, information that has been gleaned about this visit (which, as far as can be determined, is the only one he made to the United States) allows one to gain a better understanding of his priorities, his manner of operation as an entrepreneur, his interrelated connections in the realms of commerce and museums, and his tremendous energy and drive.

It is regrettable that Dresser did not leave a record of his time in the United States. It would be quite interesting to know his views on such things as the American architecture and art manufactures he observed,[67] the bizarre presidential election of 1876, and the American West where, just four months before he arrived in the United States, Sioux Indians had wiped out General Custer and his men at Little Bighorn.

What impact did Christopher Dresser have upon Americans? A number of significant outcomes directly resulted from contacts Dresser had with Americans in 1876. Due, in some small measure, to Dresser's exhortations, a combined museum and school of industrial art was established in Philadelphia and, while it did not substantially fulfil the goal of improving the artfulness of American manufactured goods, it became a well-respected institution.[68] Also, the firm of Wilson & Fenimores completed the production of the ceiling papers and wallpapers Dresser had designed and marketed them with particular intensity in 1877.[69] In addition, just before the start of its advertising campaign that year, Wilson & Fenimores opened a unique exhibition of decorative goods, the nature of which strongly suggests Dresser's guiding hand. It is described in the 16 April 1877 issue of the *Philadelphia Evening Bulletin* as follows:

> On Saturday evening last, at the invitation of Messrs. Wilson & Fenimore, No. 915 Market Street, a number of members of the Pennsylvania Museum and School of Industrial Art, the Philadelphia Art Club and members of the Press, together with several well known architects, visited the establishment of the firm mentioned to witness a private exhibition of decorative ornamentation.
>
> In the second story of the building had been fitted up seven apartments, representing parlors, libraries, studies, dining-rooms, chambers, &c., and each room was, in the ceiling and wall decorations, carpets, curtains and furniture, a model of correct taste and esthetic beauty. The ceilings and walls were all covered with paper exhibiting the new designs and coloring furnished by Dr. Christopher Dresser, of London, whose services have fortunately been secured by Messrs. Wilson & Fenimore. The decorative ornamentations were at once so novel, so artistic and so chaste, and yet so rich in general effect as to win from those present expressions of surprise and delight. Each portion of the several rooms was in perfect harmony with every other portion, and yet this harmony was chiefly attained by contrasted tints and hues of the primary colors. The style of the decoration was chiefly English, Gothic, and medieval, but in the details of ornamentation the purest forms known to ancient or modern art were utilized. The carpets were contributed to this exhibition by J.F. & E.B. Orne, the furniture by Moore, York, and Howell, the curtains by Sheppard, Arrison and Sheppard, and the gas fittings by Thackara, Buck & Co.
>
> The exhibition was, in every respect, a most delightful one, especially as it proved the progress being made in the cultivation of art ideas. The desire for purer forms of ornamental work, which was intensified by the Centennial Exhibition and subsequent causes, led Messrs. Wilson & Fenimore

> to make a close study of the work of masters, and they have succeeded in placing before the public as fine examples of decorative ornamentation as can be seen in any part of the Old World.[70]

What is particularly striking about this exhibition is that, apart from the fact that it evidently showed Dresser's ceiling papers and wallpapers to excellent advantage, its innovative arrangement of various decorative objects in realistic room settings mirrors other special exhibitions that Dresser organized, such as one for Londos & Co., in 1876,[71] and another for Dresser & Holme, in 1879.[72] Therefore, it is quite possible that the concept of the Wilson & Fenimores exhibition was Dresser's.[73]

In 1879 Dresser's decorative papers were again part of an exclusive American exhibition. In this instance, the exhibition was held in the Chicago premises of the wallpaper retailer John J. McGrath, whom Dresser had visited in 1876. The scale of the exhibition was impressive. At least 300 wallpapers by leading English,[74] French and American designers were on display, the products of many English and American manufacturers. Since papers from leading American manufacturers in Philadelphia, New York City and Brooklyn were shown, it is possible that wall and ceiling papers produced by Dresser's Philadelphia client, Wilson & Fenimores, were among them. Who designed the exhibition is not known, but it is worth noting that four room-like settings, hung with papers and further decorated with rugs, ceramic pieces and other complementary objects, constituted its central element. The novel exhibition was sufficiently notable to attract the attention of the *American Architect and Building News* and *Scientific American*.[75]

In addition to J.J. McGrath, at least one other retailer sold Dresser's wallpaper designs in the Midwest. This was the firm of J.L. Isaacs, who operated a large store, in St Louis, that specialized in home decorations. A description of the firm in the book *A Tour of St Louis*, published in 1878, notes that wallpapers were stored in

> magnificent cabinets ... which open from the walls and display the fine qualities of Dr. Dresser's art designs and French art decorations, of which Mr. Isaac is the sole agent, in the most advantageous manner. These art designs are a special feature of Mr. Isaac's business, and they are undoubtedly the handsomest wall decorations ever introduced in this country.[76]

Another outcome of Dresser's 1876 visit to the United States and subsequent visit to Japan was the acquisition of a large collection of Japanese art manufactures for Tiffany & Co. It appears that the central worth of the collection to Tiffany & Co. was, as Dresser described it, 'tutorial' in nature.[77] In other words, it would be a study collection intended to stimulate Tiffany's designers in their development of new designs for the firm. As Charles and Mary Carpenter have noted, 'The Tiffany designers used Japanese artworks both as models and as points of departure in design.'[78] This was not the firm's first exposure to Japanese art manufactures, however. It has been established that Tiffany & Co. had already been exposed to Japanese art manufactures, and had produced silver flatware and hollowware with decorative motifs inspired by Japanese models as early as the late 1860s. These designs are credited to Edward C. Moore, the firm's chief designer. However, as John Loring, Tiffany's current design director, has written, 'Between 1876 and the Paris Exposition of 1878, radical advances were made in Moore's Tiffany Japaneseque silverwares. Smooth backgrounds were replaced by a revolutionary use of *martelé*, or hammered finishes, beginning in late 1876.'[79] Loring goes on to say that 'Moore never commented on Dresser's collections and their influence on Tiffany design; but, the coincidence of date strongly suggests that Edward C. Moore and his associates had gathered considerable new design knowledge from Dresser's early-1877 shipment.'[80] Tiffany & Co.'s exciting new hollowware was exhibited at the 1878 Paris Exposition and the firm received the highest award. While the precise impact of Dresser's collection on Tiffany & Co.'s designs may never be known, for his part, Dresser saw Tiffany's success as a direct result of the artistic inspiration provided by the collection he had assembled for the firm. He stated:

> I certainly had the honour of being intrusted by
> Messrs. Tiffany & Co. with the choice of any objects
> that I might think calculated to aid in the
> development of their silversmith business; and it is
> interesting to me to know that, after a careful and
> most intelligent consideration of these objects,
> Messrs. Tiffany and Co. produced new works which
> secured for the firm the 'grand prix' at the last Paris
> exhibition.[81]

After selecting the items from Dresser's collection it wished to retain, Tiffany & Co. decided to sell the remainder at public auction.[82] The well-publicized sale began in New York City on 18 June 1877, and presented 'The Dresser Collection of Japanese Curios and Articles Selected for Messrs. Tiffany & Co.'[83] The auction comprised a staggering 1,902 lots, which consisted of ceramics, textiles, lacquerwork, metalwork, wickerwork and other items.[84] The introduction to the auction catalogue notes that 'many of the objects [in the sale] are for ordinary domestic use, but all have the quaint style, elegant and refined decoration, so marked in Japanese industry, making them real objects of art.'[85] Although the auction was not, apparently, a financial success, it generated considerable favourable publicity for Tiffany & Co. and helped stimulate greater interest in Japanese art objects in the United States.[86]

Dresser's influence on Americans also took the form of the impact of the various domestic goods he designed that Americans acquired from Britain or from American retailers who sold items designed by Dresser that were made in the United States (such as the Wilson & Fenimores paper-hangings) or items designed by Dresser that were made in Britain and imported into the United States (such as carpets and wall and ceiling papers). Another example of the latter is a tin candlestick holder that is included in the present exhibition. Made in England by Perry, Son & Co., of Wolverhampton, it bears the label of an American retailer that reads: 'F.A. Walker & Co.,

158. Tin candlestick holder designed by Christopher Dresser, which bears the label of Boston retailer F.A. Walker. Private Collection.

Boston/Dr. Dresser's Design'.[87] An example of an English-made, Dresser-designed object in an American home during the early 1880s can be seen in the book *The Opulent Interiors of the Gilded Age*. In a photo of the library in the grand Boston home of Charles A. Whittier, one can clearly see a piece of art furniture designed by Dresser, a chair manufactured by Thomas Knight & Son, of Bath, for the Art Furnishers' Alliance.[88] And in the book *Artistic Homes*, which contains remarkable documentation of the interiors of some of the most lavish homes in the United States during the same period, the author points out that the 'cove of the ceiling to the borders of the immense, oblong, octo-paneled skylight' in the magnificent personal art gallery of John T. Martin, of Brooklyn, New York, is decorated with 'one of Christopher Dresser's papers, of a pattern probably not to be seen elsewhere in this country'.[89]

A number of American designers of the latter part of the nineteenth century were undoubtedly influenced by Dresser's designs and theories of design in one way or another. Some may have incorporated Dresser's ideas into their own work, but, given the difficulty of verifying influences upon artists in the absence of their own statements in this regard, it is virtually impossible to do more than infer influences based on such things as stylistic similarities, personal connections and the like. That being said, based mainly on stylistic grounds, it is tempting to point to Dresserian ideas in the work of a number of Americans whose creations are emblematic of the Aesthetic Movement, such as the aforementioned architect Frank Furness (who also designed furniture), and the furniture makers the Herter Brothers, furniture maker Daniel Pabst, and the expatriate artist James McNeill Whistler, among others.[90]

Finally, Dresser probably influenced the largest number of Americans through the books and articles he wrote about such things as the principles of design, the ornamentation of homes and the arts of Japan. His books were reviewed by American writers, and he was frequently quoted, and treated as a highly respected authority, by American trade journals that were read by designers, manufacturers and others who wished to stay abreast of the latest trends. As a Philadelphia journalist observed in 1877, Dresser's 'publications of portfolios of colored plates are the basis of many a successful decorator's and upholsterer's reputation'.[91] As well, he was known to the readers of books and periodicals that were created in response to the craze for interior decoration that emerged in the United States during the 1880s.[92] There was a demand, particularly among middle-class women, for information about decorating techniques and materials, and, in this atmosphere, writers often invoked Dresser as an authority on these matters. For example, in a section about choosing wallpaper in her book *Woman's Handiwork in Modern Homes*, Constance Cary Harrison quotes a pertinent passage from Dresser's *Principles of Decorative Design*.[93] She also states that among the wallpapers sent to the United States by 'well-known manufacturers in England ... those of Morris and Dresser, are familiar in our houses'.[94] Articles by Dresser himself were published in American periodicals aimed at amateur decorators and designers. For example, *Art Amateur*, a publication 'devoted to the cultivation of art in the household', printed his article 'The Decoration of Our Homes', and the *Decorator and Furnisher* printed 'Ceilings, Walls and Hangings: Some Modified Views by Dr. Dresser'.[95]

During a lecture he gave in 1874, Dresser stated that he 'had the honour of preparing for the American Government a report on design, or pattern, as applied to objects and to houses, with a view to their decoration.'[96] The report, which appears to have been written in connection with the Vienna Exhibition of 1873, has never been found, so we cannot know its precise substance nor can we adduce the impact it may have had on American officials and others who read it. Nevertheless, if it is true that Dresser wrote such a report at the request of the government, this alone speaks volumes about the respect that influential Americans held for him at the time when their nation was striving for greater success in manufacturing.

Without a doubt, all that Dresser did during his visit to the United States in 1876, along with the objects he designed and the books and articles he wrote, combined to produce a palpable impact on the way that many Americans appreciated beauty in everyday objects for the home. Certainly, he was, as a reporter for the *New York Times* wrote in 1877, 'one of the most perfect specimens of art intellect which England shipped to the United States for exhibition at Philadelphia.'[97] He was that, and more.

CHAPTER
6

Dresser and Japan

WIDAR HALÉN

159. Ikkeisai Yoshiiku (1833–1904).
*The Prosperity of an English Trading
Company in Yokohama*, details, colour print
from woodblocks, 1871. Metropolitan
Museum of Art, New York. The print shows
a trade fair held by Jardine Matheson and
Company. The artist was an almost exact
contemporary of Dresser.

C hristopher Dresser's lifelong efforts to promote Japanese art and influences in the West culminated in his visit to Japan in 1876–7. This was
the first tour of the country since the opening of Japan (1854) by a
European designer, and his recollections, published under the title *Japan: Its
Architecture, Art and Art Manufactures* (1882), provided one of the most thorough treatments of the subject and became a vital impetus to the Japonism
movement.

Dresser's involvement with Japanese art follows the three main phases of
Japonism in the West. At first he was attracted by the cheer novelty of Japanese
art, but he soon recognized its distinct aesthetic qualities and finally he reached
an awareness and understanding of its artistic criteria. Although he recalled
having been familiar with the Japanese Arita patterns from childhood,[1] these
were probably the Arita patterns on Western porcelain and it was not until later
in his career that he began to incorporate Japanese ideas and devices into his
writings and designs. He certainly had access to Japanese art as a student at the
School of Design, where his tutor Octavius Hudson included Japanese study
samples in his lectures.[2]

The Museum of Ornamental Art (later South Kensington Museum) had
acquired their first Japanese lacquer and porcelain from the dealer William
Hewitt in 1852,[3] and in 1854 they enlarged their collection with 37 samples of
Japanese artefacts from the first sales exhibition of Japanese art at the Old
Water-Colour Society in London.[4] Dresser, who studied at the museum, was
certainly aware of these acquisitions and in 1861 he included Japanese examples in his lectures 'The Art of Decorative Art', published in book form the year
after. He illustrated and classified Japanese lotus motifs as belonging to 'the
most exalted grade of ornament'.[5]

Dresser was one of the first artists in Europe to respond seriously to Japanese
art, and even at this early stage he had begun to promote Japanese art and
challenge the condescension prevalent among many contemporary critics. By
comparing the Japanese lotus motifs to the Greek anthemion and other leaf
ornaments, Dresser showed that Japanese art had authentic connections with
other styles. Thus he contributed to remove the false hegemonic barriers

between Western and Oriental art in general. He encouraged a more serious study of Japanese art and aesthetics, which in turn helped to dethrone historicism and to modernize art in the West.

The Japanese section of the 1862 International

Later in life, in 1878, Dresser stated that Japanese art had been fundamental in forming his 'art character'. He underlined that Sir Rutherford Alcock had played a vital part in this when in 1862 he had allowed him to make about 80 drawings of

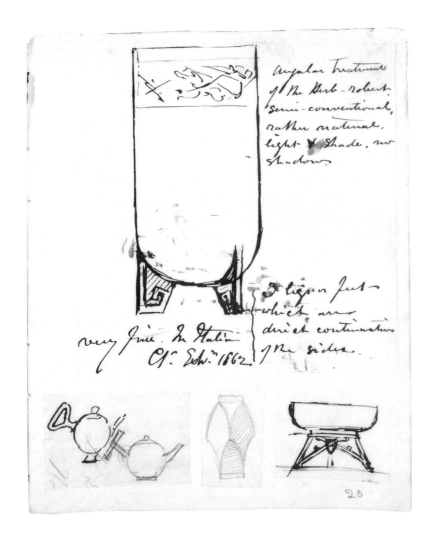

Exhibition, organized by the British minister to Japan, Sir Rutherford Alcock, was one of the most influential events in the history of Japanese art in the West. Among the post-exhibition buyers were the South Kensington Museum, William, Hewitt & Co., Murray Marks & Co. and Farmer & Rogers, where Arthur Lasenby Liberty was employed at this time.[6] In 1875 Liberty set up his own shop in Regent Street, and it was from him and from Murray Marks that early Japan enthusiasts, such as Dresser, William Burges, James M. Whistler, Edward W. Godwin, William Morris, Richard Norman Shaw and Dante and William M. Rossetti, made their first purchases of Japanese art objects.[7]

the Japanese collection he exhibited and that he also acquired some of these objects at the close of the exhibition: 'To these treasures which I thus became possessed of I have almost constantly been adding, till now my house is rather a museum than a comfortable abode for civilised beings. Feeling the beauty of these objects I have done what I could to encourage their introduction into this country.'[8]

In *Development of Ornamental Art in the International Exhibition* (1862) Dresser referred to some of the first Japonism objects in the West, which in fact he may have designed himself. He described some ebonized furniture of the kind he later

160. Dresser's sketchbook, p.20, showing drawing for Minton's China Works, vase from 1862 (see plate 161) and spherical teapots. The book contains 105 similar pages dated 1861–5. Ipswich Museum.

161. Minton's China Works. Three-legged blue porcelain vase, 1862. The Birkenhead Collection. The dated drawing for this vase is in Dresser's 'Ipswich' sketchbook (see plate 160).

designed for his Art Furnishers' Alliance, 'of quaint and unique Japanese character' exhibited by A.F. Bornemann & Co. of Bath, and some Minton porcelain vases 'enriched with Chinese or Japanese ornament'.[9] We have not been able to connect Dresser's name with this furniture company, but we do know that he worked for Minton's, and drawings in his sketchbooks from this period concur with some of the Minton vases shown at the exhibition in 1862 (plate 160).

Although several artists responded positively to Japanese art in the early 1860s, few, if any, were able to discern its aesthetic criteria, but Christopher Dresser was an exception. In 1863 he lectured on 'The Prevailing Ornament of China and Japan' at the Architectural Association. In three anonymous articles entitled 'Japanese Ornamentation' he treated the same topics and art objects as in his lecture.[10]

Like several other writers at the time, Dresser underlined the similarities between the art of feudalistic Japan and that of medieval English art, which was fashionable at the time. This was meant to justify and make Japanese art more appealing, but Dresser also dealt with the more striking differences such as asymmetry and the irregular grouping and 'rigid flatness' of ornaments and diaper patterns.[11]

Generally Dresser found that Japanese art theories were similar to his own, but he also warned against the imitative tendencies in early Japonism, chiding some French designers by saying 'they have taken the form, but have not perceived the sentiment of which the shape is but a shroud.'[12] Sceptical to this kind of Japonism, Dresser encouraged artists to consult the available literature on Japanese art, in order to arrive at a more accurate interpretation.[13]

Dresser's discourse on Japanese art and Japonism reveal a remarkable insight that is quite lacking among other contemporary writers on the subject, whose attractions were governed by curiosity rather than by an analytical appreciation. Dresser strove to comprehend the basic aesthetics of Japanese art, and he concluded his articles with a consideration of symbolic, religious forms that had not previously been apprehended in the West. In Japanese crests, grotesques and cloud-patterns Dresser discerned the 'abstract ornament in conventional form' that he had recommended in *The Art of Decorative Design* in 1862.[14] He believed that these kinds of ornaments would liberate the designers from the allegorical symbolism favoured by most Victorians, and lead to a renewal of decorative art in Europe.

This new development was well on its way by the time of the Paris International Exhibition in 1867. The Goncourt brothers proclaimed 'Japonaiserie forever',[15] and Dresser in his review of the exhibition endorsed their view in his appraisal of the Japanese stand: 'Such an acquaintance with Eastern art could scarcely fail to influence the ornamentation of objects in this country.'[16] His own perception of Japanese aesthetics became vitally enlarged and he particularly stressed the educational value of Japanese bronzes, cloisonné vessels and lacquer furniture, which he claimed was 'not anywhere surpassed'.[17] It was the Japanese metalwork and their bronze teapots that intrigued him most, and following the exhibition he tried to persuade English manufacturers to produce similar tea-services in bronze, but was unsuccessful.[18] His sketchbook from the time contains drawings of kettles and 'sugar basins in bronze' with beads on the sides and angular tripod legs (plate 161). These were reproduced in Dresser's 'Principles of Decorative Design' articles of 1871 (published in book form in 1873) and illustrated his demand for steadiness and functionalism.[19] They were eventually produced in electroplate by Elkington's, who engaged Dresser as a designer in the mid-1860s, but the dating of these objects is uncertain since they only occur in a company pattern book of 1885.

Dresser himself is known to have exhibited several of his designs at the exhibition in Paris in 1867, notably his new range of enamel painting on porcelain for the Minton factory. They comprise at least 12 vases and some 12 different borders, and most of his shapes and designs are in the Japonism style, which characterized much of his ornamentation from this time onward. Dresser probably began designing for Wedgwood around 1867, since his first designs for them were exhibited in Paris as well – pilgrim bottles, hanging vases and several borders for tableware and toiletware. Most of the patterns were in the Japonism manner, and several similar creations were exhibited at the International Exhibition in London in 1871. Here Dresser also showed his first works for the Minton's Art Pottery Studio, which existed from

1869 to 1875. Many of the shapes are identical to the ones he used at the main Minton factory, but the so-called semi-humorous designs are different and convey a strong Japanese feeling with studies of 'cats meeting and parting', 'grotesque ornaments with frogs, flowers etc.' and powerful compositions of cranes, ducks, beetles, grasshoppers and other insects.[20]

Japanese art was featured extensively at the International Exhibitions in London in 1871, 1872 and 1873. In 1871 some 'drab coloured, rough and unglazed earthenware'[21] was on view and it had a profound impact on Dresser. He also mentioned 'some specimens of Japanese earthenware, which are formed of coarse dark brown clay' in his own collection.[22] These displayed the 'bold art-effects' he so much admired, and evidently inspired the unglazed pottery he designed for Wedgwood, Watcombe Terracotta and Linthorpe Art Pottery. Dresser also showed some of his Japan-inspired textiles at the International Exhibition in 1871. These were wool and silk damasks made by James W. & C. Ward, and displayed 'the broken diapers, irregular powderings and strange key patterns' that he admired in Japanese ornamentation. Dresser was far ahead of his time in assimilating these asymmetrical and layered compositions, which became a characteristic of his own ornamentation and can be seen in numerous designs for carpets, textiles, wallpapers, porcelain and surface decorations.

By 1872 *The Builder* magazine enthusiastically announced the arrival of 'The Japanese Craze', and in the same year the Iwakura mission visited London. It was headed by two of the most famous creators of modern Japan: Iwakura Tomomi and Okubo Toschimichi. They had proposed a larger show of Japanese artefacts for the International Exhibition in London in 1873, and asked Christopher Dresser and Sir Philip Cunliffe Owen, the director of the South Kensington Museum, to assist them.[23] Sakata Haruo, a young official of the Japanese Government, personally delivered the Japanese objects for this exhibition, which also featured some coarser household ceramics shown at Dresser's recommendation.[24] Sakata remained in London as a student at the Royal School of Mines, returning to Japan in 1876, when he was appointed Dresser's escort during his visit to that country.

It was probably his personal contacts with Japanese officials that in 1873 inspired Dresser to organize the establishment of a large warehouse for imported goods from Japan and the Far East in conjunction with Charles Reynolds & Company.[25] Within a decade the new company, called Londos, had developed into the 'first and largest importer of Japanese art in Britain'.[26] Dresser was engaged

162. Londos & Co. advertising including motto 'In Pursuit of Beauty', *Furniture Gazette* (8 July 1876). NAL.

as art adviser and the company subsequently established branches in Japan, China, Persia, Morocco and Paris. The magazine *House-Furnisher and Decorator* praised Dresser's eagerness 'In Pursuit of Beauty', which was his motto and which also adorned Londos's advertising material (above). This slogan became virtually synonymous with

Japonism and the Aesthetic movement, and was subsequently adopted by Dresser's friend in New York, Louis C. Tiffany.[27]

Dresser appears to have been at the peak of his energies in 1873. He also visited the International Exhibition in Vienna that year, and supplied

163. Japanese art metal work imported by Dresser & Holme, *Furniture Gazette* (22 May 1880). NAL.

JAPANESE ART METAL-WORK.
Imported by DRESSER & HOLME, Farringdon Road.

164. *The Japanese Village at Alexandra Park, Muswell Hill, London* in *The Alexandra Palace Guide* (1875–6). NAL.

designs for several British manufacturers. Minton's, for example, showed some of his Japan-inspired cloisonné on porcelain, notably a new range with high-relief insect and grotesque decorations.[28] In his review of the exhibition Dresser dealt particularly with Japanese porcelain and cloisonné enamel work, whose influence he claimed had led to new industries in Europe.[29]

Dresser's review of the Vienna Exhibition also reiterated his great admiration for Japanese teapots, and he regretted that 'while the kettle is an object of use in every house in the land, we have to go to Japan to learn how to make one as it should be'.[30] He marvelled at the variety of materials and eccentric shapes used in Japanese metalwork, and he was particularly intrigued by the exposure of rivets and joints of various metal belts – an artistic device he incorporated in his own subsequent metalwork. The 'square kettles and round kettles and polyhedric kettles' shown in Vienna provided the impetus for several of the innovative kettles and teapots produced by Dresser in the late 1870s and '80s.

His sources were certainly also the Japanese art metalwork imported by his companies in the late 1870s (left), but above all it was the art work he studied during his tour of Japan that made a fundamental and lasting impact on his artistic mind.

Following his visit to Vienna in 1873, Dresser announced a new importing company, the Alexandra Palace Company, naming himself art director and Sir Edward Lee as managing director. The aim was to offer Japanese objects for sale at a Japanese village to be built in Alexandra Park, at Muswell Hill in north London. This Japanese village, which had been shown at the Vienna Exhibition, presented the British public with their first real view of Japanese architecture (left). The newly founded Japanese company Kiritsu Kosho Kaisha supplied the goods offered for sale. Dresser was involved with the venture until at least 1879, and his Japanese village provided yet another stimulus to the development of the Cult of Japan. In 1874 the *Art Journal* stated that 'Fashion has declared for Japanese art',[31] and by the mid-1870s this fashion had influenced the décor and taste of ordinary British households.

Dresser's *Studies in Design* (1874–6) incorporated a number of Japan-influenced designs that could easily be adapted to surface ornamentation in Victorian interiors, and his 'greeenery-yallery' and subdued colour schemes made a profound impact on decorators.[32] Above all, Dresser's fresh publication advocated 'newness of design' and he particularly recommended the students to study Japanese art and ornamentation.

En route to Japan in the autumn of 1876 Dresser visited the Centennial Exhibition in Philadelphia in the USA, and promoted his ideas in a series of lectures at the newly founded Pennsylvania Museum and School of Industrial Art. In his lecture on 'Art Museums' he referred to the South Kensington Museum as a model, but he lamented the fact that it had discontinued the practice of purchasing Oriental and Japanese art, which was of such vital importance to British designers and manufacturers.[33]

The hint was taken by the Americans, and notably by Charles Louis Tiffany and his son Louis Comfort, whom Dresser befriended during his stay. Tiffany had launched some popular silver designs in the Japanese style in the early 1870s, and now commissioned Dresser to bring back a vast collection of artefacts from Japan, amounting to some 8,000 objects. They were delivered to Tiffany's in April–May 1877,[34] and several of these artefacts provided the main impetus for the Japanesque creations of Tiffany and their chief designer, Edward C. Moore, as well as for many of the designs of Louis C. Tiffany and his interior decorating firm, Associated Artists. The sales catalogue of the collection also mentions an impressive 'translucent enamel screen, one of four taken from the emperors palace and valued at four thousand dollars',[35] which evidently provided Tiffany and his friend John La Farge with inspiration for the stained-glass screens and windows in the Japanese style they created in the later 1870s.[36]

Several American scholars have acknowledged Dresser's impact upon American Japonism. David Hanks, for instance, in paying tribute to Dresser, said that 'he acted as a catalyst for the influence of Japanese art on American manufacturers and designers.'[37] David A. Taylor has demonstrated in this publication that Dresser's presence in the US was met with great interest by trade and public alike.

By 1876–7 Dresser's role in the Japonism movement was almost as prominent in the United States as in Britain. Japanese manufacturers were now fully aware of the commercial potential of their products, and actively stimulated the Western market. The Centennial Exhibition in Philadelphia featured the largest Japanese stand ever mounted in the West, and much attention was given to the ancient porcelain, earthenware and stoneware exhibited by Dresser's trading affiliate, the Kiritsu Kosho Kaisha Company.

The increasing interest in Japanese earthenware, as distinct from the earlier fascination with porcelain, marked a change in critical interest. The British reporter Roger Soden-Smith praised precisely this kind of ceramics, which were collected by Dresser during his tour in Japan, namely Awata, Awaji, Banko, Raku, Tamba and Takatori wares. This kind of coarser-bodied ceramics with running glazes or simple salt glazing later influenced his production of Linthorpe Art Pottery in Hull. Shioda Makato's *Catalogue of Japanese Ceramics at the Centennial Exhibition* provided a model for Western collectors. Dresser himself relied heavily on Shioda, whom he also consulted while in Japan.[38]

As a result of Dresser's friendly connections with the Japanese Commissioners in 1876, a representative collection of Japanese pottery from the Centennial Exhibition was donated to the South Kensington Museum in exchange for a number of British contemporary artefacts collected by Dresser, which were presented to the Tokyo National Museum.

Leaving Philadelphia, Dresser travelled to San Francisco and from there left for Japan in the company of the Japanese Commissioners Sekisawa Akiko and General Saigô Tsugumichi. They arrived in Yokohama on 26 December 1876. According to Dresser the aim of his trip was threefold: to instruct the Japanese in modern industrial techniques; to bring the South Kensington Museum donation to the National Museum in Tokyo; and finally to enlarge his own and Tiffany's Japanese collection.[39]

Dresser was granted a semi-official status during his visit, and was asked by the Home Minister, Okubo Toschimichi, to act as adviser on the modernization of their art industries. The Emperor Meiji honoured him with an audience and offered to reimburse his travel expenses. He also allowed him to travel freely in Japan and to examine the imperial collections in Nara and in Kyoto, a rare privilege granted to few foreigners.

During his travels around the country Dresser was accompanied by two young officials of the Home Office: Sakata Haruo and Ishida Tametake. Ishida was asked to report to the government about the value of the trip, and his account, published in book form as *Dresser Hokoku* (1877), dealt with some 70 different forms of art industry commented on by Dresser. It emphasized Dresser's respect for traditional aesthetics and suggested ways of adapting modern methods of manufacturing. Ishida's report, together with Dresser's *Japan, its Architecture, Art and Art-Manufactures*, provided the most substantial coverage of contemporary Japanese art and industry up to that date, and had a considerable impact on the arts and industries in Japan.

During his 1,700-mile-long travels, Dresser visited about 75 different potteries and porcelain makers. He also inspected metalwork and iron companies, contributing particularly advice to the development of these industries in Osaka and in Sakai. Ishida, in his report, recalled that Dresser also examined the manufacture of bamboo and basketry, furniture, lacquer, textiles, embroideries, enamels, toys and paper, and that he was particularly concerned with the indiscriminate importation of European goods.[40]

Dresser was genuinely interested in Shintoism, and he frequently stressed that his personal collecting interests were based on the religious symbolism apparent in Japanese art. While visiting Nara, he participated in many discussions about Shintoism. His guide, the director of the National Museum, Machida Hisanari, took him to a Shinto dance ceremony, and he also had the rare privilege of inspecting the imperial collections in the Shosoin in Nara. He was particularly struck by the beauty of a modest water-jug whose spout was raised to the top of the orifice and covered by a flat lid, and by a heater of saké with a long straight handle.[41] These objects inspired some of his first heating vessels and decanters for Elkington's and for Hukin & Heath. A range of cruets, condiment sets, glass-stands and toast-racks produced in the late 1870s also convey the Japanese simplicity and constructional honesty he so much admired. Perhaps they were inspired by Japanese metal or lacquer stands, and strangely they also bring to mind the fences, railings and temple-gates (*torii*) that Dresser had studied while in Japan.

Dresser was certainly highly inspired by all the religious sites he visited, and a highlight was the ancient Shinto shrines at Isé. In Kyoto he profited greatly from conversations with Akamatsu Renjo, a priest who played an active role in the separation of Shintoism and Buddhism in the 1880s.[42] Dresser in his religious speculations concluded that Buddhism had made the Japanese receptive to a more sophisticated worship of nature, which was expressed in ornamentation of a naturalistic kind. In Shinto art, however, the ancient ideals of simplicity, utility, perfection of finish and constructional honesty were retained.[43] These aspects were to have a great influence on Dresser's own principles and designs, and in fact changed his entire artistic oeuvre.

His meetings with Japanese artists, connoisseurs and priests undoubtedly had a catalytic effect on Dresser, and enabled him to reach a more profound understanding of Japanese art and architecture. They also helped to promote Anglo-Japanese trade. During his trip he established further contacts for Londos and founded his own importing firm in conjunction with the Bradford businessman Charles Holme. Holme subsequently wrote perceptively about Japanese art, and founded *The Studio* magazine in 1893. The new company became known as Dresser & Holme and was established in Kobe by Dresser's sons, Louis and Christopher, in 1878. Louis returned to Britain in 1882, but Christopher married a Japanese woman and his descendants lived in Kobe until 1980, when the last of the line, Stanley Dresser, died.

During his travels Dresser amassed a vast collection of Japanese art objects. He may be counted as one of the first systematic Western collectors of Japanese artefacts and his interests covered all kinds of objects from household goods to bamboo utensils, textiles, ceramics, metalwork and architectural ornaments. His studies of the historical growth of forms from the primitive to the sophisticated went beyond the taste and interest of most Japonists. The famous American collectors Edward Sylvester Morse, Ernest Fenollosa and William Sturgis Bigelow, however, appear to have been among the first to adopt Dresser's attitude to collecting. They had certainly heard about the Tiffany collection before they left for Japan in

1877–8, and Morse and Bigelow began amassing Japanese ceramics and tea-ware of the cruder kind admired by Dresser. Like Dresser, these collectors had an eye for all forms of Japanese art, and they undertook similar researches on architecture, fine art, sculpture, ceramics and religion. Morse also made a name with his book *Japanese Homes and Their Surroundings* (1886), which was the first serious treatment of the subject to appear after Dresser's *Japan* of 1882.

The collecting attitudes among Victorian Japonists remain to be thoroughly analysed, but scholars seem to agree that the Americans generally demonstrated a higher level of cultural involvement. Dresser, however, was considered an outstanding exception to the 'pervasive cultural blindness' of the British.[44]

When Dresser returned from Japan, in the summer of 1877, he continued to enlighten the British public about Japanese art and architecture, and offered his expertise to various academic societies, manufacturers and dealers. He gave a number of lectures throughout the country, and leaders of fashion such as the critic George A. Sala and the Prince and Princess of Wales supported his campaign.[45] In 1877 Dresser organized a Japanese exhibition shown at the interior-decorating firm Jackson & Graham. The collection, which was presented with a catalogue by Dresser, contained some 2,800 objects that were chosen to be 'suggestive for the British manufacturers'.[46]

The following year he used samples of Japanese woodwork from the Jackson & Graham collection to illustrate his lecture on 'The Art Manufactures of Japan' for the Royal Society of Arts. His introduction dealt with the artistic value of Japonism, saying that it had 'done as much to improve our national taste as even our schools of art and public museums'. He even stressed that his own encounter with Japanese art had had a more profound effect on him than the education he had received at the School of Design.[47]

The grand display of Japanese art and culture at the Paris International Exhibition in 1878 provided Dresser and other Japonists with fresh inspiration, and by October that year the *Furniture Gazette* was announcing the Anglo-Japanese as 'the style of the coming season': 'Everything is already Japanese. The most progressive tradesmen in Regent Street [Liberty] sells Japanese bric-a-

165. Ebonized doorpanel for a wardrobe from Bushloe House, Leicester, 1879–80. Joseph Holtzman Collection, New York.

brac. All the curiosity shops display Japanese trinkets. Some decorators and art-furniture makers are not content unless their productions are as good imitations of Japanese work as can be found.'[48] Dresser, however, abhorred this imitative style and he advocated a more careful sifting and recasting of inspirational sources, which infused a fresh vigour into his designs.

The majority of his own furniture in the Anglo-Japanese style was done late in the 1870s for the Art Furnishers' Alliance and for his solici-

166. Dresser's Japanese lattice and geometrical patterns, delineated by Richard A. Boyd, *The British Architect* (1879). NAL.

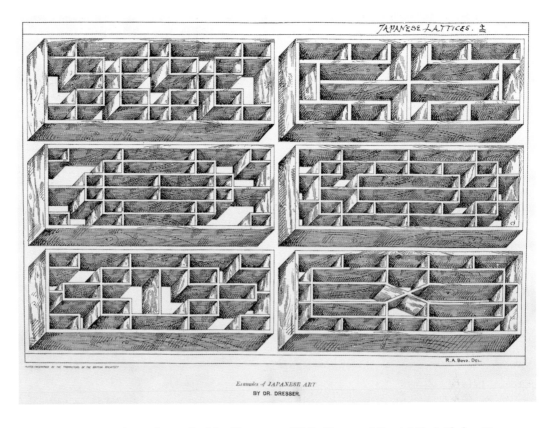

JAPANESE LATTICES.

R. A. BOYD. DEL.

Examples of *JAPANESE ART*
BY DR. DRESSER.

tor Hiram B. Owston's residence, Bushloe House, near Leicester. It was characterized by a play with solid and voids as well as contrasting and irregular shapes, combined with ebony and lacquer tints. In the cabinet panels he often used lattice panels and leather-paper in the Japanese style, or Japanese motifs in gold, olive and vermilion lacquer colours. Two wardrobes from Bushloe House, one decorated with stylized owls and the other with semi-humorous frogs, convey Dresser's love for grotesque imagery (plate 165). During his stay in Japan, Dresser had acquired a model book of Japanese furniture, and clearly he adapted both constructional and decorative details into his own original furniture.[49] His furniture clearly offered one of the boldest alternatives to ordinary Victorian design, and was perhaps regarded as too advanced by most people.

Dresser's so-called genuine Japanese room, which was a gift from Makimura Masano, the Governor of Kyoto, was exhibited at the jeweller Edwin W. Streeter's New Bond Street premises in 1878 and attracted considerable attention in the press.[50] It may well have influenced Edward W. Godwin's Anglo-Japanese designs for James M. Whistler's White House and Frank Miles's Chelsea House executed in the same year. The show of Dresser's lattice panels and other Japanese woodwork at the Architectural Association in 1878 undoubtedly made an impact on British architects. The lattice panels, which Dresser recommended for their versatility, became a popular feature in furniture and in many interiors (above).[51]

Clearly, Dresser rebelled against the constraints of Western conformism and continued to search for new ideas. In September 1878 he canvased the adaptation of Japanese ceilings to European architecture. His article on 'Works from Japan' described four model ceilings from Shogun Tokugawa's castle and shrine in Tokyo, which were in his possession and which after his death in 1904 were acquired by the V&A.[52] These coffered ceilings probably served as prototypes for several of the Anglo-Japanese ceilings that gained popularity in Britain in the 1880s and '90s. Dresser himself had incorporated similar ceilings in his decorations for Allangate Mansion (plate 167) in the early 1870s, but it was not until the turn of the century that the simplicity of Japanese interiors began to influence Western architects such as Charles Rennie Mackintosh and Frank Lloyd Wright.

By 1879 Dresser had become the most active

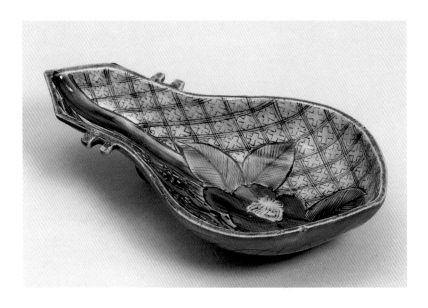

were freely adapted from various historical sources, most of the shapes, decorations and glazes were certainly influenced by Japanese ceramics, and two existing photographs of the pottery show the walls hung with Japanese silks and pictures.[54] The influence in fact was a two-way affair, which Robert Lee has observed: 'It is interesting to note that the Japanese were large buyers of the products of Linthorpe ... It has been stated, however, that some of the Japanese purchases of Linthorpe Ware have found their way back to Britain as Japanese Ware.'[55]

Dresser fell ill during 1881–2 and he retired from most of his commitments, including the Linthorpe Art Pottery and Dresser & Holme. Charles Holme continued the business of the

168. Japanese dish, bought for the South Kensington Museum from the Londos warehouse, 1877. V&A: 600–1877.

LEFT

167. Painted and coffered drawing room ceiling and cornice in Allangate, Halifax, designed by Christopher Dresser for Thomas Shaw, c.1870.

and well-known exponent of Japonism in Britain. When he opened his importing company, Dresser & Holme, in London that year, the event was attended by Sir Rutherford and Lady Alcock and other dignitaries, who all agreed, 'we seem to have left England and have been transported to Japan, so completely orientalized was everything around us'.[53] The showrooms contained the most diverse collection of Japanese artefacts, including Shiba and Hizen porcelain, Makudzu ceramics, ivorywork, lacquer objects, silver and bronze-work, iron kettles, lattice panels, screens and samples of Dresser's own Linthorpe Art Pottery, which contrasted nicely with their Japanese counterparts.

Linthorpe Art Pottery had been founded on Dresser's initiative in Middlesbrough in August 1879, and the first contemporary commentaries compared it to Japanese ceramics. Although shapes and decorations

LEFT

169. Japanese bronze kettle, c.1870, bought for the South Kensington Museum from Samuel Bing, 1875. V&A: 1882–1876.

ABOVE RIGHT

170. Japanese Raku pottery three-legged urn, bought for the South Kensington Museum from the Londos warehouse, 1877. V&A: 604–1877.

latter company, however, and his stand at the Furniture Trades Exhibition in 1883 was acclaimed as 'the most novel and striking feature of the exhibition'.[56]

Dresser & Holme were shareholders and suppliers of Japanese goods to the Art Furnishers' Alliance, which Dresser founded in June 1880 with George H. Chubb (producer of locks and metalwork), Edward Cope (lace manufacturer), John Harrison (director of Linthorpe) and Sir Edward Lee.[57] Evidently, the Art Furnishers' Alliance was intended to promote his own designs, together with a broad variety of Japanese goods. The stationery designed by Dresser was in the Japanese style, and the company clearly hoped to encourage the 'Japanese Mania', as one critic termed it in 1880.[58]

In 1882 Dresser lectured on 'Japanese Art Workmanship' in Liverpool and in Glasgow on the occasion of the opening of a 'Loan Collection of Oriental Art', which included objects from the South Kensington Museum, the Duke of Edinburgh's collection, and 1,150 items received as part of an exchange between the Glasgow Art Gallery and the Tokyo National Museum.[59] This last collection has been mistaken for the one sent by Dresser to Glasgow on his return from Japan, but the latter in fact went to a private collector, Robert Balfour, who lent the objects that illustrated Dresser's lecture. His introductory remarks criticized the indiscriminate fashion for Japanese bric-a-brac, which, he said, had resulted in nonsensical Japanesque products and converted many homes to mere curiosity shops.

The main part of Dresser's lecture, however, explored how the 'two prevailing systems of religion' – Shintoism and Buddhism – had shaped Japanese art and architecture.[60] This aspect was treated at greater length in *Japan, its Architecture, Art and Art Manufactures*, published later that year. The book was generally described as the first Western attempt to treat the art-manufactures and architecture of Japan as a serious academic subject. The *New York Times* review, entitled 'Wonders seen in Japan, Dr. Dresser's unrivalled and curious experience', particularly praised the section on architecture: 'Accordingly, although every part of this book is valuable, the architectural chapters of it, and especially the illustrations they contain, are inestimable. Japanese architecture is scarcely understood at all in Europe as yet.'[61]

Although British and American architects fell under the influence of Japanese architecture and design during the 1890s, Japanese architecture had in fact been almost entirely neglected by Western scholars. Even Sir Rutherford Alcock had proclaimed that 'the Japanese have no architecture',[62] and this fatal lack of insight permeated Western opinion. As late as 1893 William Morris still believed that 'the Japanese have no architectural, and therefore no decorative instinct'.[63] Dresser seriously tried to attempt to correct this view in his

book, which stands apart from the general literature on the subject.

Throughout the 1880s Dresser assiduously continued his study and promotion of Japanese architecture and ornamentation. His untiring efforts to enlighten the Architectural Association made a lasting impact on contemporary Victorian architects, and it was largely due to Dresser that Japanese architecture became the object of serious studies in Britain and the USA.

Never tired of lecturing on Japanese art and architecture, Dresser in 1884 addressed the Architectural Association, and stressed the importance of understanding Buddhist and Shinto aesthetics. Using Shinto's sacred symbol, the mirror, as an example, he spoke of the purist attitude in Japanese art and architecture, and urged the need for simplicity and purity in the West. He also showed a number of photographs of constructional details, drawing particular attention to the soundness of the bracketing under the curved Japanese roof.[64] By this date the *Journal of Decorative Art* commented that the influence of Japonism on the arts in Britain 'has been like the infusion of new life into a torpid body'.[65]

One of the final manifestations of the cult of Japan in Britain was Gilbert and Sullivan's highly popular operetta, *The Mikado* (1885). It prompted the creation of a Japanese village at South Kensington, which was opened by Sir Rutherford Alcock on 10 January 1885. This ambitious enter-

171. Japanese teapot, bought for the South Kensington Museum from the Londos warehouse, 1877. V&A: 603–1877.

prise consisted of five streets crowded with stalls and workshops inhabited by more than 200 Japanese people. The *Cabinet Maker* announced it as 'Japan in England' and referred to Dresser as the Japan expert *par excellence*:

> Dr. Dresser has given clear descriptions of the talent and painstaking methods of Japanese artisans and artists, but, after all is said and done, such things must be seen to be believed, and doubtless a sight of the clever workers of Kensington will be a revelation to the majority of the people.[66]

Dresser's call for a more serious study of Japanese art was given further impetus by the interest generated by the village, and was finally answered in the late 1880s and '90s by such collectors and writers as Ernest Hart and William Anderson. The British collectors Marcus B. Huish and James Bowes, however, were less successful in their endeavours, and their respective publications 'Japan and its Art Wares'[67] and *Japanese Pottery* (1890) were criticized as misleading by the American Japonists Ernest Fenollosa and Edward Morse. The latter dismissed Bowes's entire work, concluding with a statement that would have met with Dresser's approval: 'How far may one go astray who undertake to study the products of a country from just the opposite side of the globe.'[68]

Dresser, Morse and Fenollosa all had the advantage of first-hand studies in Japan, and they have been called the first Western scientific interpreters of Japanese art and culture. Dresser, in particular, stressed the benefits of utilizing methods similar to those practised by botanists, zoologists and linguists in classifying various branches of Japanese art. He was fully aware, however, that controversies and myths still hampered the development of scholarship. To a certain extent, similar attitudes dominate Western studies of Japanese art to this day, but the writings of Dresser, Fenollosa and Morse have made a valuable contribution.

Dresser's *Modern Ornamentation*, published in 1886, added further weight to the movement, as one critic wrote: 'We think that the work will be suggestive and useful, chiefly in those designs which have their motif in Japanese precedents, for in that direction we much prefer Dr. Dresser's work.'[69] However, Dresser's ornaments were rather too modern for some critics. *The Builder*, for example, described the Japan-inspired 'Evening' pattern with beetles, moths and spiders as 'inherently vicious'.[70] It was not until 1904, the year of Dresser's death, that Alphonse Mucha popularized surprisingly similar insect designs in his *Formenwelt aus dem Naturreiche*. It was only then at the brink of Modernism that the influence of Dresser's *Modern Ornamentation* had a tangible effect upon contemporary art, but few if any artists credited his pioneering work as their source of inspiration.

For more than 30 years Dresser had been a main spokesman for Japanese art, and his ideas gained increasing support in Britain towards the end of the nineteenth century. Several British artists, such as Mortimer Menpes, George Henry and Edward A. Hornel, travelled to Japan in the late 1880s and became exponents of the Japonism style in painting. Dresser's friends Sir Alfred East, Arthur Liberty and Charles Holme also toured Japan in 1888–9, visiting several of Dresser's associates.[71]

Towards the end of the century Japonism became the focus of more analytical and critical attention. The *Art Journal* in 1889 quoted a German designer as saying that 'we were all bewitched' and that 'English Art had become more strongly influenced by the art of Japan than that of any other European country'.[72]

Another German intrigued by the almost mystical impact of the Cult of Japan in Britain was the critic Petter Jesse. His influential articles 'Der Kunstgewerbliche Geschmack in England' treated Japonism as a serious topic, and he called Dresser, whom he described as the 'head of a famous studio outside London', the successor of Owen Jones.[73]

Above all the so-called 'Anglo-Japanese' style also fuelled the increasing interest in English architecture and design on the Continent, which was epitomized in Herman Muthesius' *Die Englische Baukunst der Gegenwart* (1900–04). Unfortunately the ageing Dresser did not participate in the public debate on Japonism around the turn of the century. His adherence to this style, however, clearly led to his detachment from traditional Western attitudes, and generated a new artistic vernacular that anticipated the Modern Movement. When he died in 1904, the obituary that appeared in *The Builder* recalled his lifelong passion for Japan and the East: 'He was a most genial companion and interesting talker and never tired of discussion on Art and the habits of the nations of the East, trying to trace their histories by their ornamental forms as a philologist does by their language.'[74]

In 1876 Dresser went to the United States and then on to Japan (see chapter 6), returning in April 1877. His conception of decorative design underwent a fundamental change and the work of this period is his most outstandingly innovative. He moved from the relatively subservient roles of commercial designer and art advisor to leading manufacturers into a more controlling position with more obscure firms who would allow him to dictate the – often highly experimental – form of his designs. Many of the products are signed, with a facsimile signature 'Chr Dresser' or the legend 'Designed by Dr C Dresser'.

172. Page from Dresser's record books, showing shapes for metalwork and ceramics. Now destroyed the pages were reproduced in Pevsner (1937).

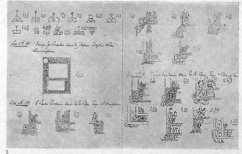

fabric designs anything between 10 and 20 guineas. Incidentally it should be noticed that most of the manufacturers for whom he worked are still in the front rank in 1937, a striking proof of that continuity of development characterizing a country in which copper coins with the head of young Victoria are valid to the present day. There are Crossley's and Brinton's in the carpet trade, and Minton's in the ceramics industry; Elkington, Hukin & Heath, Dixon's in the metal trades; Barlow & Jones, Turnbull & Stockdale, Warner & Sons, Tootal's, Wardle's in fabrics; Jeffrey's and Essex's, Sanderson's and John Line's in wall-papers.

As to Dresser's style, one has to differentiate between structural and ornamental problems. He was at his best when he had to shape objects, but he was more popular as a surface decorator. His early handwriting comes out clearly in a design for linoleum dating probably from the seventies.* It is still very similar to what ornament there is in his early books, and also to his *Studies in Design*, a portfolio of the seventies. Qualities to be stressed are a peculiar sombre colour-scheme of night-blue backgrounds with olive-brown, olive-green and gold, and certain spiky forms of wilful expression, which have scarcely any dependence on the past. This is also what makes some of the pottery which he designed in the same decade look so unusual amongst the ordinary period imitation then in fashion. There is no doubt a strong will and an original brain behind these designs.† The colour is harsh and rather crude, with unblended blues, greens, reds and gold.

The same harshness and wilfulness, not to say ruthlessness, is expressed in Dresser's designs for metal-work. I said before how much

* Comparable to linoleum designs in the account book for 1874.

† I cannot say that I have found the same appeal in what I have seen of Dresser's production for Mr. Harrison's Linthorpe Pottery at Middlesbrough for which he worked in the late seventies and the early eighties.

Designs by Christopher Dresser. 1, tea kettle in copper. 2, vase in " Clutha " glass, about 1880–90. 3–4, cruet sets, 1877–78. 5–7, pages from Dresser's account books for 1881, showing designs for lace curtains and metal-work. The headpiece on page 188 is a dinner-plate design, about 1870–80.

After Japan: Dresser and the Art Furnishers' Alliance
1877–1883

DRESSER & HOLME LONDON

173. Dresser's sample pages for the projected scheme to revive the Derbyshire flourspar industry. Holme papers. V&A.

In 1878 Dresser, in partnership with the Bradford businessman Charles Holme (1848–1923), established this wholesale warehouse in the Farringdon Road to import Oriental goods. Holme was born in Derby, the younger son of George Holme, a successful silk manufacturer. Charles entered the family firm, but moved to Bradford in 1871 to set up his own woollen business. In 1873 he was inspired by a lecture given at the Bradford Chamber of Commerce by the traveller Robert Barkley Shaw, who was the first Englishman to enter East Turkestan, when he went to investigate the possibilities of trading there. Charles Holme arranged to exchange Bradford-manufactured goods for craft goods from Turkestan. He later expanded his activities to India, China and Japan. It is not known how Dresser and he met, but it must have been through the Bradford textile manufacturing fraternity. Before he left Japan in 1877, Dresser arranged for his son Christopher to act as his agent in Kobe, and it was through

this means that Dresser & Holme was supplied. The Holme papers, recently acquired by the V&A, give insights into the minutiae of the operation, in particular an enterprise of Dresser's that came to nothing. He wanted to revive the Flour-spar or 'blue-john' industry in Derbyshire and he wrote a report and made designs, which were costed and samples manufactured, but failed to find any retail interest in the products. The costing sheet is illustrated with little sketches by Dresser (above) of the proposed shapes, with their fanciful names and cost price. These things must exist, in one example at least, and they have not as yet been identified. Dresser also used the business as a conduit for the products of the Linthorpe Art Pottery. A traveller's report among the Holme papers, on pottery samples presented to leading retailers in London – who almost without exception condemned the products, largely on the grounds of cost – may well refer to Linthorpe wares.

HUKIN & HEATH (later Heath & Middleton) BIRMINGHAM AND LONDON

Dresser was appointed art adviser to the established Birmingham manufacturing silversmith and electroplating firm of Hukin & Heath (founded 1855) in about 1878, the date the first of his designs was registered by the company. The firm specialized in novelty items for the luxury market and they were anxious to find a new direction. In 1879 they set up a London showroom at 19 Charterhouse Street, round the corner from the Dresser & Holme warehouse, and exhibited the new designs there. In the same year the firm entered a mark at Goldsmiths' Hall. A report in the *Furniture Gazette* on 23 August 1879 marked Dresser's arrival: 'The Firm have secured the services [of Dr Dresser] in

order to be reliable in point of design.' Dresser's strikingly original designs were stamped with a facsimile of his signature in addition to the firm's maker's mark. Fortunately, Dresser's designs were registered with the Patent Office, since the firm's design books, in which they were also recorded, were destroyed in the 1950s. Dresser was responsible for selecting Persian and Japanese articles to be copied through the electrotyping process by the firm. Hukin & Heath were creditors of the Art Furnishers' Alliance and so probably supplied the shop. The firm went on using the designs until about 1900.

174. Silver sugar basin, rolled edges and handle, with spoon,
marked Heath and Middleton, hallmarks for 1883.
Private Collection.

OPPOSITE 175. Cruet set, electroplate and glass, stamped '
Designed by Dr C Dresser', marked H&H, registered 1878.
Constance R. Caplin, Baltimore.

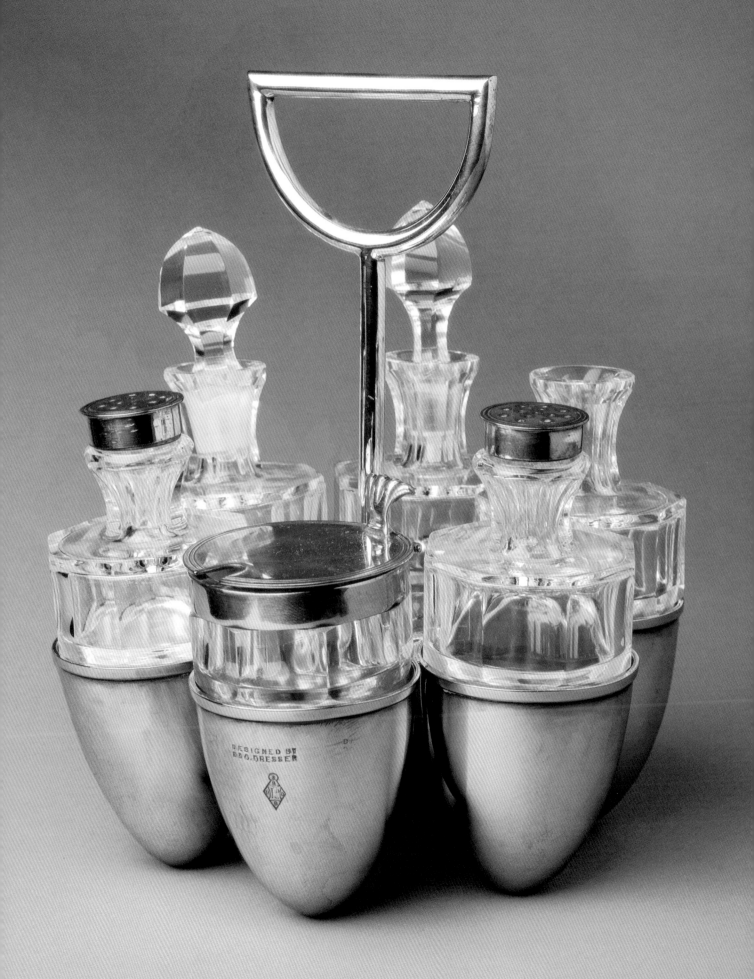

176. Three-piece teaset,
electroplate and ebony,
stamped 'Designed by
Dr C Dresser', registration
mark for 1878. The Andrew
McIntosh Patrick Collection.

177. Toast rack,
electroplate, registered
1881. The Andrew
McIntosh Patrick Collection.

178. Letter rack, electroplate, marked H&H. Cooper-Hewitt, National Design Museum.

179. Holder for six drinking glasses with carrying handle, electroplate and glass, stamped 'Designed by Dr C Dresser', marked H&H, 1887, design registered 1878. The Andrew McIntosh Patrick Collection.

180. 'Crow's-foot' decanter with amphora-shaped body,
electroplate and glass, stamped 'Designed by Dr C Dresser',
marked H&H, 2045, design registration mark for 1879.
The Andrew McIntosh Patrick Collection.

181. Three decanters (left to right): silver and glass
with ebony handle, marked Heath and Middleton,
London hallmarks for 1882–3; electroplate and glass
with ebony handle, c.1881; silver and glass with ebony
handle, marked Heath and Middleton, London hallmarks
for 1882–3. The Andrew McIntosh Patrick Collection.

182. Teapot, silver with bone and enamel-set lid,
stamped 'Designed by Dr C Dresser', Birmingham
hallmarks for 1878, design registration mark for 1878.
The Andrew McIntosh Patrick Collection.

OPPOSITE 183. Decanter, electroplate
and glass with ebony handle, c.1880.
The Andrew McIntosh Patrick Collection.

184. Oil and vinegar cruet with carrying handle, silver and glass, stamped 'Designed by Dr C Dresser', marked H&H, 1953, design registration mark for 1878. The Andrew McIntosh Patrick Collection.

185. Water-pot and teapot, decorated with engraved Japanese motifs, from a signed five-piece teaset.

186. Large soup tureen with ladle, electroplate with ebony handles and knob, stamped 'Designed by Dr C Dresser', marked H&H, 2123, design registration mark for 1880. The Andrew McIntosh Patrick Collection.

187. Small tureen with ladle. The Andrew McIntosh Patrick Collection.

JAMES DIXON & SONS SHEFFIELD

Dixon's was an early nineteenth-century firm of Britannia-metal workers and silversmiths, founded around 1806. In 1848 they secured from Elkington's a licence for the new electroplating process. They were yet another of Dresser's employers to have been involved with Cole's 'Summerly' venture. In 1873 they opened a London showroom at 37 Ludgate Hill and from 1879, as photographs of electroplated wares in their costing book of that year reveal, they were obtaining designs from Dresser. The first one to be registered by the firm dates from 1880. Between 1879 and 1882 Dresser sold about 37 designs to the firm, not all of which were put into production. In 1885 the firm issued a trade catalogue that included many of Dresser's models. Their showroom, like that of Hukin & Heath, was in the same neighbourhood as the Dresser & Holme warehouse. Dixon's supplied silver to Elkington & Co. and Howell, James & Co., and electroplate to Tiffany in New York – all firms with which Dresser had connections. Dresser's teapot designs for Dixon's are the most radical and uncompromising of his career. They broke his most cherished rules about the economical use of costly materials and ease of production. The Dixon designs secured for him his posthumous reputation as a proto-modernist, but in many cases their origins lie in Japanese forms, observed by Dresser during his time there in 1876–7.

189. Three-piece teaset, electroplate, stamped with a facsimile signature 'Chr Dresser', registered design, 1880. Private Collection.

188. Decanter, electroplate and glass, stamped with a facsimile signature 'Chr Dresser' and marked 'James Dixon & Sons', c.1880. The Birkenhead Collection.

152

190. Toast and egg rack with carrying handle, electroplate, stamped with facsimile signature 'Chr Dresser', marked no. 115, *c*.1879. Crabtree Farm.

191. Decanter, electroplate and glass, stamped with facsimile signature 'Chr Dresser', marked 'James Dixon & Sons 2548', *c*.1879. Constance R. Caplin, Baltimore.

192. Toast rack, electroplate. Ellen and William Taubman Collection.

193. Toast rack, electroplate and ebony, stamped with a facsimile signature 'Chr Dresser', marked 'James Dixon & Sons 963', *c.*1879. The Andrew McIntosh Patrick Collection.

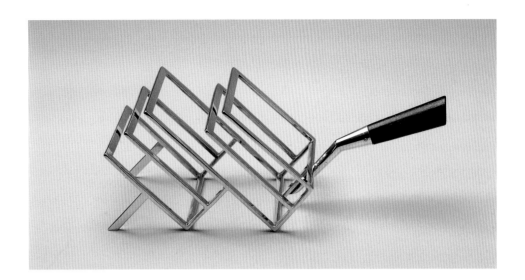

194. Three-piece teaset, electroplate and ebony, stamped with a facsimile signature 'Chr Dresser' and marked 'James Dixon & Sons 2278', design registered 1880. The Andrew McIntosh Patrick Collection.

OPPOSITE 195. Toast rack, electroplate, illegible marks, 1879. The Andrew McIntosh Patrick Collection.

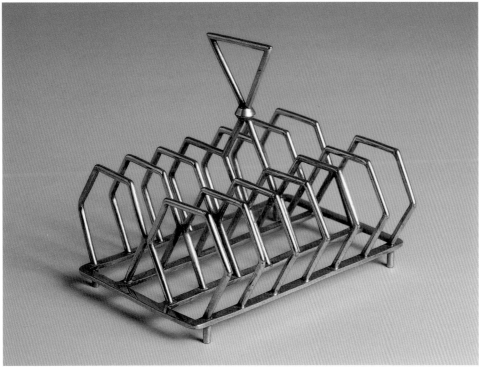

196. Toast rack, electroplate, marked 'James Dixon & Sons, no. 68', c.1879. Harry Lyons.

197. Toast rack, electroplate, marked no. 72, c.1879. Harry Lyons.

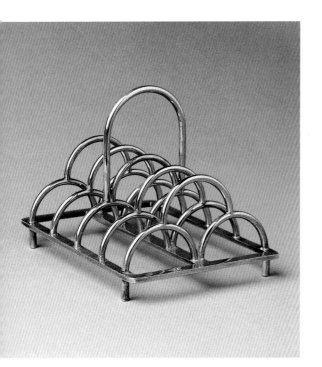

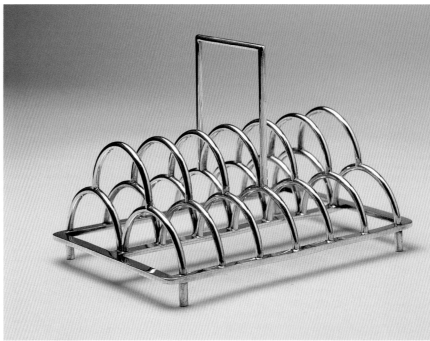

ABOVE 198. Toast rack, electroplate. Constance R. Caplin, Baltimore.

ABOVE RIGHT 199. Toast rack, electroplate, stamped with a facsimile signature 'Chr Dresser', *c*.1880. The Andrew McIntosh Patrick Collection.

RIGHT 200. Half-spherical teapot, electroplate with an ebony handle, stamped with a facsimile signature 'Chr Dresser', design registered 1879. Private Collection.

201. Three-piece teaset.
The Fine Art Society.

202. Sample page from
the Dixon costbook
showing the teapot
reproduced at plate 4.
Sheffield Public Library.

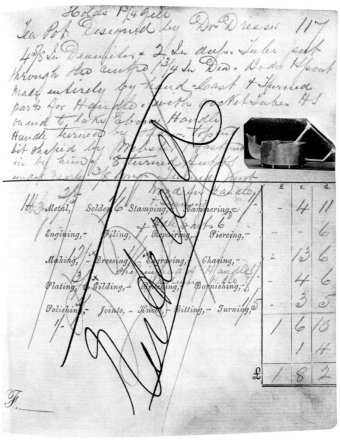

203. Decanter, electroplate and glass, stamped with a facsimile signature 'Chr Dresser' and marked 'James Dixon & Sons', *c.*1879. Harry Lyons.

204. Page from one of Dixon's record books showing a range of jugs and decanters, many in fashionable historicist styles, and including an example of plate 203 (left). Sheffield Public Library.

205. Page from one of Dixon's record books showing a range of jugs and decanters, many in historical styles such as the Neo-Renaissance, and including an example of plate 206 (right). Sheffield Public Library.

RIGHT 206. Silver decanter with engraved decoration. Ellen and William Taubman Collection.

LINTHORPE ART POTTERY MIDDLESBROUGH

Linthorpe was set up at Middlesbrough, in Teesside, in 1879 as an art pottery to produce original art wares and to provide employment for up to 100 staff. John Harrison, a businessman and admirer of Dresser, who was the owner of land with a deposit of red brick clay, funded the visionary enterprise. It was intended both to relieve the plight of the local unemployed and to utilize the native clay. The value of this humble material would have been brought home to Dresser by his experiences in Japan, where he was particularly struck with the beauty of the rough Raku teawares. Dresser acted as art director to the firm until 1882. In 1880–81 the pottery was available through Dresser & Holme. Linthorpe supplied Liberty's and Howell, James & Co., as well as Dresser's Art Furnishers' Alliance. On Dresser's recommendation, Henry Tooth, an artist who had worked as a boy in the local brickworks and whom Dresser had met on the Isle of Wight, was brought in as manager in spite of the fact that he had no experience of this trade beyond a few months apprenticeship in 1878 at the Derbyshire potters, T.G. Green. Tooth left in 1883 to establish the Bretby Art Pottery at Woodville in Derbyshire with William Ault (see below). The Linthorpe Art Pottery closed after Harrison's death in 1889. The shapes devised by Dresser for Linthorpe show most clearly his experience of non-Western design: Japanese, Peruvian, Mexican and Moroccan. Even when the source material is identified the shapes and glaze effects remain as some of the most radical and original of his career. The pottery produced during his involvement with the firm is marked with his facsimile signature impressed and the initials 'HT' for Henry Tooth.

208. Earthenware jug, impressed signature, marked no. 551 HT. Private Collection.

207. Earthenware jug, impressed signature, c.1880. The Birkenhead Collection.

OPPOSITE 209. Large three-legged earthenware vase, sunflower and sunray motif, Linthorpe mark, c.1880. David Bonsall, Image Bank Ltd.

LEFT 210. Unglazed earthenware pitcher with upturned spout, impressed signature, marked 'Linthorpe 685', *c.*1880. David Bonsall, Image Bank Ltd.

211. Japanese-style earthenware bowl. Private Collection.

LEFT 212. Earthenware bowl with pierced and raised flower and leaf decoration, *c.*1880. Private Collection.

RIGHT 213. Earthenware cylindrical 'Owl' spill vase, marked no. 175 HT, *c.*1880. Private Collection.

214. Earthenware flask-shaped vase with incised ornament, impressed signature, marked 'HT' c.1880. Private Collection.

215. Japanese-style earthenware vase, impressed signature, marked no. 331, c.1880. Private Collection.

216. Three 'Peruvian' bridge-spouted earthenware pitchers, impressed signatures, (left) marked no. 613 Ht; (centre) marked no. 296 HT; (right) marked no. 347 HT, all c.1880. Private Collection.

218. Earthenware vase, with inverted trumpet-shaped base, impressed signature, marked no. 223 HT, *c*.1880. Private Collection.

217. Large ceramic vase, impressed signature, marked no. 827 HT, *c*.1880. Private Collection.

219. Earthenware 'Peruvian' spouted pitcher, impressed signature, marked no. 335 HT, *c*.1880. Private Collection.

220. Earthenware vase with white-glazed Japanese 'mons'
or badges, impressed signature, c.1880. The Birkenhead Collection.

221. Cylindrical earthenware vase, impressed signature,
marked no. 536 HT, c.1880. Private Collection.

222. Long-necked
earthenware pitcher
inspired by ancient Roman
glass vessels, impressed
signature, *c*.1880. The
Birkenhead Collection.

RIGHT 225. Earthenware four-
legged vase with four tubular
chambers and openwork body,
impressed signature, *c*.1880.
The Birkenhead Collection.

BELOW 223. Earthenware plate with
raised decoration of a spread-winged
bird among flowers, impressed
signature, *c*.1881. The Birkenhead
Collection.

BELOW RIGHT 224. Design for a plate
similar to plate 223. Minton Museum
and Archives.

227. Earthenware jug with round stopper, impressed signature, *c*.1880. The Birkenhead Collection.

226. Earthenware jug with angled neck, illustrated in the Dresser cost book, p. 140, *c*.1883. The Birkenhead Collection.

228. Earthenware jar and cover with mottled glaze, impressed signature, marked no. 277 HT, *c*.1880. Private Collection.

229. Terracotta moon-flask, impressed signature, marked 'Linthorpe'; terracotta vase with incised decoration, impressed signature, marked 'Linthorpe 270', both *c*.1880. David Bonsall, Image Bank Ltd.

230. Three-legged earthenware vase with streaky glaze, impressed signature, marked 'Linthorpe 281', *c*.1880. David Bonsall, Image Bank Ltd. Compare with the shape of the Minton vase, plate 130.

231. Earthenware pitcher with upturned lip, impressed signature, marked no. 611 HT, *c*.1880. Cooper-Hewitt National Design Museum.

OPPOSITE 234. Earthenware dimpled double-gourd vase with angled neck, impressed signature, marked no. 326 HT, *c*.1880. Michael Whiteway.

232. Earthenware sake bottle, impressed signature, marked no. 341, *c*.1880. Private Collection.

233. Earthenware 'Peruvian' vase, impressed signature, marked no. 393 HT, *c*.1880, with ancient Peruvian pottery bridge-spouted vessel, *c.* AD1500. Cooper-Hewitt National Design Museum.

BENHAM & FROUD LTD LONDON

A firm of copper and brass manufacturers, recorded from 1860 at 40–42 Chandos Street, Charing Cross. They exhibited at international exhibitions in Paris (1855) and London (1862). Dresser designed sporadically for the firm from about 1872 (a registered design for a coalbox) until 1893. The most distinctive designs are for vessels, such as kettles and teapots, as well as trays, fire-irons and candlesticks, in a combination of brass and copper patterned with rivets, reflecting Dresser's experience of Japanese metalwork. Benham & Froud supplied the Art Furnishers' Alliance with brass-mounted wooden coalboxes, dishes and candlesticks, kettles and teapots, which are documented by photographs on the archives of Chubb's, safemakers and locksmiths, and principal shareholders of the venture.

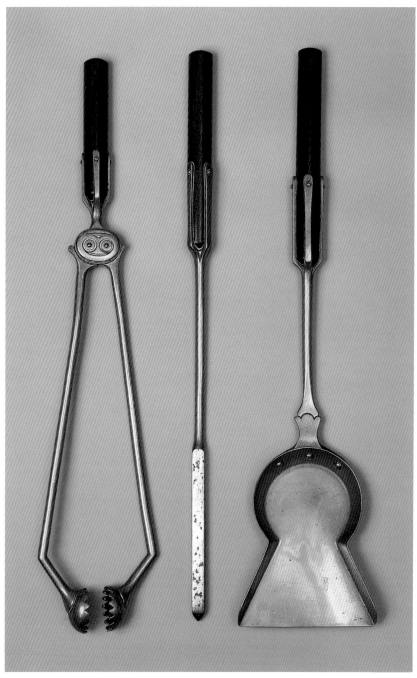

235. Set of three wooden-handled brass fire-irons, orb device trademark for Benham & Froud, c.1880. Private Collection.

OPPOSITE 236. Copper and brass rivetted kettle with cut-out base frieze in the Japanese style, c.1880. The Andrew McIntosh Patrick Collection.

237. Copper tray with mixed metal 'peacock and flower' overlay, trademarked for Benham & Froud c.1885. The Birkenhead Collection.

RIGHT 238. Copper and brass candlestick with cut-out decoration on the base, possibly made by Benham & Froud, c.1880, and sold through the Art Furnishers' Alliance. Private Collection.

239. Kettle on stand. The Andrew McIntosh Patrick Collection.

OPPOSITE 240. Copper and brass watering pot
or ewer, trademarked for Benham & Froud,
c.1885. Harry Lyons.

241. Copper and brass kettle with wooden handle,
trademarked for Benham & Froud, c.1885.
The Birkenhead Collection.

RICHARD PERRY, SON & CO. WOLVERHAMPTON

The firm specialized in the japanned and tin ironwares for which Wolverhampton was famous. Dresser's connection with the firm dates from 1883, with a registered design for a brass and wood candlestick, inspired by Japanese lacquered wood objects – specifically a type of drum used in Noh theatre, dating from the eighteenth century. Perry's London retail outlet was at 72 New Bond Street, and one of Dresser's designs for them, the 'Kordofan' candlestick, was retailed through Liberty's. Dresser's association with Perry's was closest to his ideal of bringing distinguished design to the most modest domestic items.

243. Painted metal and wood candlestick, marked 'Dr Dresser's Design' and Perry trademark, registration mark 112571, c.1890. Private Collection.

242. Copper jug with papier-mâché insulating jacket, marked 'Dr Dresser's Design', c.1883. Ellen and William Taubman Collection.

244. Painted metal candlestick, marked 'Dr Dresser's Design', *c*.1883. Private Collection.

BELOW 245. (Left) 'Japanned' metal and brass 'Kardofan' candlestick with a wooden handle, marked 'Dr Dresser's Design', registered 1883; (right) painted metal chamber stick, marked 'Dr Dresser's Design', *c*.1883. The Andrew McIntosh Patrick Collection.

ART FURNISHERS' ALLIANCE CO. LONDON

Dresser's ideas on merchandizing, which he had put into practice in a number of ventures, both wholesale and retail, crystalized with this association of manufacturers, brought together to supply 'whatever is necessary to the complete artistic furnishing of a house'. Dresser was the art director and the company directors were George Hayter Chubb, John Harrison of the Linthorpe Art Pottery, Edward Cope and Sir Edward Lee. Coverage in the *Cabinet Maker* gives some indication of the scope of the scheme. The furniture was supplied by Chubb's and manufactured by the cabinet-making firm Knight of Bath. Photographs in the Chubb archive give an idea of the choice available from the Alliance. Many of the models date from earlier in Dresser's career; some items went on to form part of the stock of Liberty's after the failure of the Alliance in 1883. Oriental artefacts were supplied by Arthur Liberty and Dresser & Holme; silver and plate by Hukin & Heath and Dixon's; metalwares by Benham & Froud; pottery by Linthorpe. A number of Dresser's employers supplied wallpapers (Lightbown, Aspinall & Co., Jeffrey & Co., Scott Cuthbertson and Arthur Sanderson); carpets (Brinton & Lewis), linoleum (Frederick Walton) and glass (Sowerby): many of them were also shareholders. William Cooke, one of the largest shareholders, registered a number of wallpaper designs during the brief period of the Alliance's activity, and these may be assumed to have formed part of the stock in the shop at 157 New Bond Street (plates 253, 254). The Alliance went into liquidation in 1883 and the stock was auctioned off in August of that year.

246. Chair in ebonized wood with gold panels and detail, illustrated in the Thomas Knight of Bath catalogue, *c.*1880. The Birkenhead Collection.

247. 'Egyptian' chair, ebonized wood.
V&A: W.35-1992.

248. Armchair of triangulated construction, polished wood, illustrated in the Thomas
Knight of Bath catalogue, made for the Art Furnishers' Alliance, c.1880. Private Collection.

OPPOSITE 249. Ebonized wood chair, illustrated in the Thomas Knight of Bath catalogue, made for the Art Furnishers' Alliance, c.1880. Private Collection.

RIGHT 250. Painted wood Japanese-style fan or face-screen with an owl, c.1880, a variant of an illustration to *Studies in Design* (1874–6). The Birkenhead Collection.

251. Board with samples of brass door furniture, Chubb's for the Art Furnishers' Alliance. The Wolfsonian-Florida International University, Miami Beach, Florida. The Mitchell Wolfson, Jr. Collection.

BELOW 252. Ebonized wood coalbox with gilded detail, c.1880. The Birkenhead Collection.

BELOW 253. William Cooke & Sons. Jade green geometric wallpaper pattern, sample, 368741, registered 20 August 1881. Public Record Office. William Cooke was one of the largest shareholders in the Art Furnishers' Alliance. This is the strongest evidence for Dresser's involvement in the firm, which appears to go back to the 1860s.

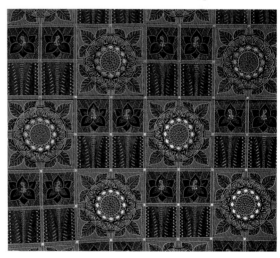

254. William Cooke & Sons. Gold and black Japanese-style wallpaper sample, 368742, registered 20 August 1881. Public Record Office. Both these papers were registered during the lifetime of the Art Furnishers' Alliance.

Dresser in Context

SIMON JERVIS

255. Henry Wyndham Phillips
(1820–68). *Portrait of Owen Jones*,
oil on canvas, 1856. RIBA Library
Drawings Collection, London.

When the 1871 census was taken, Christopher Dresser, described as 'Architect and Ornamentist', was living with his wife, nine children, aged from four to fifteen, and five servants at Tower Cressy in North Kensington, a part of London where villas and terraces for the professional and commercial classes were encroaching on the mansions and gardens of the noble and the rich (plate 33).[1] Given his lower-middle-class origins, Dresser's move in 1868 to this imposing albeit hamfisted house, itself the creation of the notable Victorian engineer Thomas Page,[2] must have seemed to set the seal, at the age of 34, on a story of almost runaway success. His claim to the Society of Arts in 1871 that 'as an ornamentist I have much the largest practice in the kingdom' echoes the confident image in the Linnean Society's photograph of their Fellow, which itself brings to life the *New York Times*'s 1877 evocation of Dr Christopher Dresser, self- proclaimed 'art adviser' extraordinary, black of beard and bright of eye (plate 2).[3]

Nemesis, inevitably, followed hubris. Dresser's appointment in 1879 as Art Director of the newly founded Linthorpe Pottery, his taking on the art editor-ship of the *Furniture Gazette* in 1880, his pivotal role as 'Art Manager' of the Art Furnishers' Alliance at its ambitious inception in the same year, and his publi-cation in 1882 of *Japan, Its Architecture, Art and Art Manufactures*, combined with a continued activity as a lecturer and as the leader of a large and produc-tive design studio – all this reflects an almost frenetic level of engagement. The involvement with the *Furniture Gazette* ended promptly in January 1881, a bare year after its commencement, to the enjoyment of the rival *Cabinet Maker and Art Furnisher*.[4] In 1881 Dresser claimed to have been seriously ill, and in 1882 he lost his role at Linthorpe. In 1883 Llewellyn Jewitt pronounced: 'Of late the works, untrammelled by the former conventionalities, and casting off the rigid severity of angular outlines on the one hand and grotesque combinations, absurdities and distortions on the other, have entered on another, newer, and far more graceful and effective phase of art'.[5] Also in 1883 the Art Furnishers' Alliance collapsed, a liquidator's sale being held in August, and in that same year Dresser moved from Tower Cressy to Wellesley Lodge, in outer-suburban Sutton. Such a series of setbacks had evidently necessitated retrenchment.

The events of the early 1880s did not, however, constitute a wholesale debacle. In 1885 Elkington & Co. registered a remarkable series of designs for silver and silver-plate, a considerable expression of faith, even if the designs themselves, comparable to others supplied to Dixon & Sons and Hukin & Heath in the late 1870s, may be earlier. Admittedly, Dresser's swansong, *Modern Ornamentation*, issued in 1886 by Batsfords, who were by then the publishers of Lewis F. Day and of Thomas Cutler's *A Grammar of Japanese Ornament and Design* (1882), was a lack-lustre restatement of earlier themes.[6] But reviving fortunes were no doubt behind a move in 1889 to Elm Bank, in Barnes, and thus about as close to central London as Hammersmith, whence Dresser had ascended to Tower Cressy and Kensington in 1868.

From the late 1880s to Dresser's death in Mulhouse in 1904, at the age of 70, his design studio continued to be active and productive. Clutha glass, made by James Couper & Sons of Glasgow, and sold by Liberty's, must have seemed innovatory on its launch in 1888 for its exploitation of a whole range of 'accidental' effects, bubbles, streaks, marbling, metallic flecks and so on, and for a free asymmetry derived from prototypes such as Persian rosewater sprinklers, and going far beyond Dresser's relatively rigid prescriptions for glass in *Principles of Decorative Design* (1873).[7] But Linthorpe pottery, if its high metallic sheen is overlooked, provided precedents, both as to forms and through the random mingling of coloured glazes. Henry Tooth's Bretby Art Pottery, founded in 1883 at Church Gresley in Derbyshire, carried on Dresser's Linthorpe manner, which was evidently still marketable in 1893 when William Ault, Tooth's former partner, signed a contract under which Dresser would provide new designs for his Swadlincote pottery, to be stamped 'Dr Dresser', as well as receiving a yearly retainer for inspection, instruction and criticism, an arrangement similar to that instituted at Linthorpe 15 years earlier.[8] The account of Dresser in the mid-1890s selling patterns based on the scarab, which he had incorporated into designs for Mintons in about 1870, some 25 years earlier, to the Lancashire wallpaper manufacturer Henry Lightbown further suggests that Dresser, although an energetic and effective salesman, and still decided in his opinions, was then living off his creative capital.[9] As for his

studio it seems at the end to have been principally devoted to the production of flat pattern for wallpapers and textiles, few of which were designed by Dresser himself; indeed its output had much in common with the commercial studio founded in 1880 by Arthur Silver, a pupil of H. W. Batley, who was trained by B.J. Talbert.

In 1899 *The Studio, An Illustrated Magazine of Fine and Applied Art*, whose first volume, published in 1893, had included articles by or about Aubrey Beardsley, Frank Brangwyn, Walter Crane, A.H. Mackmurdo and C.F.A. Voysey, included, surprisingly, an appreciation of Christopher Dresser, by then aged 65.[10] Its publication is easily explained by the circumstance that *The Studio*'s backer, Charles Holme (1848–1923), who, incidentally, lived in William Morris's Red House, had in 1879 been Dresser's partner in the import of Japanese wares. The tone of 'The Work of Christopher Dresser' is painfully *de haut en bas* in its condescension to 'not the least but perhaps the greatest of commercial designers imposing his fantasy and invention upon the ordinary output of British industry'. The old accusations, 'a certain spiky uncomfortability' and 'fondness for angularity' surface, but Dresser is given full credit for his 'regard for materials', his 'extraordinary acquaintance with the practical details of modern industries', the continued soundness and pertinence of the theories and advice contained in his *Principles* and his pioneering interest in Japan. The idea that William Morris was 'not only the greatest but the only leader of the movement ... to raise the national level of design' is scotched, and the role of Dresser, in that crusade, as the 'figurehead' of professional trade designers is underlined. Dresser must have been gratified by such recognition, but can hardly have been pleased to have been placed quite so firmly in the commercial, professional, trade pigeon-hole, a middle-class Martha to his contemporary William Morris's Mary.

The trajectory of Dresser's career may be seen to follow a classic pattern, which led vigorously upwards until about his 50th year, when he overreached himself and was forced to retreat, but which culminated in two decades of quieter achievement, a period during which he pursued commercial success and his own personal style of design, although never abandoned, ceased to be a dominant factor in his studio's output, still less the

256. William Morris.
Watercolour design
for the 'Pomegranate'
wallpaper, 1864.
Private Collection.

focus of evangelism. A quiescent, if not extinct vol-
cano? So it seems. And at the end, still evidently
active, the domestic tyrant and the design pundit
seem to have been in balance with the bibulous
lover of plants and gardening, ever the botanist,
and the authority on and student of Oriental art.

Twentieth-century posterity has insisted, and
twenty-first-century posterity no doubt will focus
on Dresser's identity as an 'industrial designer'
avant le lettre.[11] The case is a good and plausible
one, but it needs to be modulated in two respects:
first, it has to be underlined that imposing
anachronistic labels has its risks; and second it
must be recognized that knowledge of 'industrial
design' in the nineteenth century is still in its
infancy. Dresser may have had precursors and con-

temporaries of whom little or nothing is so far
known, who could equally be saluted as primordial
'industrial designers'. (There was a time when
Chippendale, who published, was regarded as the
only important mid-eighteenth-century furniture
designer and producer; new knowledge teaches
otherwise.) The point about anachronism also
needs to be laboured. Dresser, although a product
of the School of Design, who included the word
'design' in the titles of three of his five principal
books, did not usually present himself as a
designer, preferring 'architect' and 'ornamentist',
his favourite titles apart from 'doctor' and 'professor', or such labels as 'artist', 'art advisor', 'art
director', 'art editor', 'art manager' or 'decorator'.
These terms are closely related to contemporary

combinations such as 'art-industry' or 'art-manu-factures' and it needs to be recalled that the term 'industrial designer', now so entrenched, is not of immemorial coinage, and that the 'art' component, now discarded, was still current, albeit on its final wane, when in 1937 Pevsner published both his *Enquiry into Industrial Art in England* and the article on 'Christopher Dresser, industrial designer', which rescued Dresser from oblivion.

'Ornament has always arisen out of architecture': Dresser's 1873 dictum, echoing Ruprich-Ruppert's 1863 'le premier des décorateurs, c'est l'architecte!', demanded that he, proud ornamentist, should also describe himself as an architect.[12] Since anyone was at liberty to make this claim until the introduction of compulsory registration in 1931, the description was, legally speaking, no imposition, but nor was it convincing; Dresser had neither trained nor practised as an architect. Looking backwards, however, architects, a profession at the top of the artistic pecking order, had often taken a leading role in design innovation. Daniel Marot, William Kent and Robert Adam are the supreme exemplars, and Soane's statement, made in 1812, 20 years after Adam's death, that 'manufacturers of every kind felt, as it were, the electric power of this revolution in art' was no exaggeration.[13] The architect John Buonarotti Papworth (1775–1847) was not an innovator to compare with Adam, but he designed for a whole spectrum of manufactures, including furniture, silver, stained glass, lighting, glass and textiles, and his promotion in an 1834 lecture of 'the art of ornamental design' no doubt helped to bring about his short-lived appointment in 1837 as part-time director of the new School of Design.[14] In the next generation, that preceding Dresser, the architect A.W.N. Pugin was equally, if not more, versatile and productive, while Sir Matthew Digby Wyatt – the scion of an architectural dynasty, who was closely associated with the mid-century movement for design reform – designed carpets, wallpapers, tiles and cast-iron public conveniences. It is also worth noting that architects continued to design for manufacturers in the post-Dresser generation; a case is Charles Robert Ashbee, an Arts and Crafts grandee, who stated in 1911: 'I have designed for manufacturers of pianos, bedsteads, wall papers, clocks, cast-iron ware, furniture, pottery, metal work, organs and printed books.[15]

Another context for Dresser, to set alongside architect-designers, is provided by those designers, often with artisan backgrounds and sometimes autodidact, who emerged from the world (frequently the provincial world) of the drawing school: Thomas Sheraton, and Peter and Michael Angelo Nicholson, father and son, may stand as exemplars. Yet further precursors were the shadowy designers who worked more-or-less exclusively for one branch of industry or even for one firm. George Haité, father of George Charles Haité (1855–1924), and Charles Hudson, both of whom designed for Swaisland's, the shawl printers of Crawford in Kent, in the 1840s, and James Huntington, who was said in 1861 to be selling more designs to English paper-stainers than all the French designers put together, are among these unsung backroom servants of industry.[16] There were, of course, other species of designer, including sculptors such as Flaxman and painters such as Stothard, but in the Dresser context the architect, the drawing-master and the designer for industry, sometimes the product of a confined, even inbred, monoculture, are the crucial ingredients.

Dresser's years at the School of Design, from Somerset House in 1847, when he was 13, to the end of his studies at Marlborough House in 1854, aged 20, stamped him for life. There he developed the botanical interests that were to be dominant up to the late 1860s and that remained central to his thinking on ornament. But there too he made contact with the teachers and mentors who were to influence him and with some of the manufacturers who were to employ him. Among the former may be numbered the painter, designer and teacher Richard Redgrave, whose *Report on Design* at the 1851 Great Exhibition, published in 1852, Dresser praised in 1862 and quoted in 1873; Gottfried Semper, the great German architect, designer and theorist, who was in London from 1850 to 1855; Ralph Wornum, the future keeper of the National Gallery, who was employed by the School of Design from 1848 to 1854, and whose *Analysis of Ornament* was long the standard textbook on the subject; and Matthew Digby Wyatt, secretary of the Executive Committee of the Great Exhibition, who was responsible, with his friend Owen Jones, for the courts devoted to various historic styles in the Crystal Palace, when it was re-erected at Sydenham in 1853.

In parenthesis it is worth adding that Dresser

257. Owen Jones. Design
sample of woven wool
and silk fabric imitating
gold-printed flock
wallpaper for Jackson
& Graham, Oxford Street,
London, registered
4 January 1868.
Public Record Office.

of the *Grammar of Ornament* (1856), for which
Dresser supplied the plate on leaves and flowers,
and in which Jones included an extra principle, 'All
ornament should be based upon a geometrical
construction'; Jones, the productive and versatile
designer of, *inter alia*, books, tiles, mosaics, textiles,
graphics, wallpapers, carpets, silver, furniture and
interiors: all these and other aspects of Jones made
a deep impression on Dresser. But there were significant differences between the two. Jones was the
son of a celebrated Welsh antiquary, not an
obscure excise officer; he received a full architectural training under the learned and distinguished
Lewis Vulliamy; he travelled widely when young,
visiting Egypt and Spain, where he carried out the
original research that underlay his magnificent
Alhambra (1836–45); he was in contact with
advanced French and German theorists and translated Seroux d'Agincourt; a member of the Arts
Club, a friend of Henry Cole, and of George Eliot
and G.H. Lewes, and a gold medallist of the Royal
Institute of British Architects – Jones moved in
exalted circles. It would probably come as a surprise to Christopher Dresser to discover that,
around the turn of the twentieth century, his own
works should command more public attention
than the even greater achievements of Owen
Jones, his master.[20]

There is in the numbered paragraphs of
Dresser's *The Art of Decorative Design* (1862) and in
the very title of his *Principles of Decorative Design*
(1873), whose first sentence invokes the importance of 'true principles of ornament', an echo of
Pugin, and of 'decorative laws', more than a hint
of that systematic pursuit of certainties that came
to animate the School of Design and that inspired
Owen Jones's principles. In 1862 Dresser, aged 28,
wrote of having arrived at 'a knowledge of the
laws which govern the production and combination of ornamental forms' after 15 years of study
and research.[21] There is a touch of Gradgrindian
dogmatism in this approach, understandable in
view of Dresser's education, his youth, and the
endorsement provided by repeated approaches
from 'manufacturers of the greatest eminence
desiring designs for their respective
manufactures'.[22] In 1873, aged 39, Dresser was
still successful, but his *Principles of Decorative
Design* show little evidence that all around him
there was emerging what Batley in 1882 called 'a

had contacts in the scientific world, who informed
his theories of decoration, including the botanists
John Lindley (1799–1865), a juror in 1851, and
Sir William Hooker (1785–1865), director of Kew
Gardens from 1841, John Tyndall (1820–93), professor of natural philosophy at the Royal Institution, and George Wilson (1818–59), appointed
director of the nascent Scottish Industrial Museum
in 1855:[17] in 1873 Dresser quoted the last-
named's observations on the nautilus shell as a
demonstration 'of the perfect compatibility of the
highest utility with the greatest beauty'.[18]

Owen Jones, however, was without doubt the
greatest influence on Dresser, who paid heart-felt
tributes to Jones not only after his death in 1874,
when Dresser was a member of the Owen Jones
Memorial Committee, but also during his lifetime.
Thus Dresser wrote in 1862: 'The excellency of
these works [the Alhambra and Greek courts in the
Crystal Palace at Sydenham, and Saint James's
Hall] calls loudly to us as a nation to do honour to
Mr Owen Jones, who created them'.[19] Jones, the
colour theorist and practitioner, well acquainted
with the writings of Chevreul and Field; Jones, the
formulator of correct principles of design, printed
for the School of Design in 1852; Jones, the creator

258. Henri-Auguste Fourdinois (1830–1907).
Cabinet, ebony with inlay of box, lime, holly, pear,
walnut, mahogany and marble, manufactured in
Paris, 1861–7. V&A: 721–1869. Bought for the
South Kensington Museum from the Paris 1867
exhibition for £2,750.

more comfortable, easy, a more wooden and less stony style', and the splendid plates of *Studies in Design*, published from 1874 to 1876, and avowedly dating from 'the last fifteen years' (that is, some could be as early as 1861, if not 1859), look backwards rather than forward.[23] And when in 1880 Dresser initiated his art editorship of the *Furniture Gazette* by reprinting 13 of Owen Jones's principles, he nailed his colours firmly to that mast, fashioned in 1852. It may be added that, whereas the medium of *Modern Ornamentation* (1886) was influenced by the present in its employment of delicate hatching and tonal gradations, the message of the designs themselves is again weighted towards Dresser's past. Only two of the 50 plates were described as Japanese, whereas 23 are based on Islamic ornament, Persian, Arabian, Indian and so on. To that number may be added others, including a 'Venetian' design of Moresque character, and an unexpected 'Italian Renaissance' design, which,

like so many of the others, seems a variation on Islamic themes initiated by Owen Jones.[24] The next largest category is of 'Mediaeval' or 'Gothic' designs that recall the style of the 1860s.

Dresser's consistency with regards to both principles and styles no doubt reflects integrity and constancy; but a measure of intransigence may also be suspected. His dislike of Renaissance ornament was one constant. He was probably unaware that the illustration he used towards the beginning of *Principles* (1873) to convey the excitement of 'sharp, angular or spiny forms' was derived from a plate of ornament, published in 1615 by Étienne Carteron (*c.*1593–1633), in the *cosses de pois* style, a descendant of the Renaissance grotesque.[25] Also in 1873 Dresser singled out for criticism a virtuoso Fourdinois cabinet purchased by the South Kensington Museum from the 1867 Paris Exhibition for the prodigious sum of £2,750; it displayed refined mannerist grotesque and Moresque ornament.[26] Indeed South Kensington's weakness for the Renaissance never ceased to annoy Dresser, and it is thus consistent if odd to find Ariosto, a quintessentially Renaissance poet, imprisoned in a Gothic decorative scheme in *Studies in Design* (1876), that particular plate almost certainly designed by J. Moyr Smith.[27] In 1870 an almost exact contemporary of Dresser, Marc Louis Emanuel Solon (1835–1913), began to work for Minton's, where he remained until 1904, the year of Dresser's death. Solon's *Inventions Décoratives* (1866) are an example of the elegance and creativity of contemporary French designers working in a style largely inspired by Renaissance or mannerist prototypes.[28] Trained at Sèvres, Solon was a sophisticated exponent of the French *Néo-Grec* style, which also utilized Greek elements and relished angularity and geometry. 'Angularity' was indeed singled out by Dresser in a candelabrum by Miroy Frères, which he saw and admired at the Paris 1867 Exhibition.[29] Was he aware that it was in this tainted style? And as for geometry, César Daly (1811–94), the founder and editor of the *Revue générale de l'architecture* (1840–90), who was an admirer of Owen Jones and, as did others, spotted the significance of the Japanese display at the London 1862 Exhibition, based his analysis of architectural history and progress on geometry: in 1851 he greeted Matthew Digby Wyatt's *Specimens of Geometrical Mosaics of the Middle Ages* with an enthusiastic

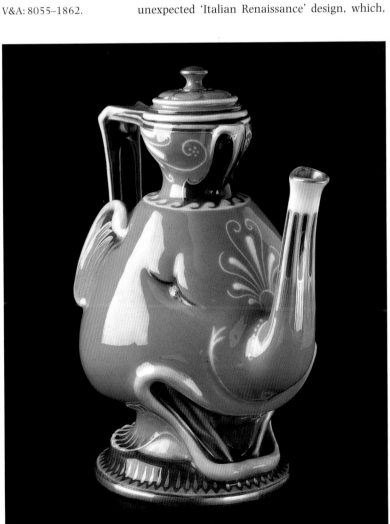

259. Sèvres. Porcelain coffee-pot, designed by Marc-Louis-Emanuel Solon (1835–1913), shown at the London 1862 exhibition and published in Solon's *Inventions décoratives* (Paris, 1866). V&A: 8055–1862.

'What taste! What luxury! What elegance!'[30] Despite these affinities Dresser would surely not have approved of a pamphlet, *Industrial Art* (1890), in which the accomplished French designer Albert Willms, who had been head of Elkingtons' design studio since 1859, stressed the French contribution to British design.

Dresser admired German science: 'The Germans are greater thinkers than we are'.[31] But there is little sign that he had a deep acquaintance with design developments on the Continent, beyond the objects he noticed as worthy of praise at exhibitions, such as the cloisonné enamels of 'Barbedien' [*sic*] and Christofle, and the glass of Lobmeyr, and which he sometimes used, as with Austrian carpets at the Vienna 1873 Exhibition, as a stick with which to beat the low standards of British manufacturers.[32] None of the foreign objects that Dresser admired was Gothic in style. Indeed Dresser is not often thought of as a Goth, and would usually be placed, like Owen Jones, in a broadly opposite, even opposing camp. In Dresser's 1862 categorization of the different grades of ornament as 'embodiment of mental power' 'later Gothic' scores low:

> The Greek, the Moorish, the early English, much of the Indian and mediaeval, many features in the Japanese, and some parts of the Egyptian and the Renaissance
>
> Much of the Egyptian and Chinese, and a few features in the Greek and Japanese
>
> A great portion of the middle-age work, especially the later Gothic, and many parts of the Chinese and Indian
>
> Much of the Pompeian and our modern floral patterns.[33]

However if 'Gothic' is allowed a wider meaning, embracing such of Dresser's terms as 'early English', 'mediaeval' and 'Christian', this style will be seen to be prominent among his published designs, second only to Islamic in *Modern Ornamentation* (1886), as has been noted, and the largest identified category in *Studies in Design* (1876). (In *Principles of Design* (1873) Dresser himself describes how the term 'Gothic' is popularly used to embrace styles prevalent from the twelfth to the sixteenth centuries)[34]. The 1862 *Art of Decorative Design* is more preoccupied with botanically and geometrically derived principles of ornament than with historic styles, but nonetheless the influence on its

illustrations of *Floriated Ornament* (1849), in which A.W.N. Pugin, the great Gothic architect of the previous generation, disposed 'natural leaves and flowers in geometrical forms', is patent.[35]

In 1873 Dresser described how Sir Gilbert Scott (1811–78), William Burges (1827–81, Dresser writes 'Burgess'), George Edmund Street (1824–81) and others were lending Gothic 'nobility of expression, truthfulness of structure, and suitability to our special requirements'.[36] At this point all three architects were still active and creative and Dresser's statement was thus not inaccurate. But Scott was 62, Burges 46 and Street 49, all considerably older

260. George Edmund Street (1824–81). Sedilla in the chancel of Saint-James-the-Less, Westminster, 1859. Charles Handley-Read noted in 1968 that 'Street anticipated Dresser's style of 1862'.

than Dresser, and all working in a style fully forged in the 1850s. Also in 1873, significantly, Scott's eldest son, George Gilbert Scott junior (1839–97), a closer contemporary of Dresser, was building Leamington Vicarage in the Queen Anne style. That High Victorian Gothic should have appealed to Dresser is not surprising: honesty in construction, and truth to materials, geometrical design, clean forms, and radical formalization, sometimes amounting to abstraction, were common goals. Moreover there was a zest, a vigour, even a degree of violence, in much Gothic ornament, which found an echo in Dresser's own inventions. Many of the designers and architects who reached maturity in the 1860s, Dresser's contemporaries, commenced as vigorous Goths. A few examples must suffice; the 1861 bookcase by Richard Norman Shaw (1831–1912), shown in the Mediaeval Court of the London 1862 Exhibition, and his Holy Trinity, Bingley, of 1864; Northampton Town Hall and its furniture and decoration (1861–4) and Congleton Town Hall (1864–7), by E.W. Godwin (1833–86);[37] and *Gothic Forms Applied to Furniture, Metal Work and Decoration for*

261. Bruce J Talbert.

(a) side ornament for a wall-cupboard from
Gothic Forms Applied to Furniture
(London, 1868). Michael Whiteway.

(b) diaper pattern, Christopher Dresser, from *Studies in Design* (London, 1876). Michael Whiteway.

(c) James W. & C. Ward, design sample for registration with the patent office. Public Record Office.

Domestic Purposes (1868) by Bruce J. Talbert (1838–81). However, all three designers were to move to a more 'comfortable, easy' style, or range of styles, in the 1870s or earlier. Charles Locke Eastlake's *Hints on Household Taste in Furniture, Upholstery and Other Details* (1868, but based on articles published from 1864 to 1866, well before Dresser began in 1870 to publish the articles in the *Technical Educator* which became his *Principles*) captures the moment of transition, including as it does an eclectic mix, including the Knole sofa, and a Windsor chair, alongside stolidly Gothic designs mainly by Eastlake himself. In *Principles* Dresser vigorously attacked an X-framed armchair from Knole, illustrated by Eastlake, as 'essentially bad and wrong' for its defective construction.[38] In fairness it should be added that he also instances an armchair designed by Eastlake (although 'slightly altered' by Dresser, its back being rendered simpler, but heavier) as a 'correctly formed work'.

To demonstrate his personal theories on the correct construction of chairs Dresser included several of his own designs in *Principles*. Constructionally correct these may be, but they are also wilfully eccentric and clumsy. They anticipate several chairs produced in about 1880 for the ill-fated Art Furnishers' Alliance project, which make the toughest chairs by a Goth such as William White appear, if not elegant, at least handsome (perhaps E.W. Pugin's 'Granville' chair is of a rival ungainliness).[39] There is here a purblindness, a deficient sense of proportion, also apparent in Dresser's 1873 demolition, on highly principled grounds, of Burges's 'Yatman' cabinet, made in 1858, and shown in the Mediaeval Court at the London 1862 Exhibition, which entirely misses the point that this was a joyful archaeological *jeu d'esprit*.[40] Although Dresser published on the Paris 1867 Exhibition, it is revealing that when he came to single out models for metalwork in *Principles* all his illustrations were of Gothic objects shown in 1862 or in that manner, including Skidmore's Hereford Cathedral screen, designed by Scott.[41]

The inclusion in the 1862 Exhibition of Sir Rutherford Alcock's pioneering 'Japanese Court' further underlines the significance of that exhibition for Dresser. William Burges, whose pupil, Josiah Conder (1852–1920), settled in Japan in 1876 and who himself took a Japanese pupil,

262. William Burges, the 'Yatman' cabinet with painted panels by Edward Poynter, made by Harland & Fisher for Mr H.G. Yatman of Haslemere, 1858, and shown at the London 1862 exhibition. Dresser remarked 'The windows on the roof ... degrade the work to a mere doll's house' (*Principles of Decorative Design*, 1873). V&A: c.217–1961.

263. Sir George Gilbert Scott (1811–1878). Hereford Cathedral screen, painted iron, made by Skidmore of Coventry and shown in the London International Exhibition of 1862. V&A: M.251–1984. 'One of the finest examples of artistic metalwork with which we are acquainted' (Christopher Dresser, *Principles of Decorative Design*, 1873).

Kingo Tatsuno, in 1880, wrote in 1862: 'Truly the Japanese court is the real mediaeval court of the Exhibition',[42] and Burges chaired the meeting of the Architectural Association in 1863 at which Dresser spoke on Japanese ornament.[43] During the later 1860s William Eden Nesfield, Richard Norman Shaw, Thomas Jeckyll and Burges's close friend, E.W. Godwin, were leaders in the adoption and free adaptation of Japanese motifs. An interesting case is that of George Ashdown Audsley (1838–1925) and his brother William James Audsley, whose *Sermon on the Mount* (1861), a virtuoso chromolithographic performance in the Gothic style, was praised by Dresser in *The Art of Decorative Design*, which illustrates two Audsley motifs in colour. In 1870 they published the catalogue of a collection of Japanese enamels shown in Liverpool, the first of a series of works on Japanese art.[44] But the Audsleys' *Polychromatic Decoration as Applied to Buildings in the Mediaeval Styles* (1882) still presents vigorous Gothic ornament of a High Victorian character, some of it borrowed from J.K. Colling (1816–1905), whose *Art Foliage for Sculpture and Decoration* (1865, reprinted 1878) contained

vigorously formalized ornament, which must have appealed to Dresser. Colling, it may be noted, supplied the text to the wide-ranging *Suggestions in Design* (1880) by John Leighton (1822–1912), whose *On Japanese Art* (1863) was the first book on this subject to appear in Britain. There is no question that Dresser played a leading part in relation to Japan, as merchant and importer, and as two-way ambassador, propagandist and elucidator, particularly in the American context. But the very radicalism of, for example, his metalwork designs of around 1880, many using Japanese models, can be interpreted as a continuation of that taste for geometry, formalization and angularity that was particularly a feature of advanced Gothic in the 1860s, and that is already present in Dresser's Ipswich sketchbook of that period. Dresser's most idiosyncratic designs are not Gothic, but his style is closely analogous to 1860s Gothic and, as has been noted, even in 1886 many of his published designs were explicitly Gothic. Another close comparison is to be found in the style of ornament favoured by Alexander 'Greek' Thomson, a Scottish equivalent of *Néo-Grec*, geometrical, formalized and angular.[45] B.J. Talbert, Daniel Cottier and J. Moyr Smith all had links to Thomson, and the decorations of Thomson's Queen's Park Church (1869), on which Cottier collaborated and which Ford Madox Brown admired, are fully worthy of Dresser.[46]

Many of the best known designers active in the 1860s and '70s were provincials, often Scots: E.W. Godwin from Bristol, Talbert from Dundee, Cottier and Moyr Smith from Glasgow, Richard Charles from Caernavon, and G.A Audsley from Elgin, of whom all but Cottier and Charles received architectural training outside London. Dresser, in London from the age of 13 and trained at the School of Design, stands a little apart. It may be suspected that the excellent links he established with manufacturers from the late 1850s onwards owed more to contacts made through the school than to his Scottish birth or Yorkshire origins. As the leader of a successful and commercial design studio he had to some degree to respond to fashion; he was one competitor among many. For example Jeffrey & Co., the wallpaper manufacturers, employed Owen Jones, William Burges, E.W. Godwin, B.J. Talbert, C.L. Eastlake, Walter Crane, Lewis F. Day and Albert Moore, as well as Dresser.[47] Moreover, although such linkages and overlaps are difficult to pin down, it is clear that, just as manufacturers could employ a wide range of designers, named or anonymous, those who worked for design studios might be promiscuous. J. Moyr Smith worked for Dresser but, although they were friendly in 1868, Dresser's virtual absence from Smith's *Ornamental Interiors Ancient and Modern* (1887), which gives considerable prominence to Talbert, may reflect an eventual resentment at lack of recognition;[48] perhaps Talbert, for whom Smith also seems to have worked, was more generous. Dresser himself seems to have borrowed from Talbert: Talbert, who owned Dresser's *Principles*, as well as works by Colling, the Audsleys and Viollet-le-Duc, and 'Art Furniture by Godwin', that is William Watts's 1877 catalogue, may well have reciprocated.[49] Dresser's design world was to some extent a continuum, and he was not always in a position to pursue his own style.

In 1863 Warington Taylor, the business manager of Morris, Marshall, Faulkner & Co., founded in 1861, observed that William Morris 'disliked flowers treated geometrically stiffly in patterns' and wrote

264. Edward William
Godwin. 'Egyptian' chair,
birch with a caned seat,
*c.*1880. Ellen and William
Taubman Collection.

disapprovingly of how, in Dresser's patterns, 'the leaves and flowers are distorted into the most painful geometrical harsh forms'.[50] John Ruskin, whose chapter in *The Stones of Venice* (1853) 'On the Nature of Gothic Architecture' made an indelible impression on Morris, kept a copy of J. Moyr Smith's *Studies for Pictures* (1868), dedicated to Dresser and with a title-page replete with jagged Gothic ornament, 'as an example of distortion in modern mind'.[51] Dresser conducted an anti-Ruskin polemic in *The Art of Decorative Design* and Moyr Smith followed suit in *Ornamental Interiors* (1887), where he recommended James Fergusson's *Handbook of Architecture* (1855) as an antidote to *The Stones of Venice*. *The Studio*'s 1899 reduction of Dresser to, as it were, Morris's ambassador to the commercial middle classes and to industry, is the distorted mirror-image of Dresser's and Moyr Smith's characterization of Ruskin as a meddling amateur or Smith's suggestion that Morris's Daisy wallpaper, designed in 1862 and issued in 1864, was only successful because created by the poet of *The Earthly Paradise* (1868, 1870) – by implication another rich amateur. Why did oblivion overtake Dresser? It must be simply that his style had gone out of fashion and his didactic works had been superseded. Why did the same not happen to Morris? Poet, politician, propagandist, as well as designer and manufacturer, Morris enjoyed friendships with many of his greatest contemporaries; he inspired the next generation and enjoyed fame and influence at home and abroad before and after his death. He was simply the bigger man: in Lydgate's words 'Comparisouns doon offte gret greuaunce'.

Dresser's oblivion and his rescue thence followed a pattern familiar in Victorian designers: an article by Pevsner (1937); prominent inclusion in the great Exhibition of Victorian and Edwardian Decorative Arts (1952) organized by Peter Floud at the V&A; serious appraisal in Alf Boe's *From Gothic Revival to Functional Form* (1957); and a first specialized article by Shirley Bury, who had been one of Floud's colleagues in 1952, in 1962. Thenceforward, starting with Richard Dennis's and John Jesse's exhibition at the Fine Art Society in London in 1972, Dresser has been the subject of an international succession of exhibitions, for instance Cologne (1981), London (1979), London (1999) and Milan (2001), and of publications, notably two major books by Widar Halén (1990) and by Stuart

Durant, the doyen of Dresser studies (1993). Dresser's own works have been reprinted, commencing with *Principles of Decorative Design* in London in 1973 and *The Art of Decorative Design* in New York in 1977, and he has featured conspicuously in most general books and exhibitions on late nineteenth-century design (and not only in these: Bevis Hillier included objects by Dresser in his 1971 Minneapolis exhibition, *The World of Art Deco*). It may indeed be that the Dresser 'industry' is only surpassed by those devoted to Pugin and to Morris.

There are nonetheless indirect links between Morris and Dresser. At the 1862 London Exhibition, so important to Dresser, he approved of a chair designed by Morris's close friend Philip Webb (1831–1915), a pupil of Street; its 'constructive peculiarity', the sloping struts supporting its back, Dresser noted as a 'hint' that might be 'attended to'.[52] In *Principles* he praised a chair from Talbert's *Gothic Forms* (1868) with a comparable detail, and versions of this are incorporated into his own designs for Egyptian and five-legged chairs, and into chairs made for the Art Furnishers' Alliance.[53] Also in 1862 Dresser singled out table glass designed by Webb for James Powell & Sons of Whitefriars for its 'simplicity of treatment'.[54] Perhaps there is here a foretaste of the usually simple forms of Clutha glass, and indeed of Linthorpe pots, whose 'purity of art treatment' was commended by Llewellyn Jewitt in 1883.[55]

Much of the admiration Dresser now commands leads back to his silver and electroplate designs, which seem so uncannily and seductively to anticipate Modern design and have, perhaps inevitably, been posthumously canonised as proto-Modern 'classics'. They are indeed a striking vindication of Dresser's approach to design, as evinced in his diagrams, at once theoretical and practical, of the correct angles for pouring, first published in 1862, and his observations of 1873 on metalwork manufacture, particularly with regard to achieving stiffness and economy in sheet metal. Perhaps, as one who was forgotten during the heroic years of Modernism, Dresser makes an appropriately ironic Post-Modern hero. But would it not be more illuminating if the 'pioneer' mythology were henceforward set aside and Dresser and his remarkable and varied achievements, not all of them admirable, were to be appreciated and understood in his and their own complex contexts?

In the mid-1880s, after the collapse of the Art Furnishers' Alliance and when his career was at its lowest ebb, Dresser made up an album of designs, presumably as a sample book to solicit commissions from manufacturers. The designs cover his career to date, with ceramics, stained glass, wallpaper, textiles and floor-coverings all included. They have a value beyond their place in illuminating Dresser's efforts to find employment in the wake of the Alliance disaster, in that they enable firm attributions to be made among the unsigned work of Dresser's earlier career. They also demonstrate the most important feature of his career at this point: that he had returned perforce to his earlier practice as an 'ornamentist' or pattern-designer and running his studio to supply the manufacturing trade.

265a.

265b.

265 a–g. Watercolour patterns for stained glass, textiles and ceramics from an album of designs, entitled 'Original Designs by Christopher Dresser' and bearing an inscription 'Chr. Dresser/ Wellesley Studio/ Sutton: Surrey'.
The Metropolitan Museum of Art, New York.

Dresser's Later Designs
1883–1904

265c.

265d.

265e.

265f.

265g.

ELKINGTON & CO. BIRMINGHAM

In 1885 this old-established and immensely successful Birmingham firm of silver and electroplate manufacturers registered with the Patent Office and put into production a series of designs by Dresser. The second volume of the firm's design books (now in the V&A) includes about 24 drawings for domestic wares, tea-sets, sugar bowls, claret jugs, kettles, cruet stands, baskets, a tureen and a tankard, designed by him. The drawings are all annotated with Dresser's name and model and design registry numbers, and date from 1881–93. Elkington's success was greatly enhanced by the foresight of the founder in taking out one of the earliest patents for the electrodeposition process in 1836. A comercially viable method of production was patented in 1840. Electroplate rapidly superseded Sheffield plate, the popular eighteenth-century silver substitute, and Britannia metal, a cheap alloy. A number of the Dresser designs were produced in electroplate. It is hard to be precise about the exact extent and date-span of Dresser's early connection with the firm, but he seems likely to have drawn their attention in the 1860s to the revived cloisonné techniques being employed with such success in France, and to have promoted the use of Japanese-style metal-working methods. The firm exhibited at all major international exhibitions from 1851.

ABOVE RIGHT 266. Electroplate and glass cruet. Constance R. Caplin, Baltimore.

RIGHT 267. Silver and silver-gilt milk jug, marked 'Elkington & Co.', registration no. 22865 for 1885. The Andrew McIntosh Patrick Collection.

OPPOSITE 268. Electroplated pitcher, marked 'Elkington', registered 1885. Private Collection.

269. Electroplate and glass cruet set, marked 'Elkington', registered 1885. The Andrew McIntosh Patrick Collection.

270. Electroplated three-piece tea set, marked 'Elkington', registered 1885. Private Collection.

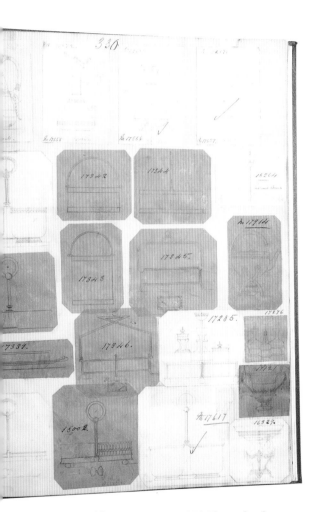

271. Detail from a page of designs in Elkington's silver pattern book, showing the jug at plate 272. Photo courtesy of Birmingham Library.

272. Electroplated jug, marked 'Elkington 17558', registration no. 22872, dated 1885. The Andrew McIntosh Patrick Collection.

LEFT 273. Electroplated soup tureen with ebonized handles, marked 'Elkington & Co.', 1885. The Wolfsonian-Florida International University, Miami Beach, Florida. The Mitchell Wolfson, Jr. Collection.

275. Electroplated coffee pot, registration mark for 1885. Private Collection.

274. Silver jug with ebony handle, hall-marked for 1885. Private Collection.

BELOW 276. Electroplated conical sugar bowl. David Bonsall, Image Bank Ltd. Variants of the design are included in the 'Ipswich' sketchbook, about 1864. In *Principles of Decorative Design* (1873) an exaggerated form is illustrated, fig. 149. See also plate 7 on p. 14.

277. A page of designs from Elkington's silver pattern book, showing the sugar bowl at plate 276. Photo courtesy of Birmingham Library.

JAMES COUPER & SONS GLASGOW

Dresser's designs for an 'art glass' range for this Glasgow industrial glass manufacturer were sold under the trade name 'Clutha', the ancient name of the River Clyde, which runs through Glasgow. The 'Clutha' trademark was resgistered by Couper's in 1888. The firm exhibited the new glassware in 1890 at the third show mounted by the Arts and Crafts Exhibition Society, described as 'specimens of Clutha glass, designed by Christopher Dresser'. The designs draw on ancient Roman and Near Eastern forms (similar to the shapes used at the Linthorpe pottery), and the technique exploits 'accidental' effects in its use of bubbled and randomly streaked glass, in shades of green, brown, golden yellow and pink with metallic flecks and opaque white striations. The glass was retailed through Liberty's and the pieces bear the mark 'DESIGNED by C D REGISTERED' with the 'Clutha' trademark in mock-Celtic script and the lotus-flower trade mark of Liberty & Co. The 'Clutha' range was advertised by Liberty throughout the 1890s.

278. Four glass vases, marked 'Designed by C.D.' all *c*.1890. The Birkenhead Collection.

279. Two glass vases, marked 'Designed by C.D.', *c*.1890. The Birkenhead Collection.

OPPOSITE 282. Vase with etched glass, *c.* 1980.
Collectionn of Sheri Cyd Sandler.

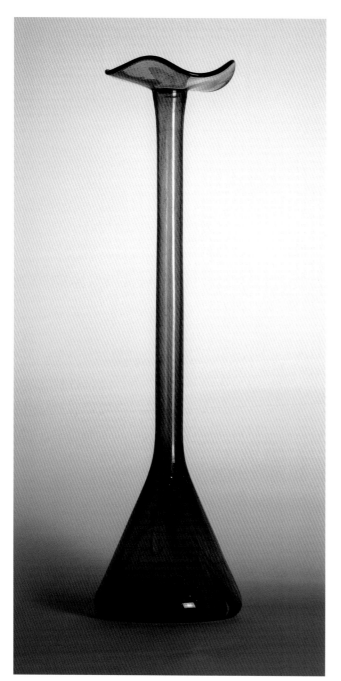

280. Long-necked glass vase, marked 'Designed by C.D.', *c.*1890.
Private Collection.

281. Large glass vase, marked 'Designed by C.D.', *c.*1890.
The Birkenhead Collection.

AULT POTTERY SWADLINCOTE, DERBYSHIRE

The Ault Pottery was founded in 1887 in competition with
Linthorpe by William Ault, former partner of Henry Tooth in the
Bretby Pottery. In 1889, when Linthorpe closed down after John
Harrison's death, the moulds were sold by public auction and a
number were acquired for the Ault firm. These models were
produced by the company at least until Dresser's death in 1904.
In 1893 Dresser signed a contract with the firm to supply designs
and he specified that the pieces should bear his signature in
facsimile. At this very late stage in his career he produced some
remarkable new shapes, notably the 'Goat's Head', 'Tongue' and
'Face' vases, with brilliantly coloured glazes.

283. Three earthenware vases, all marked with
Dresser's impressed facsimile signature, all *c.*1893.
Private Collection.

284. Three yellow earthenware vases, 'Goat'
and 'Tongue' models, marked with Dresser's impressed
facsimile signature, *c*.1893. The Birkenhead Collection.

285. Frog earthenware vase, marked with Dresser's
impressed facsimile signature, *c*.1893. Private Collection.
This vase belonged to Christopher Dresser.

287. Bridge-spouted 'Peruvian' earthenware pitcher
with streaked and dribbled glaze, marked with Dresser's
impressed facsimile signature and no. 288, c.1893.
Private Collection.

OPPOSITE 286. 'Basket' earthenware vase, marked
with Dresser's impressed facsimile signature, c.1893.
Harry Lyons.

288. Large four-handled
earthenware vase,
marked with Dresser's
impressed facsimile
signature, c.1893.
Private Collection.

289. Two earthenware
twist vases, marked with
Dresser's impressed
facsimile signature,
c.1893. Private Collection.

290. Two earthenware
vases, marked with
Dresser's impressed
facsimile signature,
c.1893. Harry Lyons.

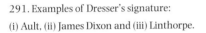

291. Examples of Dresser's signature:
(i) Ault, (ii) James Dixon and (iii) Linthorpe.

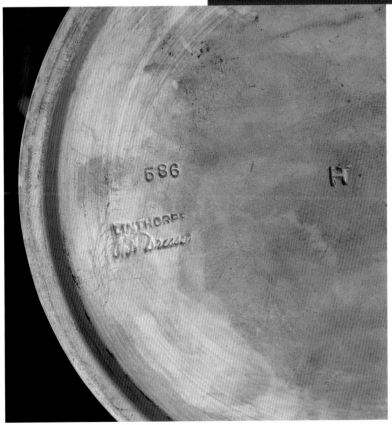

CHRONOLOGY

CYNTHIA TROPE

Historical events are in roman; events in Dresser's life are in **bold**.

1809
Birth of Owen Jones, designer, writer, architect, mentor to Christopher Dresser.

1812
Birth of Augustus Welby Northmore Pugin, architect, designer.

1819
Birth of John Ruskin, critic, essayist and reformer.

Birth of Alexandrina Victoria (Queen Victoria) of Great Britain.

Birth of Albert, prince of Saxe-Coburg-Gotha. He is to become Victoria's consort.

1825
Stockton and Darlington Railway opens. It becomes the first railway for passengers and freight pulled by steam engine.

1833
Birth of Edward William Godwin, architect, designer.

1834
Christopher Dresser is born on 4 July in Glasgow, Scotland, third child of Christopher and Mary (Nettleton) Dresser.

Birth of William Morris, designer, craftsman, political activist.

The *Exposition des Produits de l'Industrie Française*, the first large-scale industrial exhibition, takes place in Paris in what is now place de la Concorde. There are nearly 2,500 exhibitors.

1836
Contrasts; or, a parallel between the noble edifices of the fourteenth and fifteenth centuries, and similar buildings of the present day; shewing [sic] *the present decay of taste* by A.W.N. Pugin is published by John Grant.

1836–7
G.R. Elkington and Henry Elkington are granted a series of patents relating to the new electrodeposition process for plating base-metal. In 1837, to exploit the process, they form a partnership with Pugin's metalworker, John Hardman; experiments with electroplating conducted by John Wright and Alexander Parkes culminate in 1840 in a commercially viable method that is duly patented by Elkington; this process revolutionizes the trade and brings plated wares within the reach of a vastly expanded public.

1837
Victoria becomes queen of Great Britain.

The Government School of Design opens at Somerset House, Strand, London, following deliberations during 1835–6 of a Select Committee on Arts and Manufactures appointed by Parliament.

1839
Louis-Jacques-Mandé Daguerre invents the daguerreotype process.

William Henry Fox Talbot invents the photographic negative.

The Copyright of Design Act makes it possible to secure copyright for designs.

1840
Queen Victoria marries Albert of Saxe-Coburg-Gotha.

1841
The True Principles of Pointed or Christian Architecture by A.W.N. Pugin is published by John Weale.

1842–5
Plans, Elevations, Sections and Details of the Alhambra by Owen Jones is published by the author: the earliest British book printed in colour, by chromolithography.

1844
Glossary of Ecclesiastical Ornament and Costume by A.W.N. Pugin is published by Henry G. Bohn.

1845
The Condition of the Working Classes in England by Friedrich Engels is published in Leipzig.

1847
Christopher Dresser, aged 13, enters the recently established Government School of Design, Strand. He studies at the school over the next seven years.

Richard Redgrave (1804–88), painter and design reformer, is appointed headmaster of the School of Design. Dresser attends his two lectures on 'The Importance of Botany to the Ornamentist' in 1849.

Henry Cole (1808–82), design reformer, inaugurates 'Felix Summerly's Art-Manufactures' to 'promote public taste' and encourage commissions of its artists' cooperative members to design household objects for reproduction.

1849
Floriated Ornament: a series of Thirty-one Designs by A.W.N. Pugin is published by Henry G. Bohn.

The Seven Lamps of Architecture by John Ruskin is published by Smith, Elder & Co.

Henry Cole and Richard Redgrave found the *Journal of Design and Manufactures*.

1850–51
The School of Design awards Dresser a place as one of 15 student exhibitioners; his design for a tea service is shown in January 1850. Dresser receives four prizes in all, for 'a Tea Service to be Printed', 'a Breakfast Service to be painted', 'a Dessert Service to be painted' and 'designs for Dresses upon a Geometric basis'.

1851
The Great Exhibition of the Works of Industry of All Nations is held in London.

1851–2
Dresser attends lectures by the chemist Dr Lyon Playfair at the School of Mines, Jermyn Street, London. Attributes his 'love for the natural sciences' to these presentations; decides to specialize in botany.

1851–3
The Stones of Venice by John Ruskin is published by George Allen.

1852
The School of Design becomes part of the new Department of Practical Art with Henry Cole appointed as general superintendent; this develops into the Department of Science and Art at the South Kensington Museum. Botanist Dr John Lindley lectures at the Department of Practical Art on 'The Symmetry of Vegetation'. Dresser is awarded a scholarship for textiles and 'art painting'.

Redgrave publishes his 'Supplementary Report on Design', a critical overview of design at the 1851 exhibition. (His design ideology is published officially as *Manual of Design* in 1876.)

Following the success of the Great Exhibition, a Museum of Manufactures is established; by 1857 it is re-named the South Kensington Museum, and in 1899 it becomes the Victoria and Albert Museum, as it is known today. Cole would remain associated with the museum until 1875.

Death of A.W.N. Pugin at the age of 40.

1853
Exhibition of the Industry of All Nations is held in New York.

Dresser is awarded student medals for 'ornament painted in colours', 'applied design' and designs in the 'woven fabric class'. He wins a prize from textile manufacturer Liddiard for 'best design to be printed on cambric' and is awarded another scholarship.

Four ships of the US East India Squadron, commanded by Commodore Matthew Perry, enter the harbour of Uraga to establish trade with Japan – a country that has been isolated from the outside world since the seventeenth century.

1854
Dresser receives his final scholarship on 4 March, and finishes his studies at the School of Design.

Dresser marries Thirza Perry of Maidley (now Madeley), Shropshire, on 24 May. They establish their first household at 4 Swiss Cottages, Black Lion Lane, Hammersmith; they eventually have 13 children – five boys and eight girls.

Dresser is appointed lecturer on botany at the Female School of Design (then called the Metropolitan School, Gower Street).

Joseph Paxton's Crystal Palace from the Great Exhibition of 1851 is re-built and opened at Sydenham, with a special rail link constructed from Victoria Station. The building is enlarged and filled with plaster replicas of historical interiors and exteriors: Owen Jones's Alhambra Court is especially admired.

Treaty of Peace and Amity between the US and Japan (Kanagawa Treaty) signed, reopening Japan to foreigners after more than 200 years of seclusion. Similar treaty with Great Britain concluded within the year.

1855
Dresser receives his first appointment as a botany lecturer at the School of Design on 25 August (he lectured on botany and art-botany until 1869).

Dresser files an application for and receives a patent for 'Improvements in the mode of effecting what is called nature printing'.

Exposition Universelle is held in Paris.

1856
The *Grammar of Ornament* by Owen Jones is published by Day & Son. It includes Dresser-designed Plate No. XCVIII, illustrating the 'geometrical arrangement of flowers'.

1857–8
Dresser writes a series of 11 articles in the *Art Journal*, 'Botany, as adapted to the Arts and Art Manufacture'.

1859
On the Origin of Species by Means of Natural Selection by Charles Darwin is published by John Murray.

The Rudiments of Botany, Structural and Physiological by Dresser is published.

Unity in Variety as Deduced by the Vegetable Kingdom by Dresser is published by James S. Virtue.

Dresser receives honorary doctorate *in absentia* in botany from the University of Jena, Germany, for these two seminal books on botany and a short paper on the organs of plants.

1860
Popular Manual of Botany by Dresser is published by Adam and Charles Black.

Dresser is elected a fellow of the Edinburgh Botanical Society.

Dresser is appointed professor of botany at St Mary's School of Medicine, the London Hospital Medical College and the Royal Polytechnic Institute.

Dresser unsuccessfully applies for chair of botany at University College, London.

Dresser and his family move to St Peter's Square, Hammersmith, where Dresser establishes his studio.

1861
Dresser is elected to the Linnean Society.

Dresser starts teaching at the School of Design at South Kensington, where he continues to 1868.

Dresser presents a series of lectures to the Society of Arts on the subject of decorative art (subsequently published as *The Art of Decorative Design*, 1862).

Albert, the prince consort, dies.

1862
International Exhibition is held in London. The Mediaeval Court includes exhibits by William Burges, Richard Norman Shaw, J.P. Seddon, Dante Gabriel Rossetti, G.E. Street and William Morris. The Japanese collection of Sir Rutherford Alcock is shown – the first public exhibition of Japanese art in Britain.

The Art of Decorative Design by Dresser is published by Day & Son.

Development of Ornamental Art in the International Exhibition by Christopher Dresser is published.

1866
Hints on Household Taste by Charles Locke Eastlake published by Longmans, Green & Co.

1867
Exposition Universelle held in Paris.

Dresser exhibits ceramic designs for Minton and Wedgwood, and cast iron for Coalbrookdale at the Paris Exposition. He writes a series of articles on the exhibition for *The Chromolithograph*.

Gothic Forms Applied to Furniture, Metalwork and Decoration for Domestic Purposes by Bruce Talbert is published by S. Birbeck and Bruce Talbert.

Japan's last shogun, Tokugawa Yoshinobu, relinquishes political authority to Mutsuhito (Emperor Meiji). Start of the Meiji (enlightened peace) period.

1868
Dresser and family move to a large house, Tower Cressy, Aubrey Road, Kensington, where they live until 1882.

Emperor Meiji moves from Kyoto to Tokyo (formerly Edo), now the capital of Japan.

1869
US transcontinental railroad is completed.

1869–70
Dresser designs interiors for Allangate House, Halifax, for Thomas Shaw MP.

1870
Dresser is elected to membership in the Society of Arts.

1870–73
Dresser writes a series of articles for the *Technical Educator* (eventually compiled and published as *Principles of Decorative Design*, 1873).

1871
Japan's Iwakura mission starts an 18-month tour to study the social systems of the US and European countries.

Dresser exhibits porcelain, Coalbrookdale cast iron and carpets by Crossley's under his own name as designer.

1873
Principles of Decorative Design by Dresser is published by Cassell, Petter & Calpin.

Dresser participates in the *Weltausstellung* (International Exhibition), held in Vienna, Austria.

Dresser becomes art advisor to the Alexandra Palace Company, importer of Japanese art.

Dresser designs metalwork for manufacturer Benham & Froud (until 1893).

1874
Death of Owen Jones.

Dresser designs Bushloe House, Leicester, for his solicitor, Hiram B. Owston.

1874–6
Studies in Design by Dresser is published by Cassell, Petter & Calpin.

1876
United States Centennial International Exhibition, Philadelphia.

1876–7
Dresser visits US and Japan. October 1876, Dresser departs from Liverpool, England, and arrives in Philadelphia by 30 October. He delivers three lectures, the first on the occasion of the founding of the Pennsylvania Museum and School of Industrial Arts. He visits the *Centennial Exhibition* where his designs for wallpapers, ceramics and carpets are shown. He supplies Philadelphia-based wallpaper

manufacturer Wilson & Fenimores with wallpaper designs. By 19 November Dresser arrives in Chicago to see retailers John J. McGrath and W.H. Hudson. Dresser travels across US by rail, arriving in San Francisco on 27 November. He joins Sekisawa Akiko and General Saigō Tsugumichi, Japanese Commissioners to the *Centennial Exhibition*, for the voyage to Japan.

Dresser spends just over three months (26 December 1876–3 April 1877) travelling throughout Japan, studying its art, architecture and design, observing manufacturing processes and techniques for a variety of wares. On behalf of the South Kensington Museum he delivers a group of European decorative arts objects to the Imperial Museum in Tokyo. Dresser advises the Japanese government on modern industrial production and offers comment on various art manufactures.

1877
Patent applications for wallpaper designs filed with the US Patent Office on 17 March; patents (numbers 9,975–9,987, by patentee Christopher Dresser, assigned to Wilson & Fenimores) registered on 15 May.

William Watt's *Art Furniture Catalogue* showing E.W. Godwin's designs.

1878
Exposition Universelle is held in Paris. Dresser serves as a juror for Class 22 (wallhangings).

1879
Dresser & Holme, importer of Japanese art, is founded; Dresser's sons Louis and Christopher are stationed in the Japan office, in Kobe (Dresser senior is involved until 1882).

John Harrison establishes the Linthorpe Art Pottery, Middlesbrough (Dresser acts as art director to the firm until 1882).

1880
Dresser appointed art editor of the *Furniture Gazette*.

The Art Furnishers' Alliance is founded.

1882
Japan, Its Architecture and Art Manufactures by Dresser is published by Longmans, Green & Co.

1883
The Art Furnishers' Alliance is dissolved.

Dresser moves to Wellesley Lodge, Brunswick Road, Sutton, Surrey.

1884
Dresser designs ceramics for Old Hall Pottery, Hanley, Staffordshire (until 1886).

1886
Modern Ornamentation by Dresser is published by the Wellesley Studio.

Death of E.W. Godwin.

1888
Dresser designs 'Clutha' glass for John Couper & Sons (until 1900).

1889
Exposition Universelle is held in Paris.

Dresser moves from Sutton to a house in Barnes, overlooking the River Thames.

1890
William Ault (Ault & Co.) buys moulds of Dresser designs at the liquidation sale of the Linthorpe Art Pottery.

1893
Founding of *The Studio*, a magazine devoted to the arts and illustrated by photolithography.

World's Columbian Exposition is held in Chicago.

1896
Death of William Morris.

1899
The last article about Dresser during his life is published by *The Studio* (run by Dresser's old collaborator Charles Holme).

1900
Exposition Universelle Internationale is held in Paris.

Death of John Ruskin

1901
Death of Queen Victoria.

1904
Dresser dies while on a business trip in Mulhouse France, to consult with wallpaper manufacturer Jean Zuber.

1905
Dresser's effects and property, including many Asian wares, are sold.

1936
Art historian Sir Nikolaus Pevsner rediscovers the design work of Christopher Dresser and includes him in *Pioneers of the Modern Movement from William Morris to Walter Gropius*, published by Faber & Faber.

1937
Pevsner's article 'Christopher Dresser, Industrial Designer' appears in the *Architectural Review*, LXXXI.

1952
Dresser's work is displayed prominently in the *Exhibition of Victorian and Edwardian Decorative Arts* at the Victoria and Albert Museum.

1962
Shirley Bury's article 'The Silver Designs of Christopher Dresser' appears in *Apollo* magazine.

1972
Dresser is the subject of the exhibition *Christopher Dresser, 1834–1904* at the Fine Arts Society, London.

1981
The exhibition *Christopher Dresser, Ein Viktorianischer Designer* is held at the Kunstgewerbemuseum, Cologne, Germany.

1991–3
Italian metalwork manufacturer Alessi (founded 1921) produces objects based on, or reproducing, Dresser designs (including cruet sets, teapots, toast racks) for its 'La Tavola Di Babele' and 'Archivi' series as part of its 'Officina Alessi' line.

2001–2
The major exhibition, *Christopher Dresser. A Designer at the Court of Queen Victoria*, is mounted at Triennale, Milan.

2004
Shock of the Old: Christopher Dresser, the first major museum exhibition devoted to Dresser, is mounted by Cooper-Hewitt, National Design Museum, Smithsonian Institution, in New York. A version entitled *Christopher Dresser; Art and Industry* is shown at the Victoria and Albert Museum.

NOTES

FOREWORD

1. Pevsner (1937), p. 183–6.

2. Anon (1952).

3. Dennis and Jesse (1972).

4. 'The Work of Christopher Dresser', *The Studio* (November 1899), vol. 15, pp. 104–14.

5. Henry Cole (1808–82), who founded the *Journal of Design and Manufactures* in 1849 and is believed to have first coined the phrase 'art manufacturer'.

6. Bisland, Elizabeth. 'Proposed Plan of the Cooper Union Museum for the Arts of Decoration', pamphlet printed in 1896, pp. 6, 8, and Hewitt, Eleanor Garnier, 'The Making of a Modern Museum', pamphlet published in 1919.

7. Gere and Whiteway (1993) and Whiteway (Milan, 2001).

CHAPTER 1

1. Details of extensive research on Christopher Dresser's life undertaken by Harry Lyons can be found in Lyons (1999). His encyclopedic knowledge of the minutiae of Dresser's life and career has been put unstintingly at our disposal, and this account is immeasurably the richer for it.

2. One of the very few glimpses of Dresser's childhood, this autobiographical information comes from a letter published in the *Journal of the Society of Arts*, 17 March 1871; quoted in Halén (1990), p. 10, and in full in Durant (1993), p. 9.

3. Harry Lyons (op. cit. note 1) has painstakingly analysed Dresser's sources of income, from scholarships and prize money, throughout his years of studying, but his parents must have had to support him to an extent.

4. For a full account of the Schools and the National Art Training Schools, see: Bell, Quentin. *The Schools of Design* (London, 1963).

5. Wainwright, Clive. 'The Making of the South Kensington Museum, I; The Government Schools of Design and the Founding Collection, 1837–51', *Journal of the History of Collections* (2002), vol. 14, no. I, p. 4. For a detailed account of Henry Cole and the development of education and collecting at South Kensington, see: Bonython, Elizabeth, and Anthony Burton. *The Great Exhibitor, the Life and Work of Henry Cole* (London, 2003).

6. Cole, Henry. *Introductory Addresses on the Science and Art Department: No. 1. The Function of the Science and Art Department* (1857), p. 7.

7. Dresser, Christopher. 'Ornamentation Considered as a High Art', *Journal of the Society of Arts* (1871), vol. XIX, p. 352.

8. For a full account of Redgrave's design and teaching career, see: Casteras and Parkinson (1988).

9. The detail of Dresser's education, extracted from *Reports* of the Government School and his own writings, can be found in Halén (1990).

10. See: Bury, Shirley. 'Redgrave and Felix Summerly's Art-Manufactures' in Casteras and Parkinson (1988).

11. Cole, Henry. 'On the International Results of the Exhibition of 1851', speech to the Society of Arts, 1 December 1852, quoted in Whiteway (2001), p. 10.

12. Dresser, Christopher. 'Art Museums', *Penn Monthly* (February 1877), p. 119; quoted in Burton (1999), p. 33.

13. Dresser (1873), p. 90.

14. See: Floud, Peter. *An Exhibition of Victorian & Edwardian Decorative Arts* (V&A, London, exhib. cat. 1952), introduction.

15. Quoted in Burton (1999), p. 127.

16. Lyons (1999), p. 12.

17. Lyons, Harry. 'Christopher Dresser – Interior Designer', *Decoration in Buildings: The Decorative Arts Society* (1997), no. 21, pp. 22–6.

18. Dresser (1862), p. 16.

19. Jones (1856, reprinted 1986), pp. 5–6.

20. See: Morris, Barbara. *Inspiration for Design: The Influence of the Victoria and Albert Museum* (London, 1986).

21. See: Burton (1999), Chapter 5: 'The Supremacy of Henry Cole'.

22. Ruskin, John. *The Two Paths, Being Lectures on Art and Its Application to Decoration and Manufacture* (1859) in *The Works of John Ruskin* (London and New York, 1903–12), vol. 16, p. 320.

23. See: Conner, Patrick, ed. *The Inspiration of Egypt* (Brighton Museum and Art Gallery, 1983); Wilkinson, Sir John Gardner. *Manners and Customs of the Ancient Egyptians* (London, 1837), 5 vols; Thompson, Jason. *Sir Gardner Wilkinson and his Circle* (Austen, Texas, 1992).

24. This was an abridged edition, entitled *A Popular Account of the Ancient Egyptians*.

25. Holman-Hunt, W. *Pre-Raphaelitism and the Pre-Raphaelite Brotherhood* (London, 1905), vol. II, pp. 134–6.

26. Thompson, Jason. *Sir Gardner Wilkinson and his Circle* (Austen, Texas, 1992), p. 186.

27. Dresser (1873), p. 8.

28. See: Solman, David. *Loddiges of Hackney, the Largest Hothouse in the World* (London, 1995). It is easy to lose sight of the fact that Paxton, among all his other wide interests and abilities, was a top-ranking botanist.

29. Dresser (1873), p. 5.

30. For a detailed account of the founding years of the female school, see: Morse, Belinda. *A Woman of Design, a Man of Passion* (Lewes, E. Sussex, 2001).

31. *Ibid.*, p. 246.

32. Lyons (1999), p. 10.

33. Dresser (1862), preface.

34. See: *Journal of the Society of Arts* (1871), vol. XIX; (1872), vol. XX; (1874), vol. XXII; (1878), XXVI. The articles deal with ornament and applied art and the influence of the East, particularly Japan.

35. In the preface to Dresser (1873) the author reports on a visit to a 'provincial town hall' where he notes evidence of his design ideas being put into practice.

36. Dresser (1873), p. 56.

37. See: MacDonald, Sally. 'Gothic Forms Applied to Furniture; The Early Work of Bruce James Talbert', *Furniture History* (1987), vol. XXIII, pp. 39–66. Like Dresser, Talbert worked for Jackson & Graham, Brinton's, the carpet manufacturers, the Coalbrookdale iron foundry and Jeffrey & Co., wallpapers.

38. The album is now in the Metropolitan Museum in New York, plates 265 a–g.

39. Dresser (1874–6), p. 37.

40. Dresser, Christopher. *Development of Ornamental Art in the International Exhibition: Being a Concise Statement of the Laws which Govern the Production and Application of Ornament* (London, 1862).

41. Dresser, Christopher. 'The Art Manufactures of Japan, from Personal Observation', *Journal of the Society of Arts* (1877–8), vol. XVI, p. 169.

42. See: Faulkner, Rupert, and Anna Jackson. 'The Meiji Period in South Kensington: The Representation of Japan at the Victoria and Albert Museum 1852–1912', in Impey, Oliver, and Malcolm Fairley, eds. *Meiji No Takara: Treasures of Imperial Japan* (The Nassar D. Khalili Collection of Japanese Art) (London, 1995), 1, pp. 152–95.

43. See: Bury, Shirley. 'The Silver Designs of Christopher Dresser', *Apollo* (December 1962), pp. 766–7.

44. *The Chromolithograph, a Journal of Art Decoration and the Accomplishments* (London, 1868), vol. I.

45. Dresser, Christopher. 'Eastern Art and Its Influence on European Manufacturers and Taste', *Journal of the Society of Arts* (6 February 1874).

46. Dresser (1862), p. 8.

47. Recollections of Frederick Burrows in Durant (1993).

48. Dresser, Christopher. 'The Art Manufactures of Japan', *Journal of the Society of Arts* (1878).

49. Durant (1993), p. 39.

50. *The Biographer* (15 October 1894), vol. IX, p. 97, an account presumed to have been written by Moyr Smith himself. See also: Lyons and Morley (1999), p. 14; Stapleton, Annamarie. *John Moyr Smith 1839–1912: A Victorian Designer* (Somerset, 2002), pp. 11–14.

51. Nellie Dresser was interviewed in 1952 by John Lowry of the V&A. The unpublished notes are preserved in the Furniture and Woodwork Department in the Museum.

52. *Alexandra Palace Guide* (1875), p. 7.

53. *Furniture Gazette* (20 May 1876).

54. *The Complete Letters of Oscar Wilde*, p.120.

55. The articles for the *Technical Educator* were published in book-form in *Principles of Decorative Design* (London, 1873); the passage referring to Japanese earthenwares is on p. 120.

56. See: Sato, Hidehiko. 'The Legacy of Dr Dresser in Japan', *Christopher Dresser in Japan*, p. 68; travelling exhibition, April–December 2002, organized by the Koriyama City Museum of Art, Fukushima, Japan.

57. *Journal of the Society of Arts*, vol. XXVI, p. 177.

58. *Furniture Gazette* (July–December 1879), vol. XII, p. 32.

59. In the 1905 auction of Dresser's house contents after his death there is a quantity of carved Japanese work including several ceilings.

60. 'A Japanese Room', *Art Journal* (July 1878), vol. 40, p. 158. The many other accounts of these enterprises in the *Art Journal* (1877, p. 136), the *Illustrated London News* and the *Furniture Gazette* (both 15 June 1878) and the *Art Journal* (8 July 1878) are somewhat confusing, but the extensive coverage suggests they were exciting to the public.

61. Halén (1990), p. 85.

62. Allwood, John. *The Great Exhibitions* (London, 1977), p. 57. After the exhibition closed, 78 wagons of exhibits were sent to the Smithsonian Institute in Washington, including the remarkable ethnic objects from Peru. The installation of the Ethnographical galleries at the British Museum is discussed in chapter 4.

63. *Cabinet Maker and Art Furnisher* (1 July 1881), pp.1–2.

64. Godwin's scheme for the Society is discussed in detail by O'Callaghan, John. 'The Fine Art Society and E.W. Godwin', in *FAS 100* (Fine Art Society, London, 23 March–30 April, 1976); and by Reid, Aileen. 'The Architectural Career of E.W. Godwin', in Soros, Susan Weber, ed. *E.W. Godwin, Aesthetic Movement Architect and Designer* (2000), pp. 169–71.

65. Lyons (1999), footnote 63.

66. 'The Works of Christopher Dresser', *The Studio* (1899), vol. XV, pp. 104–14.

67. Godwin, E.W. *The Architect* (23 December 1876); quoted in Adburgham, Alison. *Liberty's: A Biography of a Shop* (London, 1975), p. 21

68. See: Hillier, Jack. 'Japanese Art and the Fine Art Society', *FAS 100* (London, 1976), p. 24.

CHAPTER 2

1. Dresser, Christopher. *The Popular Manual of Botany* (Edinburgh, 1860) p. 5.

2. Ruskin, John. *Letters of John Ruskin to Charles Eliot Norton* (Boston and New York, 1904). See letter dated 17 June 1870.

3. See: Wiener, Martin J. *English Culture and the Decline of the Industrial Spirit, 1850–1980* (Cambridge, 1981). Wiener's overriding thesis is that Britain was never entirely at ease with industrialization.

4. *Journal of the Society of Arts* (10 February 1871), XIX, no. 951, pp. 217–16.

5. The regulations relating to the School of Design appear in the published British Parliamentary Papers. These are to be found in their most accessible form in *British Parliamentary Papers. Industrial Revolution. Design* (Shannon, 1968–70), 4 vols.

6. See: Flachat, Stéphane. *L'Industrie. Exposition de 1834* (Paris, 1834).

7. See: 'Foreign Schools of Design: Report from Mr Dyce', *Parliamentary Papers* (1840) (98) vol. XXIX. Dyce visited the Gewerbe-Institut and the Bau-Akademie in Berlin, the École Gratuit, founded in 1767, and the École de St. Pierre in Lyons. (See also note 5.)

8. See: Snodin, Michael, ed. *Karl Friedrich Schinkel: A Universal Man* (New Haven and London, 1991). Since 1819 Schinkel had been a member of Technische Deputation für Gewerbe (the Prussian state body for fostering trade and industry) which published a journal, *Vorbilder für Fabrikanten und Handwerker* (Berlin, 1821–37). This consisted principally of engraved and chromolithographic plates as exemplars for manufacturers and designers. The earliest instruction manual associated with the Prussian design education system is: Bötticher, C.G.W. *Dessinateur-Schule: Ein Lehrkursus der Dessination der gewebten Stoffe; als Handbuch für den Lehrer so wie als Leitfaden für den Selbstunterricht* (Berlin, 1839). Carl Bötticher (1806–99) was a protégé of both Schinkel and Peter Beuth (1781–1853), the civil servant, who was in charge of advancing the cause of industrial design in Prussia.

9. Dyce, William. *The Drawing Book of the Government School of Design* (London, 1842) was issued in six parts. The plates illustrating 'Dyce's outlines' were executed in a novel manner: by copper strips set in wooden blocks. Some of the folio-sized plates showing classical ornament were lithographed by Thomas Shotter Boys, the leading contemporary lithographer, after Dyce's drawings.

10. Pugin, A.W.N. *Floriated Ornament: A Series of Thirty One Designs* (London, 1849; a later edition was published in 1875). Dresser used the same simple colour schemes as Pugin for some of the designs in *The Art of Decorative Design* (London, 1862). Pugin did not take his plants from nature – as did Dresser – but tells us he took them from Tabernae Montanus' (Jacob Theodor Bergzaben) *Eicones Plantarum … omnis generis* (Frankfurt, 1590), the process of adapting a simple woodcut being an obvious shortcut in representing plants.

11. Muthesius, Hermann. *Der Zeichenunterricht in den Londener Volkschulen* (Gotha, 1900). This had previously appeared in the education journal *Pädagogischen Blättern für Lehrerbildung*. Hermann Muthesius (1861–1927) was a Prussian state architect. In 1896 he joined the German embassy in London where he was delegated to study developments in British architecture and design. His *Das Englische Haus* (1904–5) is still the best account of British domestic architecture during the ascendancy of the Arts and Crafts movement. Muthesius was among the key players in the Deutsche Werkbund.

12. See: 'Hindrances to the Progress of Applied Art', *Journal of the Society of Arts*, XX, pp. 435–43.

13. See: The British Association for the Advancement of Science's *Portfolio of Lithographic Drawings of the Principal Manufactures Exhibited at the Birmingham Exposition 1849* (Birmingham, 1849).

14. The *Journal of Design and Manufactures* was edited by Richard Redgrave (see following note). It was a vehicle for those concerned in raising the standard of British design. Among the reformers who contributed to it were Dyce, Owen Jones, Pugin and Matthew Digby Wyatt.

The journal was opposed to the current naturalism in ornamental design. The *Journal of Design* was far more down-to-earth in its presentation than Schinkel's and Beuth's *Vorbilder für Fabrikanten und Handwerker*. Over 200 samples of fabrics or wallpapers were mounted in the *Journal of Design* and provide a remarkable record of reformist design.

15. See: Casteras and Parkinson (1988). This provides a balanced view of Redgrave and includes much detail of his role in British design education.

16. See: Gonse, Louis, ed. *L'Art à l'Exposition de 1878* (Paris,1879). See: Duranty. 'Revue des arts asiatiques': '*Les tissus sont les œuvres les plus importantes de l'Inde. Elle est la mère des étoffes; la Perse est sa seule rivale, car la Chine et Japon*', p. 539. Louis-Émile-Edmond Duranty (1833–80) was a novelist, a *réaliste*, and friend of Degas.

17. See: Desmond, Ray. *Sir Joseph Dalton Hooker: Traveller and Plant Collector* (Woodbridge and London, 1999).

18. Dresser, in a letter, dated 20 September 1860, requesting a testimonial from Sir William Jackson Hooker of Kew in support of his candidature for the Chair of Botany at University College London, refers to two native species of orchid that he had earlier given to Dr Joseph Hooker – *Epipactis purpurata* and *Orchis fusca* – both of which were collected in Kent. In a letter of 25 September, in which he thanked Sir William for the testimonial, Dresser refers to a *Neotia spiralis*, another native orchid, which he had collected on Box Hill in Surrey. (Archive of the Royal Botanic Gardens, Kew.) Significantly, John Lindley, whose lectures at Marlborough House Dresser would have attended in November 1852, was the leading British authority on orchids. (See: Stearn, William T., ed. *John Lindley, 1799–1865: Gardener, Botanist and Pioneer Orchidologist* (Woodbridge, nd [1999]).

19. The first students of the School of Mines were enrolled in November 1851. The school was housed in the same building as the Museum of Practical Geology in Jermyn Street, off Piccadilly. In the wake of the 1851 Exhibition there was an increased awareness of international competition in industry. Much pressure was placed on the government to fund higher education in science and technology – the School of Mines was an important outcome. Here chemistry, as well as geology, mineralogy, chemistry, general natural history, physics, applied mechanics, metallurgy and mechanical drawing, were taught and diplomas awarded. A wide range of students attended, including many 'working men', government officials and army officers. Albert, the Prince Consort, attended lectures at the institution. T.H. Huxley was among the many distinguished lecturers to be associated with the School of Mines. The institution now forms part of the Imperial College of Science.

20. See: Reid, Wemyss. *Memoirs and Correspondence of Lyon Playfair, First Lord Playfair of St Andrews, P.C., G.C.B., LL.D., F.R.S., &c.* (New York and London, 1899).

21. Dresser adhered to Lindley's injunctions throughout his career. Lindley concluded his three lectures thus: 'the nearer nature is approached, the nearer we approach to that which is beautiful ... With regard to conventional designs, general truth is quite sufficient; and provided the principle of symmetry, equipoise ... are sufficiently regarded it matters little in what particular manner the representations of vegetable forms are given. It is, however, indispensable that the parts should bear a certain relation to each other, and that relation must be what actually exists in nature. Let this be attended to, and it is impossible that any great fault can be committed.' pp. 50–51.

22. Scott, Geoffrey. *The Architecture of Humanism: A Study in the History of Taste* (London, 1914). See: Chapter V, 'The Ethical Fallacy'. Scott is especially interesting on Ruskin's *Stones of Venice* (1851–3). Scott saw Ruskin's moralizing arguments as stemming in essence from the fourth book in Plato's *Republic*. But 'the dictator's [Ruskin's] authority has long since, by his own extravagance, been destroyed. The casuistries of *The Stones of Venice* are forgotten; its inconsistencies quite irrelevant to the case', pp. 132–3.

23. George Phillips in *Rudiments of Curvilinear Design* (London, 1838–40) suggested how the spines of a sea-urchin could serve as an inspiration to pattern designers. Forbes, however, appears to have been the earliest authority to have attempted to extrapolate design principles from structures of undersea creatures. The significance of the lectures lies in the fact that we witness in them an attempt to extend the vocabulary of the decorative designer beyond the historicizing conventions of the era.

24. See: Paley, William. *Natural Theology; or, Evidences of the Existence and Attributes of the Deity, Collected from the Appearances of Nature* (London, 1802). 'There cannot be design without a designer, contrivance without a contriver', p. 12.

25. In an interview in 1969 with Frederick Burrows I learned that Dresser employed a full-time gardener and spent as much time as he could in his conservatory. Burrows described the garden as 'memorable'. Burrows was born in 1878 and joined Dresser's Elm Bank studio in 1899 as an articled pupil. He went on to study at the Royal College of Art and later became Principal of Portsmouth School of Art and subsequently a Ministry of Education Inspector of Art Schools. He was almost certainly the last link with the Dresser studio.

26. See: Arber, Agnes. 'Goethe's Botany', *Chronica Botanica* (Waltham, Mass., 1946), vol. 10, no. 2. 'In one of his notes after saying that "*Alles ist Blatt*" [Goethe] suggests that the stem is a leaf which becomes radially symmetrical [*Ein Blatt, das sich gleich ansudehnt*]', p. 78 (see also note 29).

27. DNA research is given a high priority in major botanical institutions. The discovery of the DNA structure by Watson and Crick in 1953 has resulted in the recognition of new relationships between the genera and families of plants. Conventional taxonomical views are sometimes confirmed and sometimes overturned.

28. Darwin in *The Foundations of the Origin of Species: Two Essays Written in 1842 and 1844. Edited by his Son, Francis Darwin* (Cambridge, 1909) declared that nothing was 'more wonderful in Natural History than looking at the vast number of organisms ... united by a similar type of structure. When we ... see bat, horse, porpoise-fin, hand, all built on the same structure ... we see that there is some deep bond of union between them ... Now this wonderful fact of hand, hoof, wing and claw being the same, is at once explicable on the principle of some parent forms ... every botanist considers petals, nectaries, stamens, pistils, germen [the ovary] as metamorphosed leaf ... The skulls of vertebrates are undoubtedly composed of ... metamorphosed vertebrae, thus we can understand the strange form of the separate bones which compose the casket holding man's brain'.

29. See: Dresser, Christopher. *Unity in Variety, as Deduced from the Vegetable Kingdom: Being an Attempt at Developing that Oneness which is Discoverable in the Habits, Mode of Growth , and Principle of Construction of All Plants* (London, 1859), p. 111. The title of the book indicates the thoroughly Goethean nature of Dresser's botany. Agnes Arber (1879–1960) in her *Natural Philosophy of Plant Form* (Cambridge, 1950) noted that Dresser's observation that the leaf was a 'modified branch' was an advance on the previously held view that the leaf was the ultimate unit of the plant (p. 74). Arber, a Cambridge botanist who, in her later years, became interested in the philosophical implications of science, appears to have been the first modern authority to recognize the originality of some of Dresser's botanical ideas. She seems to have been entirely unaware of Dresser's importance as a designer.

30. Plato (*c.*429–347 BCE) does not actually use the term 'archetype' in the *Timaeus*. However, he does describe how the creator desired to make all things like himself. This necessitates a plan or model. Arber (see note 29), citing the American philosopher

H.A. Wolfson, who attributed the earliest use of the term 'archetype' to Philo Judaeus, who flourished before 40 CE (p. 65).

31. See: Owen, Richard. *On the Archetype and Homologies of the Vertebrate Skeleton* (London, 1848).

32. The *Urpflanze* of Goethe should be viewed as a mental construct, rather than an actual entity. In a letter, from Naples, written to his friend Johann Gottfried Herder (1744–1803) of 17 May 1787, Goethe wrote: 'I am very close to the secret of the reproduction and organization of plants and that it is the simplest thing imaginable ... The Primal Plant is going to be the strangest creature in the world, which Nature herself shall envy me. With this model ... it will be possible to go on forever inventing plants and know that their existence is logical ... if they do not actually exist, they could, for they are not the shadowy phantoms of a vain imagination, but possess an inner necessity and truth. The same law will be applicable to all other living organisms.' (See Auden, W.H., and Mayer, Elizabeth J.W., translators. *Goethe, Italian Journey [1786-1788]* (London, 1962). The Primal Plant was to be used as a didactic device by both M.J. Schleiden and Dresser who describe it as an 'ideal plant'.

33. Many authorities were opposed to the theories of the morphologists because they appeared to contradict the doctrine of 'special creation', which asserted that God had created each species separately. John Murray in *Strictures on Morphology: Its Unwarrantable Assumptions and Atheistical Tendency* (London, 1845) declared that 'the laws imposed by the Divine Law Giver, are like Himself, unsusceptible to change, and incapable of overthrow'. The Rev. James McCosh and George Dickie in their *Typical Forms and Special Ends in Creation* (Edinburgh, 1856) regretted 'that the recent discoveries as to harmony of structure running through the whole organic kingdoms have been turned by some to improper purposes'. William Whewell in his *History of the Inductive Sciences ...* (London, 1857) attempted to provide a theistic justification for morphology: 'There is another aspect of the doctrine of the Archetypal Unity of Composition of Animals, by which it points to an Intelligence from which the frame of Nature proceeds; namely this: that the Archetype of the animal structure being of the nature of an *Idea*, implies a mind in which this Idea existed and thus Homology [correspondence of structure] itself points the way to the Divine Mind', pp. 561–2.

34. See: Dresser (1862), Chapter 11: 'Adaptation', paragraph 11. It is worth pointing out that ship design was one of the most advanced areas of Victorian technology. The vicissitudes of the construction of Brunel's and Scott Russell's *Great Eastern* –

finally launched in 1860 – excited the imagination of a whole generation.

35. See Newman, Charles. *The Evolution of Medical Education in the Nineteenth Century* (London, 1957). Linnaeus and John Lindley published works on medical botany.

36. Dresser described *The Popular Manual of Botany* (1860) as a 'ladies' book'. This was an occasional – if unflattering – way of describing an introductory or elementary work. Lindley's *Ladies' Botany; or, a Familiar Introduction to the Study of the Natural System of Botany* (London, 1834) was immensely popular and appeared in many editions.

37. Tyndall was among the most successful of all Victorian popular scientific lecturers. He lectured at the Royal Institution and in the United States. His efforts to popularize science did nothing to diminish his reputation as one of the leading scientists of the age. His publications on electricity, light and sound went into numerous editions. See: Burchfield, J.A. *John Tyndall: Essays on a Natural Philosopher* (Dublin, 1981).

38. Ernst Chladni first published his method of creating vibration patterns by stroking a violin bow at the edge of a metal plate covered with fine sand in *Entdeckungen über die Theorie des Klanges* (1787). Chladni's experiments were well known by the time Dresser advocated their use to designers in 1862. No other contemporary authority on design, however, seems to have commented upon Chladni.

39. See: Rorschach, Hermann. *Psychodiagnostik Methodik und Ergebnisse eines wahrnehmungsdiagnostischen Experiments* (Bern, 1921). Bruno Klopfer and Helen Davidson supply a brief history of Rorschach's ink-blots in *The Rorschach Technique: An Introductory Manual* (New York, 1962).

40. The phenomenon of 'figure and ground' was first described in 1920 by E.J. Rubin (1886–1951), the Danish psychologist who specialized in visual perception. This and related phenomena are, of course, likely to have been known to designers and craftsmen for a long time – at an empirical level. As, too, would have been the phenomenon of counterchange in which the interstices of a pattern can form an alternate design – M.C. Escher (1898–1972) is probably the best known exponent of counterchange.
E.H. Gombrich in *The Sense of Order: A Study in the Psychology of Decorative. The Wrightsman Lectures* (London, 1979) examines pattern and ornament in relation to theories of Gestalt perception. See also: Arnheim, Rudolf. 'Gestalt Psychology and Artistic Form' in Law Whyte, Lancelot, ed. *Apects of Form* (London, 1951; 2nd edition 1968), pp. 196–208.

41. Owen Jones, who was responsible for the Alhambra Court at the Crystal Palace in Sydenham – which consisted of plaster replicas

of fragments of the building – published a small guide for visitors: *The Alhambra Court in the Crystal Palace* (London, 1854). Here he discussed briefly the visual effects of repeat pattern: 'In surface decoration any arrangement of forms, consisting only of straight lines, is monotonous, and affords but imperfect pleasure; but introduce lines which tend to carry the eye towards the angles, and you have at once an additional pleasure. Then add lines giving a circular tendency... and you have now complete harmony', pp. 36–7. This appears to be the earliest account of how pattern is perceived. Jones presented his ideas on pattern and ornament in their fully evolved form in his *Grammar of Ornament* (London, 1856).

42. See: Dresser (1862), Chapter V: 'Analysis of Ornamental Forms'. Dresser illustrates 49 examples of tessellation and repeat. Two examples appear to derive from Japanese sources and one from an Islamic source – the majority are likely to have been known to most designers of pattern for machine production. Some designs, however, may have been devised by Dresser. Dyce illustrated some of the basic forms of repeat in his *Drawing Book* (1842). See also note 9.

43. Pugin in *Contrasts; or, A Parallel between the Noble Edifices of the Middle Ages and Corresponding Buildings of the Present Day; Shewing the Present Decay of Taste* (London, 1836; 1841) satirizes contemporary architecture – eclectic or 'pagan' – and the scientific materialism of the times with incomparably witty drawings. The work was enormously influential in advancing the cause of Gothic.

44. The survival of the Ipswich sketchbook is as remarkable as it is inexplicable. It was brought into the Ipswich Museum by an elderly man in the late 1960s. Patricia Baker, the curator of the museum, recognized its importance immediately and offered to purchase it. The reasons for its survival – when Dresser's record books had all been burned – will probably never be known. One of the pages had already been defaced by a crude drawing of a vase of flowers in ball-point.

45. The writer, as Simon Jervis points out in his essay, is likely to have been Charles Holme. (But why – knowing Dresser's fondness for the title 'Doctor' did Holme call him 'Mr'?) See note 48 for the full bibliographical reference.

46. The two compositions are 'The Evening Star' (plate XVI) and 'Night' (plate XIX). Both make use of flat and stylized (conventionalized) representations of plants. The two compositions do not appear in sketch form in the Ipswich sketchbook (see note 44). It is plausible that they actually antedate the sketchbook. It is also conceivable that the two compositions met with some approval when they were published in 1862 and Dresser was prompted

to pursue this direction – hence the more ambitious semi-pictorial sketches, based upon lines of poetry, which appear in the Ipswich sketchbook. There appears to be no precedent for the 'Evening Star' and 'Night' in British decorative art, although Philipp Otto Runge (1777–1810), the German Romantic painter, painted allegorical and symmetrically organized compositions representing *Morning*, *Midday*, *Evening* and *Night*. It is tempting to think that Dresser might have known these, but there is no evidence to substantiate such a view – although Runge's compositions were published in 1806 and again in 1807 in the form of engravings. Goethe described them as 'mysterious and charming'. (See: Gage, John. *Goethe on Art* (Berkeley and Los Angeles, 1980)). See also: Durant, Stuart. 'Aux origines de l'Art nouveau, Christopher Dresser et la science de l'ornement', *L'École de Nancy et les art décoratifs en Europe. Actes du Colloque 15,16 Octobre 1999* (Nancy, 2000).

47. In the late 1970s, when I assisted Ernst Gombrich in finding some material for his *The Sense of Order*, which was published in 1979, I made mention to him of the fact that abstractionism arose at a time when the study of ornament was at its apogee. Early twentieth-century abstract art, I suggested, could, perhaps, be considered as arising out of the work of the great nineteenth-century authorities on ornament – Owen Jones, Gottfried Semper, Viollet-le-Duc, Jules Bourgoin, et al. 'It's obvious', he replied. (I had had in mind the work of early abstract artists – Hans Arp (1887–1966), Giacomo Balla (1871–1958), Robert Delaunay (1885–1941), Sonia Delaunay (1885–1979), Johannes Itten (1888–1967), Wassily Kandinsky (1866–1944), Paul Klee (1879–1940), Franz Kupka (1871–1957), Kasimir Malevich (1878–1935), Piet Mondrian (1872–1944), Georgia O'Keeffe (1887–1986).) In the event, Gombrich broached the theme rather cautiously in *The Sense of Order* (see note 40): 'There is nothing the abstract painter used to dislike more than the term "decorative", an epithet which reminded him of the familiar sneer that what he had produced was at best pleasant curtain material. One is reminded of Michelangelo, who rebuked a correspondent for addressing him as a sculptor. The successful and those who have arrived tend to deny their poor relations … the reader … will realize that the theory of twentieth-century abstract painting owes indeed more to the debates on design that arose in the nineteenth century than is usually allowed … During these times of ferment around the turn of the century the words ornament and decorative were not yet dirty words in the criticism of painting.' (p. 62)

48. This is from an anonymous article, 'The Work of Christopher Dresser', *The Studio* (London, 1899), vol. XV, pp. 104–14.

49. Dresser's ideas on colour can be found in the *Technical Educator* 1870–72 (and in *The Principles of Decorative Design*, 1873). Dresser's description of post-1851 colour theory is probably the most accessible of all those published. His ideas are an amalgam of those subscribed to by his contemporaries, though by the 1870s the complex rules of 'colour harmony' were becoming less rigidly adhered to. Paramount among the sources for the theory purveyed by Dresser was George Field's *A Treatise on Colour …* (London, 1835). George Field (1776–1854) was principally a chemist. He was also the leading authority on pigments – and the inventor of an ingenious 'chronometer' and a 'metrochrome'. With these devices he claimed to have established the ideal proportional relationships – in terms of their surface area to produce 'harmonies' – of the three primary colours. These were three of red to five of blue to eight of yellow. The secondary colours (orange, etc.) and the tertiary colours (olive, etc.) had yet more complex relationships. Field's ideas were very widely accepted. See: Gage, John. *George Field and His Circle …* (Cambridge, 1989). Owen Jones reproduced Field's ratios in the *Grammar of Ornament* (London, 1856), see: Proposition 18. Richard Redgrave, one of Dresser's mentors, published an *Elementary Manual of Colour* (London, 1853) that relied heavily on Field. Dresser also knew the works on colour of Sir David Brewster, M.E. Chevreul and D.R. Hay. Owen Jones had made detailed – and would-be scientific – studies of the Indian fabrics at the Great Exhibition and incorporated these in his *Grammar of Ornament* Propositions. Despite conforming to the rules of the elaborate colour theory that he had learned in his youth, Dresser frequently managed to achieve considerable novelty in his colour schemes.

CHAPTER 3

1. *Journal of the Society of Arts* (17 March 1871), p. 352. The full quote reads: 'That I was intended by nature as an artist, I doubt not; but let it ever be remembered that, with the view of causing me to become one, my parents placed me at a "school of design"; as a consequence, I may not be an artist; and this I know, that after being a student there for seven years, I spent five years in continuous efforts before I succeeded in making one penny by ornamental designing. Whether I am or am not an artist, I am content to leave to the public to judge, but I may fairly say this, that I am not simply an amateur. As an architect I have as much work as many of my fellows, and as an ornamentist I have much the largest practice, etc'.

2. *Building News* (21 April, 1865).

3. 'Dr Dresser retires [from Dresser & Holme] to devote the whole of his time to his professional work as an architect and ornamentist', *Furniture Gazette* (8 July 1882). Frederick Burrows, who worked for Dresser, 1899–1901, was surprised to learn that Dresser had designed glass and metalware (apart from iron gates). Neither were carpets nor ceramics mentioned in his interview with Stuart Durant. A second member of the Dresser Studio, Cecil F. Tattersall, who worked for 10 years, 1894–1904, with Dresser referred to Dresser as designing bedspreads, tapestries, cretonnes and wallpapers. (See records of the Victorian and Edwardian Arts Exhibition, 1952 at the V&A.)

4. Dresser (1873), p. 90: 'all walls, however decorated, should serve as a background to whatever stands in front of them'.

5. List of prize-winners, Department of Science and Art, 'Reports and Documents As to the State and Progress of Schools of Design. 1850–1851'.

6. List of prize-winners, Department of Science and Art, 1853. This design was printed by Hargreaves on cambric for Liddiard and registered at the PODR. Dresser was additionally awarded prizes that year for four designs for printed fabrics. And a further prize for 'applying the principles taught by the Department to a chintz'. 'First Report of Department of Science and Arts, 1853', Appendix K, p. 355.

7. 'He [Dresser] had a tremendous knowledge of manufacturing processes'. Interview with Frederick Burrows in Durant (1993), p. 41.

8. *Ibid.*

9. *Reports of the United States Commissioners to the Paris Universal Exposition, 1867*, vol. I, p. 94.

10. See: *Reports of the United States Commissioners to the Paris Universal Exposition, 1878*, vol. III, p. 465 *et seq.*

11. *Illustrated London News* (6 September 1862), p. 275.

12. 'Dr Dresser is designing for French companies, thereby reversing the trend.' *Building News* (29 December 1865).

13. Probably including Daniel Lee, and Strines Printing Co., both Manchester, James Black, Glasgow, and Swaislands Printing Co., Kent.

14. *Furniture Gazette* (12 June 1880).

15. National Archive. BT/31/2670/14236. Jas Templeton, Glasgow is also mentioned, but this may have been for tapestries.

16. '… no class of persons in our country so thoroughly obstruct the progress of applied art … as the "buyers" … in our large retail houses … These are men utterly ignorant of … art'. From 'Hindrances to the Progress of Applied Art', *Journal of the Society of Arts* (12 April 1872), p. 436.

17. *Furniture Gazette* (8 July 1882), p. 26. The term 'architect' was loosely used at this time. I have not seen any evidence that Dresser was schooled in the engineering aspects of architecture.

18. Morris, Barbara. *Liberty Design, 1874–1914* (London, 1989), pp. 18–19.

19. Additionally, the 'Dresser' family tree held by the descendants of Sir Frederick Dresser, a late Victorian Liverpool merchant, firmly annotates Dr Christopher Dresser as a designer for Liberty – an association supported by Dresser's daughter, Nellie. V&A file, The Victorian and Edwardian Exhibition, 1952. Letter from Nellie Dresser.

20. Cecil Tattersall in his letter to the V&A, 6 September 1952 states that during the period 1894–1904 Dresser 'did no designing himself, but maintained a studio and mainly concerned himself with sales.' Frederick Burrows supports this, giving a picture of Dresser supervising the studio, rather than creating designs himself. Burrows added that Dresser's technical knowledge of machines was a 'by-word' in the studio, and implies that nothing left the studio without his authorization. 'All the time he imposed his personality upon the designs.' Interview with Frederick Burrows in Durant (1993).

21. Listed by Pevsner. See: *Architectural Review* (1937), vol. 81, p.185.

22. Bolton Museum and Art Gallery.

23. 'Many of [Tootal's] designs could be produced in England, France and Switzerland, but he would be a sanguine operator , who could hope to rival in one generation, so immense and varied production', *Reports of the United States Commissioners to the Paris Universal Exposition, 1878*, vol. II, p. 432.

24. Information courtesy of Stead McAlpin archives.

25. Information courtesy of Stead McAlpin archives. *Carlisle Journal* (30 April 1878); *Carlisle Patriot* (May 1878).

26. V&A file on the London International Exhibition of 1862, which contains a list of present and former students of the School of Design, whose designs were exhibited.

27. 'I [confess] I am not very fond of wallpapers under any circumstances. I prefer a tinted or painted wall.' Dresser (1873), p. 90.

28. *Building News* (29 December 1865).

29. Cooke established a partnership with John Trumble in 1846 in Leeds. Its business covered the North of England. Cooke split with Trumble in 1856.

30. Sugden, A.V., and Edmondson, J.L. *A History of English Wallpaper, 1509–1914* (London, 1926), pp. 233–5.

31. *Art Journal* (1860), p. 378.

32. Anaglypta catalogue, 1912.

33. Dresser (1873), p.106.

34. The *Illustrated London News* articles on wallpapers, carpets and textile hangings at the exhibition, although unsigned as was the journal's custom, carry Dresser's unmistakeable style and phraseology.

35. Sala, G.A. *Notes and Sketches of the Paris Exhibition*, pp. 271–8.

36. The Crossley Archive, Halifax, West Yorkshire. See also Lyons (1999), fig. 16.

37. *The Graphic* (3 June), 1871.

38. *Technical Educator* (1872), vol. 3, p. 250, and *Warehousemen and Drapers' Trade Journal* (15 June 1872), p. 111.

39. Victorian and Edwardian Exhibition, 1952, file in the V&A. Interview by Lowry of Nellie Dresser.

40. Mayers, F.J. *Carpet Designs and Designing* (Essex, 1934), p. 130.

CHAPTER 4

1. Dresser (1873), p. 161. In writing this article, Michael Whiteway, Charlotte Gere and Harry Lyons have provided huge quantities of information. For assistance with sources of inspiration I am indebted to Colin McEwan, Jim Hamill, Stuart Needham, Leslie Webster, Tim Clark, Judith Swaddling, Christopher Date and Gary Thorn in the British Museum, and to Colin Sheaf at Bonhams. My thanks also to Suzanne Fagence Cooper, Emma Kelly and Sachi Sen in the V&A for access to Japanese objects acquired from Londos & Co and from Bing.

2. Dresser (1874–6), pp. 8 and 3.

3. Dresser (1874–6), p. 14.

4. Dresser (1874–6), pl. XXII.

5. Westwood, J.O. *Paleographia Sacra Pictoria. The art of illuminated manuscripts. Illustrated sacred writings. Being a series of illustration of the ancient versions of the Bible copied from illuminated manuscripts executed between the fourth and sixteenth centuries* (London, 1843–5).

6. Dresser (1873), p. 13.

7. Dresser (1873), pp. 82–3.

8. He greatly admired the coffered ceilings of Japanese temples and asked for models to be made; these were presented to him after his return to England, see Dresser (1882), pp. 214–15. One of these models survives in the V&A.

9. Dresser (1873), pp. 114–15. See also, p. 48, note 1.

10. Dresser (1873), pp. 120–23, figs 97–113. For an illustration of the kind of Moroccan water vessel that inspired Dresser's designs, see Joppien (1981), fig. 21, p. 32. Joppien's account of Dresser's sources is the best and most wide-ranging to date.

11. For an example of a Persian sprinkler, see Tait, H., ed. *Masterpieces of Glass* (British Museum, London, exhib. cat., 1968), no. 161.

12. For the pen and ink design, see Joppien (1981), fig. 64, p. 62. The design is rectangular; by a simple alteration of the angle of one of the cranes it has been adapted to a square shape.

13. The V&A acquired a number of Japanese items from the 1862 International Exhibition in London. Michael Whiteway has noted that among these purchases was a flower-pot with flying cranes and waves. It was included in Audsley, G., and Bowes, J. *Keramic Art of Japan* (London, 1875), 2 vols, pl. XLVII, no. 4. Dresser knew this lavishly illustrated book and quotes from it in his paper on 'The Art Manufactures of Japan, from Personal Observation', *Journal of the Society of Arts* (1 February 1878), pp. 169–77.

14. The flying cranes design was adapted to many other shapes. For the registered designs see Public Record Office vol. BT 43/69, no. 268725 (10 December 1872). I owe this reference to Imogen Loke.

15. For a jardinière with the Minton flying cranes design, see Rudoe (1994), no. 384, pl. 144.

16. Much of the silversmiths' section is taken up with discussion of Dresser's laws governing the application of handles and spouts to vessels. This is where his original designs appear. These include two designs for conical sugar basins with zoomorphic feet that served also as handles; the pointed bases were designed to allow the dust to separate from the lumps and fall to the bottom. The simpler of these two designs was eventually produced by Elkington in electroplate in 1885 (see page 207).

17. Dresser (1873), pp. 137–8.

18. For the Japanese ironwork inlaid with gold and silver see: Harris, V. *Japanese Imperial Craftsmen: Meiji Art from the Khalili Collection* (British Museum, London exhib. cat., 1994), nos. 29–32. For a Japanese inlaid copper tray acquired by the V&A from Londos & Co. in 1881, see: Halén (2002), p. 169, no. R-13. For Bidri ware, see Stronge, S. *Bidri Ware: Inlaid Metalwork from India* (London, 1985).

19. 'Eastern Art and Its Influence on European Manufactures and Taste', *Journal of the Society of Arts* (6 February 1874), pp. 211–19. In this paper he speaks at length of Barbédienne and Christofle, noting correctly the difference in technique employed by the two Paris rivals.

20. This was separate from the *Grammar of Ornament*, published in 1856.

21. Dresser (1862), p. 169, fig. 135 (vignette from *The Preacher*) and pl. XXIV.

22. Dresser (1873), pp. 86–7, fig. 61 or Dresser (1874–6), pl. LIX bottom left and *Floriated Ornament: A Series of Thirty-One Designs by Augustus Welby Pugin, Architect* (London, 1849), pl. 10 bottom right (reprinted by Richard Dennis, Shepton Mallet, 1994).

23. Dresser (1862), pp. 38–40.

24. I am grateful to Michael Whiteway for drawing to my attention an illustration of the BM flask in Dennis, G. *The Cities and Cemeteries of Etruria*, 2 vols (London, 1884), p. 457. The flask entered the British Museum in 1850 and was among a group of Egyptian items found in an Etruscan tomb, the so-called Isis tomb, in 1827. The contents of the tomb were once in the possession of the Prince of Canino, a celebrated collector of Etruscan antiquities. The flask was one of two, with incised decoration, antelope handles and hieroglyphic inscriptions expressing New Year greetings, see *Principi etruschi: tra Mediterraneo ed Europa* (Museo Cirico Archeologico, Bologna, exhib. cat. 2000), no. 414.

25. *A Catalogue of the Most Interesting and Miscellaneous Collection of Curios Formed by the late Dr Dresser*, sold by J. C. Stevens, King Street, London, 9 May 1905, lot 215.

26. Dresser (1873), p. 151.

27. Dresser (1878), note 9, p. 169

28. One of the few pieces from his collection to have survived was acquired by the British Museum in 1980 (1980,12-17,4): it is an eighteenth-century square pottery dish with relief decoration of basket-weave pattern and orchids. On the reverse are two labels referring to 'Dr Dresser's collection'; one bears a lot number (1207) indicating a subsequent sale and it has not been possible to identify it with any of the lots in the sale of Dresser's collection because the catalogue descriptions are too brief.

29. Dresser (1874), pp. 212–14. The Japanese dress may be one of those included in the posthumous sale of Dresser's collection. Dresser illustrates the fabric in *Traditional Arts and Crafts of Japan*, fig. 189, p. 442.

30. The history of the V&A's Japanese collection is fully discussed in Faulkner and Jackson (1995), pp. 152–92.

31. Dresser had begun to sign his work prior to 1876, see Dresser (1874–6; reprint), p. 37 for references to wallpapers for Jeffrey & Co with his name printed in the margins.

32. An example of the Dresser tea-set in its box is to be seen in the V&A (M57-1979 and M65-1979); it is displayed in the British Galleries, next to an even more compact Japanese version (M39-1965).

33. Noted by Faulkner and Jackson (1995), p. 172.

34. Dixon & Sons' costing book was discussed by S. Bury in 'The Silver Designs of Christopher Dresser', *Apollo* (December 1962), pp. 766–70. It subsequently disappeared until its sale at Phillips, London, 29 March 1994, lot 187. It is now in Sheffield Public Library.

35. For examples of rectangular Chinese teapots, see: Lo, K.S. *The Stonewares of Yixing from the Ming Period to the Present Day* (London and Hong Kong, 1986), figs 114 and 96.

36. *Ibid.*, fig. 80, a late nineteenth-century teapot.

37. For Japanese drums, see: *Kazari: Decoration and Display in Japan, 15th–19th Centuries* (British Museum, London, exhib. cat. 2002), no. 36. A red-painted Perry & Son candlestick is in the British Museum, see: Rudoe (1994), no. 94.

38. For the Japanese bronze vases in the V&A, see: Halén (2002), p. 169, cat. no. R-14, height 30.5cm.

39. Dresser (1882), p. 428.

40. Dresser (1882), fig. 180, p. 425.

41. Dresser sale catalogue 1905 (see note 25), no. 5; V&A Inv. Nos. 384 and 384A-1905, ht. 40cm, illustrated in Halén (2002), p. 169, cat. no. R-15.

42. For the Minton design, see: Halén (1990), fig. 155, p. 137; for the Chubb reference, see: Collins, M. *Christopher Dresser 1834–1904* (Camden Arts Centre, London, exhib. cat. 1979), cat. 114.

43. Dresser (1882), p. 459, fig. 200.

44. The V&A bronze vase (Inv. 148-1876) is illustrated in Halén (2002), p. 169, no. R-16. See also Faulkner and Jackson (1995), fig. 11.

45. For a Seto ware bowl with crumpled rim acquired by the V&A from the Philadelphia Exhibition of 1876, see Halén (2002), p. 126, cat. no. R-6. The V&A houses Dresser's album of Japanese ceramics in his collection, acquired from his family after his death. Several pages from this are illustrated in Halén (2002), pp. 194–8.

46. See, for example, *The Edward T. Chow Collection*, Sotheby Parke Bernet (Hong Kong), 19 May 1981, lot 494.5.

47. See Forsdyke, E.J. *Catalogue of Greek and Etruscan Vases in the British Museum* (London, 1925), vol. I, no. A331.

48. For similar handles on Roman glass vessels, see Tait, H., ed. *Five Thousand Years of Glass* (London, 1991), p. 69, fig. 86.

49. For the Bronze Age prototype, see: Greenwell, W. *British Barrows: A Record of the Examination of Sepulchral Mounds in Various Parts of England* (Oxford, 1877), XCIX, pp. 308–9, ill. p. 310, fig. 134, H. 8in.; Kinnes, I.A., and I.H. Longworth. *Catalogue of the Excavated Prehistoric and Romano-British Material in the Greenwell Collection* (British Museum, London, 1985), no. 99.

50. *Saxon Obsequies, illustrated by Ornaments and Weapons discovered by the Hon. R. C. Neville in a cemetery near Little Wilbraham, Cambridgeshire during the Autumn of 1851* (London, 1852). Other important early publications included Bronze and Anglo-Saxon pottery, for example Kemble, J.M. *Horae Ferales; or, Studies in the archaeology of the Northern Nations* (London, 1863), see pp. 214–17 and pls XXIX–XXX.

51. A number of examples are illustrated in Martinez, Cruz. *Cerámica Prehispánica Norperuana*, BAR International Series 323, 1986, nos. 650–54.

52. Registration no. Sl. 728. The vessel dates from *c.*900–1470. See: Braunholz, H.J. *Sir Hans Sloane and Ethnography* (British Museum, London, 1970, exhib. cat.), p. 35, pl. 24.

53. The Peruvian displays are described with illustrations of pottery in Chambers, W. & R. *Guide to the British Museum – Historical and Perspective* (London, 1850), p. 39.

54. See: Allwood, J. *The Great Exhibitions* (London, 1977), p. 57, where there is brief mention of a display from Peru that went afterwards to the Smithsonian Museum.

55. For an example in pottery, apparently the only known example with Dresser's facsimile signature, and a unique version in silver, both in the British Museum, see Rudoe (1994), nos. 82 and 96.

56. It is interesting to note that Dresser owned Fijian objects himself, see Dresser sale catalogue 1905 (see note 25), lot 257, a Fiji food bowl.

57. Audsley & Bowes (1881), p. 259, pl. XXXII, division 4.

58. See: King, J. 'Franks and Ethnography', in M. Caygill and J. Cherry, eds. *A.W. Franks: Nineteenth-Century Collecting and the British Museum* (London, 1997), p. 152.

59. Dresser (1874), p. 217.

CHAPTER 5

1. In the writing of this essay, I have benefited from the comments and suggestions of LeeEllen Friedland, Widar Halén, Michael J. Lewis, Joanne Rasi, Michael Taft, Sylvia L. Yount and, especially, Harry Lyons.

2. Dresser's will is on file at the Principal Registry of the Family Division at First Avenue House, High Holborn, London.

3. In Dresser (1878), p. 170, the author states that he left Liverpool on 6 October. However, the 'Latest Shipping Intelligence' section of the 10 October 1876 issue of *The Times*, p. 4, reports that the *Russia* was in Queenstown, Ireland, on 8 October, which suggests that it may have left Liverpool the day before.

4. At the end of his stay in Japan, Dresser left

Yokohama on 3 April and travelled to Hong Kong aboard the steamship *Malacca*, arriving in Hong Kong on 10 April 1877. See: 'Shipping Intelligence', *Japan Weekly Mail* (7 April 1877), p. 274; 'Shipping', *China Mail* (10 April 1877). The 26 April issue of the *Singapore Daily Times* reports that Dresser, whose name is misspelled 'Dressen', was bound for Marseilles aboard the Messageries Maritimes Company's steamship *Djemnah*. The same item notes that the *Djemnah* made intermediate stops at Shanghai, on the 13th; Hong Kong, on the 19th; and Saigon on the 23rd; and arrived in Singapore on the 25th. The steamer was scheduled to leave Singapore on 26 April and follow a route that would take it to Galle (Ceylon), Aden, Suez, Port Said, Naples and, finally, Marseilles. According to *The Times*, the *Djemnah* arrived in Marseilles on 22 May. See: 'The Mails', *The Times* (24 May 1877), p. 5. Dresser's return to Europe via this route is noted in Lyons and Morley (1999), n.p. I am grateful to Mr Lyons for sharing copies of some of the items in the Asian newspapers cited above.

5. Dresser (1882b), p. 51.

6. Dresser (1878), p. 170.

7. 'Latest Shipping Intelligence', *The Times* (23 October 1876), p. 11; 'Passengers Arrived', *New York Times* (21 October 1876), p. 10.

8. 'Japan in New-York', *New York Times* (6 May 1877), p. 10.

9. 'Dr Dresser in America', *Furniture Gazette* (July–December 1876), p. 363.

10. The exhibition opened on 10 May 1876 and closed on 10 November of the same year. The number of persons who attended is estimated to have been close to 10 million, equivalent to one-fifth of the country's population.

11. 'News, Notes, and Comments', *Furniture Gazette* (January–June 1876), p. 296.

12. Founded in 1870 and opened to the public in 1872, the Metropolitan Museum of Art was strongly influenced by the philosophy and organization of London's South Kensington Museum, an institution with which Dresser had strong ties.

13. This mention of Lt. Reeve is interesting, especially because it is the only known reference to Dresser having an assistant during this trip. The list of Dresser's fellow passengers aboard the *Russia* includes a J.W.B. Reeve. This is apparently the same person since, according to records at the Royal Naval Museum, Lt. John W.B. Reeve was in service at that time. However, Reeve appears not to have accompanied Dresser to Japan, since his name does not appear on any of the other published lists of ship passengers or hotel guests that bear Dresser's name. Reeve's service record, at the National Archives, Kew, contains no information about his contact with

Dresser. For information about Lt. Reeve, I am indebted to Allison Wareham, librarian and head of Information Services at the Royal Naval Museum, and also Michael McCaughan and Harry Lyons.

14. 'The World's Display', *Philadelphia Inquirer* (30 October 1876), p. 2.

15. 'Art Industries: Lecture by Dr Christopher Dresser at the Academy of Fine Arts', *The Press* (31 October 1876), p. 2.

16. Gallaudet, Edward M. 'Governmental Patronage of Art' in Thurston, Robert H., ed. *Reports of the Commissioners of the United States to the International Exhibition Held at Vienna, 1873* (Washington, 1876), vol. II, part N, pp. 8–10.

17. The early history of the Pennsylvania Museum and School of Industrial Art is provided in the annual reports of its board of trustees. See, especially, *First and Second Reports of the Board of Trustees of the Pennsylvania Museum and School of Industrial Art* (Philadelphia, 1876–7), pp. 1–19. In later years, the museum and the school were separated. Today they operate as the Philadelphia Museum of Art and The University of the Arts' College of Art and Design.

18. Owen's background, including his extensive involvement with international exhibitions, is summarized in Burton (1999), pp. 116-17.

19. Dresser, Christopher. 'Art Museums', *Penn Monthly* (January–December 1877), p. 117.

20. Dresser wrote: 'Messrs. Londos & Co. at once arranged with me that I make for them, during my journeyings in [Japan], a typical collection of art objects such as should illustrate as fully as possible both the present and the old manufactures of Japan, and have reliable tutorial value, and Messrs. Tiffany of New York arranged with Messrs. Londos & Co. that I make a similar collection for them'. See: Dresser (1878), p. 170.

21. William Platt Pepper to Londos & Co., 18 November 1876. Dalton Dorr Letter Records, series 2, PMA Letter Press Book #1, Philadelphia Museum of Art, Archives. I am grateful to archivist Susan K. Anderson for her assistance.

22. Dresser, Christopher. 'Art Industries', *Penn Monthly* (1877), pp. 12–29; 'Art Museums', *Penn Monthly* (1877), pp. 117–29; 'Art Schools', *Penn Monthly* (1877), pp. 215–25.

23. Durant (1993), p. 28.

24. 'Art Industries', *The Press* (31 October 1876), p. 2.

25. William Platt Pepper to Londos & Co., 18 November 1876. Dalton Dorr Letter Records, series 2, PMA Letter Press Book #1, Philadelphia Museum of Art, Archives.

26. 'Art Museums', *Philadelphia Inquirer* (3 November 1876), p. 2.

27. *Ibid.*

28. William Platt Pepper to Londos & Co., 18 November 1876. Dalton Dorr Letter Records, series 2, PMA Letter Press Book #1, Philadelphia Museum of Art, Archives.

29. Lewis, Michael J. *Frank Furness: Architecture and the Violent Mind* (New York, 2001), p. 95.

30. Jones (1856). For discussions of Furness's possible design influences, see: O'Gorman, James F. *The Architecture of Frank Furness* (Philadelphia, 1973), pp. 34–8; Cohen, Jeffrey A. 'Styles and Motives in the Architecture of Frank Furness' in Thomas, Cohen, and Lewis, eds. *Frank Furness: The Complete Works* (revised edition New York, 1996), pp. 91–120; and Yount, Sylvia L. '"Give the People What They Want": The American Aesthetic Movement, Art Worlds, and Consumer Culture, 1876–1890', (Ph.D. diss., Univ. of Pennsylvania, 1995), pp. 35–51.

31. Lewis, Michael J. *Frank Furness: Architecture and the Violent Mind* (New York, 2001), p. 122.

32. *Philadelphia Inquirer* (31 October 1876), p. 5; *The Press* (31 October 1876), p. 8. During the previous week, Wilson & Fenimores ran a smaller advertisement in the *Philadelphia Inquirer* that stated only: 'Wilson & Fenimores' Paper Hangings. Our Own Manufacture. Interior Decorations. The Latest London Styles. 915 Market Street.' See, for example: *Philadelphia Inquirer* (23 October 1876), p. 5.

33. 'Dr Dresser in America', *Furniture Gazette* (July–December 1876), p. 363. These activities were also noted in Wilson & Fenimores' handbill 'To the Trade'.

34. *Ibid.*

35. The Patent Office's research facilities are located in Arlington, Virginia. I am grateful to Jim Davie, patent examiner at the United States Patent and Trademark Office and keen student of the rich history of his agency, for considerable assistance in tracking down Dresser's designs.

36. *Annual Report of the Commissioner of Patents for the Year 1877* (Washington, 1878), p. 423; *Official Gazette of the United States Patent Office* (2 January–26 June 1877), p. 834. The short article 'Dr Dresser in America', published in the 9 December 1876 issue of the *Furniture Gazette*, states that Dresser created six sets of designs for Wilson & Fenimores, with each set consisting of five individual designs for 'dado, dado rail, sides, frieze and ceiling, or thirty new and elegant designs in all'. This may have been the case, but the fact remains that only 13 of Dresser's designs were submitted for patent protection.

37. Examples of Japanese 'diaper' patterns are illustrated in Dresser (1882b), p. 266.

38. Dresser (1874–6).

39. Dresser, Christopher. 'Art Schools', *Penn Monthly* (1877), p. 225.

40. 'Tiffany's Great Sale of Japanese Curiosities', *Philadelphia Evening Bulletin* (6 June 1877), p. 4.

41. South, Erastus. 'Novelties from an Expert's Baggage', *Daily Graphic* (16 April 1877), p. 319.

42. 'Declaration', Book 16 (1876), p. 122, and 'Naturalization', Book 22 (1876), p. 161, both at the Albany County Hall of Records, Albany, New York. Henry Dresser was born on 6 August 1854. His birth certificate is accessible through the Family Records Centre, London, which is jointly operated by the Public Record Office and the General Register Office. I am grateful to Harry Lyons for information about Henry Dresser, including the lead to his presence in Albany.

43. In his will, Christopher Dresser makes it clear that his sons were expected to support themselves when they reached the age of 21.

44. *The Albany City Directory for the Year 1875* (Albany, 1875), p. 75. According to the *Directory*, Henry Dresser boarded at 82 Hamilton Street and worked at 466 Broadway. Businesses located at 466 Broadway that year were a retail dry-goods store and a job printer. Henry Dresser's name does not appear in the Albany directory for 1876, but it does in the 1877 directory. On page 78 of that volume he is listed as a clerk living at 13 Judson Street; his place of business is not given. Henry Dresser's name is not included in the Albany directories for 1878 and 1879, which may indicate that he had moved away from Albany.

45. 'Hotel Arrivals', *Chicago Tribune* (20 November 1876), p. 4. The newspaper lists 'Charles Dresser', but it could only have been Christopher Dresser, who typically signed his name 'Chr. Dresser'.

46. 'The City: General News', *Chicago Tribune* (22 November 1876), p. 8.

47. Darling, Sharon. *Chicago Furniture: Art, Craft & Industry, 1833–1983* (New York, 1984), p. 190.

48. Twyman's trips to England and France for the purpose of purchasing avant-garde decorative papers are noted in the article 'An Exhibition of Wall-Papers', *American Architect and Building News* (1879), p. 79.

49. 'Personal Intelligence', *Chicago Times* (23 November 1876), p. 6.

50. Williams, Henry T., ed. *The Pacific Tourist: Williams' Illustrated Transcontinental Guide of Travel from the Atlantic to the Pacific Ocean* (New York, 1876), p. 13. The three railroads that carried passengers from Chicago to Council Bluffs were the Chicago, Burlington and Quincy Railroad; the Chicago and North-Western Railroad; and the Chicago and Rock Island Railroad.

51. The epochal linking, by rail, of the east and west coasts of the United States took place on 29 April 1869 at Promontory Point, Utah.

52. Williams, Henry T., ed. *The Pacific Tourist: Williams' Illustrated Transcontinental Guide of Travel from the Atlantic to the Pacific Ocean* (New York, 1876), p. 9.

53. Williams, Henry T., ed. *The Pacific Tourist: Williams' Illustrated Transcontinental Guide of Travel from the Atlantic to the Pacific Ocean* (New York, 1876); Crofutt, George A. *Crofutt's Trans-Continental Tourist* (New York and San Francisco, 1874); Crofutt, George A. *Crofutt's New Overland Tourist and Pacific Coast Guide*, vol. 1 (Chicago, 1878).

54. Rae, William F. *Westward by Rail: The New Route to the East* (London, 1870).

55. 'Hotel Arrivals', *Salt Lake Daily Tribune* (25 November 1876), p. 4. Dresser probably arrived the day before.

56. Crofutt, George A. *Crofutt's New Overland Tourist and Pacific Coast Guide*, vol. 1 (Chicago, 1878), p. 126.

57. Dresser (1882b), pp. 119–20. Contemporaneous engravings of views of the sort Dresser saw from Salt Lake City are included in Crofutt, George A. *Crofutt's Trans-Continental Tourist* (New York and San Francisco, 1874), p. 83, and Williams, Henry T., ed. *The Pacific Tourist: Williams' Illustrated Transcontinental Guide of Travel from the Atlantic to the Pacific Ocean* (New York, 1876), p. 133.

58. Crofutt, George A. *Crofutt's Trans-Continental Tourist* (New York and San Francisco, 1874), p. 82.

59. 'Overland Travel', *San Francisco Chronicle* (27 November 1876), p. 3.

60. 'Hotel Arrivals', *San Francisco Chronicle* (28 November 1876), p. 4.

61. According to information provided by the hotel, which is still in operation, the Palace opened in 1875. An engraving of the hotel as it would have looked at the time of Dresser's stay is in Crofutt, George A. *Crofutt's New Overland Tourist and Pacific Coast Guide*, (Chicago, 1878), vol. 1, p. 213.

62. 'Overland Travel', *San Francisco Chronicle* (28 November 1876), p. 3; 'Hotel Arrivals', *San Francisco Chronicle* (29 November 1876), p. 4. A brief and somewhat condescending article about Saigō and his colleagues, titled 'Centennial Japs: Homeward Bound with a Full Philadelphia Outfit', was published in the 29 November 1876 issue of the *San Francisco Chronicle*, p. 1; Dresser is not mentioned.

63. *Official Catalogue of the Japanese Section. International Exhibition, 1876* (Philadelphia, 1876), p. 5. See also: Sato, Hidehiko. 'The Legacy of Dr Dresser in Japan' in *Christopher Dresser and Japan* (Tokyo, 2002), p. 59.

64. The specific nature of Saigō's assistance is discussed by Sato in his essay 'The Legacy of Dr Dresser in Japan', pp. 59–60, and also by Widar Halén in 'Dresser in Japan', see pp. 127–39 in the present publication.

65. According to the *San Francisco Chronicle*, the *City of Tokio* left San Francisco on 2 December. See: 'Additional Shipping Intelligence', *San Francisco Chronicle* (3 December 1876), p. 5. However, in Dresser (1882b), p. 3, he states that the trip was a sea voyage of 21 days, and, on p. 1, states that he arrived in Yokohama on the morning of 26 December. (A 26 December arrival by the *City of Tokio* is also noted in the 'Shipping Intelligence' column of the *Japan Weekly Mail* (30 December 1876), p. 1,192.) If Dresser's report of a 21-day voyage is accurate, and the effect of crossing the International Date Line is taken into account, then the *City of Tokio* would have left San Francisco on 4 December. However, I am inclined to accept the 2 December departure date reported in the *San Francisco Chronicle*.

66. Launched in 1874, the *City of Tokio* was 423 feet in length, with a capacity of 5,079 tons. See: Ashmead, Henry Graham. *History of Delaware County, Pennsylvania* (Philadelphia, 1884), p. 388. A fine engraving of the steamship was published during the year of Dresser's voyage to Japan. See: 'The Century: Its Fruits and Its Festival. II. American Progress', *Lippincott's Magazine* (January–June 1876), p. 143.

67. While no extended discussion of American decorative art and architecture by Dresser is available, in his lecture on 'Art Industries', delivered at the Pennsylvania Academy of the Fine Arts on 30 October 1876, he did offer generous praise and gentle criticism of American ornament, stating: 'Since I came amidst you I have seen pieces of ornament which for energy and power surpass anything I have before seen. There is a soda-fountain at the entrance to the Continental Hotel, in this city, on the back of which gold incised ornament is wrought: this ornament is most excellent. And surely in many of your buildings there is much decoration that is good, yet I cannot say that great faults do not also abound; but the edifices are often noble, and vigorous, and stately, and the shortcomings are those which are due to the smaller opportunities of study, which a new country necessarily affords, than a continent which has enjoyed a civilization of a thousand years.' (See: Dresser, 'Art Industries', p. 14.) Comments he made during the lecture that were more strongly critical appear to have been excised from the published text. According to a reporter's account of the lecture, Dresser criticized 'new

Public Buildings at Broad and Market streets' where 'he had seen two columns into which a group of figures were so jammed as to make it appear as though they were in everlasting and never-ending pain, straining and bursting in a vain endeavor to lift the enormous mass of material above them.' See: 'Art Museums: Another Interesting Lecture by Dr Dresser – The Importance of the New Art Museum in the Park –Valuable Suggestions', *Philadelphia Inquirer* (3 November 1876), p. 2.

68. It is worth noting that, at some point, the Pennsylvania Museum and School of Industrial Art published an eight-page work by Dresser titled *General Principles of Art, Decorative and Pictorial; with Hints on Color, its Harmonies and Contrasts* (Philadelphia, n.d.). A copy of this publication is in the collection of the Free Library of Philadelphia. I am grateful to Emily Lind Baker for locating it.

69. Between 16 April and 23 June 1877 the firm placed 41 display advertisements in the *Philadelphia Inquirer* about 'special patterns for interior decoration' designed by Dr Christopher Dresser.

70. 'Decorative Ornamentation', *Philadelphia Evening Bulletin* (16 April 1877), p. 8. The three firms, other than Wilson & Fenimores, that contributed to this exhibition all displayed their products at the Philadelphia Centennial Exhibition. For more information about them, see: United States Centennial Commission, *International Exhibition, 1876. Official Catalogue* (Philadelphia, 1876), pp. 113 and 117.

71. 'Art in the City', *Furniture Gazette* (January–June 1876), p. 316. See also: Lyons (1999), n.p.

72. 'Japanese Art', *Furniture Gazette* (July–December 1879), p. 22.

73. It is also a possibility that the idea of designing exhibits in this manner was inspired by the displays of several British firms, at the Philadelphia Centennial Exhibition, that placed products in settings resembling the rooms of homes. See: Yount, Sylvia L. '"Give the People What They Want": The American Aesthetic Movement, Art Worlds, and Consumer Culture, 1876–1890', (Ph.D. diss., Univ. of Pennsylvania, 1995), pp. 91–2.

74. In addition to Dresser, the English designers whose wallpaper designs were represented included J. Moyr Smith, Bruce J. Talbert, Walter Crane, William Morris, Wilberforce R. Bennett, Milford Warner, E.W. Pugin and Owen Jones.

75. 'An Exhibition of Wall-Papers', *American Architect and Building News* (8 March 1879) vol. 5, no. 167, p. 79. This article was reprinted in *Scientific American Supplement* (January–June 1879), vol. 7, pp. 2,717–18.

76. Dacus, J.A., and Buel, James W. *A Tour of St Louis* (St Louis, 1878), pp. 311–12.

77. Dresser (1878), p. 170.

78. Carpenter, Charles H., Jr, with Carpenter, Mary Grace. *Tiffany Silver* (New York, 1978), p. 185.

79. Loring, John. *Magnificent Tiffany Silver* (New York, 2001), p. 30.

80. *Ibid.*

81. Dresser (1882b), p. 221. The exposition judges' glowing report on Tiffany's silver is in Bachelet, M.L. *Rapport sur L'Orfèvrerie. Groupe III.—Classe 24. Exposition Universelle Internationale de 1878 à Paris* (Paris, 1880), p. 16.

82. See: Dresser (1878), p. 177.

83. *The Dresser Collection of Japanese Curios and Articles Selected for Messrs. Tiffany & Co.* (New York, 1877). This auction catalogue and numerous clippings of newspaper articles about the collection and the auction are in the collections of the Tiffany & Co. Archives, Parsippany, New York. I am grateful to Annamarie Sandecki, archivist at the Tiffany archives, and Janet Zapata, former archivist at the Tiffany archives, for information about these materials. Articles about the collection and the auction include: 'An Extraordinary Invoice: Rare Japanese Goods and a New Beverage', *Evening Post* (16 April 1877), p. 3; 'Quaint Japanese Curios: The Rare and Interesting Collection at Tiffany & Co.'s', *The World* (21 April 1877), p. 2; South, Erastus 'Novelties from an Expert's Baggage', *Daily Graphic* (16 April 1877), p. 319; 'Japan in New-York', *New York Times* (6 May 1877), p. 10; and 'Tiffany's Great Sale of Japanese Curiosities', *Philadelphia Evening Bulletin* (9 June 1877), p. 4.

84. Items from a collection known as the Heard Collection were also included in the sale.

85. *The Dresser Collection of Japanese Curios and Articles Selected for Messrs. Tiffany & Co.* (New York, 1877), p. 3.

86. Carpenter, Charles H., Jr, with Carpenter, Mary Grace. *Tiffany Silver* (New York, 1978), p. 185.

87. According to *Goulding's Business Directory of New York, Philadelphia and Boston for the Year 1876* (New York, [1876]), vol. II, p. 925, F.A. Walker was a dealer in 'house furnishing goods' with shops at 83 Cornhill Street and 6 Brattle Street, Boston.

88. Lewis, Arnold, Turner, James, and McQuillin, Steven. *The Opulent Interiors of the Gilded Age* (New York, 1987), photo no. 170, p. 155. Chairs of the same design are illustrated in several recent publications about Dresser, including Whiteway (2001), p. 161. I have been informed by Harry Lyons that Dresser's design drawings for this chair are in the archive of the firm of Thomas Knight & Son, which is part of the collections of the V&A.

89. [Sheldon, George W.] *Artistic Houses, Being a Series of Interior Views of a Number of the Most Beautiful and Celebrated Homes in the United States* (1883; reprint, New York, 1971), p. 139.

90. Halén has called attention to possible connections between Dresser and a number of American designers and manufacturers. See his article 'Christopher Dresser, the Centennial Exhibition, and the Anglo-American Dialogue', *Antiques* (Sept. 2001), vol. 160, no. 3, pp. 354–63. Possible connections between Dresser and Whistler are discussed in Bendix, Deanna Marohn. *Diabolical Designs: Paintings, Interiors, and Exhibitions of James McNeill Whistler* (Washington, 1995), pp. 32, 55, 58, 146, 215

91. 'Tiffany's Great Sale of Japanese Curiosities', *Philadelphia Evening Bulletin* (9 June 1877), p. 4.

92. This craze is described in Yount, Sylvia L. '"Give the People What They Want": The American Aesthetic Movement, Art Worlds, and Consumer Culture, 1876–1890', (Ph.D. diss., Univ. of Pennsylvania, 1995), pp. 203–59.

93. Dresser (1873).

94. Harrison, Constance Cary. *Woman's Handiwork in Modern Homes* (New York, 1881), p. 136.

95. Dresser, Christopher. 'The Decoration of Our Homes', *Art Amateur* (December 1884–May 1885), vol. 12, pp. 86–8, 109–10; (June–November 1885), vol. 13, pp. 33–4; Dresser, Christopher. 'Ceilings, Walls and Hangings: Some Modified Views from Dr Dresser', *Decorator and Furnisher* (1888), vol. 13, pp. 26–7.

96. Dresser, Christopher. 'Eastern Art, and Its Influence on European Manufactures and Taste', *Journal of the Society of Arts* (21 November 1873–13 November 1874), vol. 22, p. 218. A short item titled 'The English Jury at the Philadelphia Exhibition', published in the 6 May 1876 issue of the *Furniture Gazette*, p. 363, says of Dresser: 'It may be remembered that the American report on Design at the Vienna Exhibition was also from his able pen.' It is possible that this report was solicited by the United States commissioners to the Vienna Exhibition, but omitted from their four-volume published report for some reason. The commissioners' report, edited by the eminent engineer Robert H. Thurston, is titled *Reports of the Commissioners of the United States to the International Exhibition Held at Vienna, 1873* (Washington, 1876). I have diligently searched for Dresser's report among the publications of the US commissioners to the Vienna Exhibition that are in the collections of the Library of Congress, Washington, D.C., and in the 'Records of the US Commission,

Vienna International Exposition (1873)', at the National Archives and Records Administration, College Park, Maryland, but have not been successful. I have also searched microfilmed consular correspondence, for the period 1870–74, at the National Archives and Records Administration, but have not found any mention of Dresser. In addition, at my request an archivist associated with the Rare and Manuscripts Collections, Carl A. Kroch Library, Stevens Institute of Technology, searched the Dr R.H. Thurston Papers, but found nothing related to Dresser. Surely, a special prize awaits whoever finds Dresser's elusive report to the US government.

97. 'Japan in New-York', *New York Times* (6 May 1877), p. 10

CHAPTER 6

1. Dresser (1882b), preface and p. 392. For Christopher Dresser and Japan, see also Halén, Widar. *Christopher Dresser and the Cult of Japan*, unpublished dissertation (Oxford, 1988), 2 vols; Halén, Widar. *Christopher Dresser* (Oxford, 1990 and London, 1993); Halén, Widar, ed. *Christopher Dresser and Japan* (Tokyo, 2002).

2. Halén *ibid.* (1988), vol. 1, pp. 37–48, and Department of Science and Art, *Minute Books* (20 April 1854), Public Record Office, London.

3. V&A Museum, MR.nos. 33–4, 48–9, 50–51 and 689/1952.

4. Department of Science and Art, *Minute Books* (20 April 1854), Public Record Office, London.

5. *Building News* (3 January 1862), p. 8 and Dresser (1862), pp. 40 and 91.

6. Christie's auction catalogue (15 May and 1 December 1862).

7. Halén *ibid.* (1988), vol. 1, pp. 94–109 and 'Japan Mania – Collection of Japanese art around the Meiji Restoration', *ANDON* (Leiden, 1987), vol. 7, pp. 112–23, and Williams, G.C. *Murray Marks and His Friends* (London, 1919), pp. 13–43.

8. Dresser (1878), p. 169, and 'Dresser's Drawings of Japanese Porcelain in his collection' (nd), V&A (D.397-541/1905), 'Dresser's Album of Japanese "Mon" patterns', V&A (D.209-1905) and 'Dresser's Albums of Japanese Drawings' V&A (DJ.76-1905, DJ.161-168/1905, DJ.104-1905).

9. Dresser, Christopher. *Development of Ornamental Art in the International Exhibition* (London, 1862), pp. 90 and 146.

10. *Building News* (22 May 1863), pp. 387–8, and *The Builder* (1863), pp. 308–9, 364–5 and 423–4.

11. *Building News* (1863), p. 388, and *The Builder* (1863), pp. 364–5 and 423–4.

12. *The Builder* (1863), p. 308.

13. *Ibid.*

14. *Ibid.*

15. Chisaburo, Yamada, ed. *Japonisme in Art* (Tokyo, 1980), pp. 59–64.

16. Paris Exhibition (London, 1868), p. 112.

17. *Ibid.*, p.12.

18. *Building News* (1865), p. 916

19. Dresser (1873), p. 77.

20. Halén (1990), pp. 120–28.

21. *Official British Report of the International Exhibition of 1871* (London, 1871), p. 8.

22. *Technical Educator* (1871), vol. II, p. 342.

23. *Tokyo Exhibition Society Journal* or '*Kaigai Hakurankai Hanpo Sando Shiryo*' (Tokyo, 1928), vol. I, p. 77.

24. *Official Guide to the International Exhibition of 1873* (London, 1873), p. 37.

25. *Furniture Gazette* (1878), vol. X, p. 75.

26. *Pottery Gazette* (1883), p. 68.

27. *In Pursuit of Beauty: Americans and the Aesthetic Movement* (Metropolitan Museum of Art, New York, exhib. cat. 1986), p. 193.

28. Minton & Co.'s exhibition album for Vienna in 1873, Royal Doulton Minton Archive, Stoke-on-Trent, Ms. 1469.

29. *Journal of the Royal Society of Arts* (1874), vol. 22, pp. 211–21 and *Furniture Gazette* (1874), pp. 89–90, 111–12, 136–7, 159–60, 183–4.

30. *Ibid.*, p. 136.

31. *Art Journal* (1874), p. 14.

32. Halén, Widar. 'Christopher Dresser and the "Modern English Style": His Later Designs for Wallpapers and Hangings', *Journal of the Decorative Arts Society*, (1990), no. 14, pp. 10–15, and Halén, Widar. 'Christopher Dresser and the Aesthetic Interior', *Magazine Antiques* (1991), vol. CXXXIX, no. 1, pp. 256–67.

33. Dresser, Christopher. 'Art Museums', *Penn Monthly* (Pennsylvania, 1877), pp. 117–26.

34. *The Dresser Collection of Japanese Curios and Articles selected for Messrs. Tiffany & Co*, Leavitt Auctioneers (18 June 1877, New York).

35. *Ibid.*

36. Halén *ibid.* (1988), pp. 185–220, and Halén, Widar. 'Christopher Dresser, the Centennial Exhibition, and the Anglo-American Dialogue', *Magazine Antiques* (September 2001), pp. 354–63.

37. *In Pursuit of Beauty* (Metropolitan Museum of Art, New York, exhib. cat. 1986), p. 255.

38. *The Builder* (1878), p. 213.

39. Dresser (1882b), preface.

40. Tametake, Ishida. *Dresser Hokoku* (Tokyo, 1877).

41. Dresser (1882b), pp. 100–08.

42. *Ibid.*, p. 144.

43. *Ibid.*, p. 234.

44. Earle, Joe. 'The Taxonomic Obsession: British Collectors and Japanese Objects 1852–1896', *Burlington Magazine* (1991), vol. 28, pp. 864–73.

45. Correspondence between Dresser and George A. Sala, 4 July and 28 December 1877, The Brotherton Library, University of Leeds, and Dresser (1878), pp. 169–78.

46. *Art Journal* (1877), p. 136.

47. Dresser (1878), p. 169.

48. *Furniture Gazette* (1878), p. 277.

49. *Chodo Zue* (Wellcome Institute, London, 1804).

50. 'A Japanese Room', *The Times* (12 June 1878), 6f.

51. Dresser, Christopher. 'Japanese Woodwork', *The Builder* (1878), p. 654.

52. V&A museum nos. 390 and 391-1905. Dresser, Christopher. 'Works from Japan', *The Builder* (1878), p. 969, and Dresser, Christopher. *Notes on Four Japanese Ceilings*, original manuscript, V&A Museum Library. MSS.86.EE.3.

53. *Furniture Gazette* (1879), vol. 12, p. 22.

54. Le Vine, Jonathan R.A. *Linthorpe Art Pottery* (Middlesbrough, exhib. cat. 1970), p. 13.

55. Lee, Robert. 'A Forgotten Yorkshire Pottery, Linthorpe Ware', *Heathon Review* (Bradford, 1934), pp. 37–40.

56. *Pottery Gazette* (1883), p. 435.

57. Register of the Art Furnishers' Alliance Co., 10 February 1882, Public Record Office, London.

58. *Cabinet Maker* (1880), p. 64.

59. *Catalogue of a Loan Collection of Oriental Art at the Corporation Galleries* (Glasgow, 1882).

60. 'Japanese Art Workmanship', *Furniture Gazette* (1882), vol. 17, pp. 223–9.

61. *New York Times* (17 December 1882), p. 6.

62. Alcock, Rutherford. *The Capital of the Tycoon* (London, 1863), p. 279.

63. *Arts & Crafts Essays by Members of the Arts & Crafts Exhibition Society* (London, 1903, pp. 28–33.

64. 'Some Features of Japanese Architecture and Ornamentation', *The Architect* (1884), pp. 384–6.

65. *Journal of Decorative Art* (1884), p. 494.

66. *Cabinet Maker* (1885), p. 181.

67. *Art Journal* (1885–6).

68. Earle, Joe. 'The Taxonomic Obsession: British Collectors and Japanese Objects 1852–1896', *Burlington Magazine* (1991), vol. 28, pp. 864–73.

69. *British Architect* (1886), vol. 25, p. 157.

70. *The Builder* (1887), vol. 52, p. 492.

71. *Journal of the Society of Arts* (1890), vol. 38, pp. 673–86, and *Art Journal*, 1892, pp. 154–8.

72. *Art Journal* (1889), p. 330.

73. *Kunstgewerbeblatt* (1892), pp. 1–3, and Halén, Widar. 'Ornamentation Seen as High Art: The Pioneering Work of Owen Jones and Christopher Dresser', *Scandinavian Journal of Design History* (1990), vol. 1, pp. 35–46.

74. *The Builder* (1904), p. 610.

CHAPTER 7

1. These details copied from the microfilm of the census in Kensington Public Library.

2. Boase, G. C. 'Thomas Page (1803–1877)', *Dictionary of National Biography* (London, 1895–6), pp. 42–3.

3. Quoted in Halén (1990), p. 31.

4. See Durant (1993), p. 36.

5. 'Improvements in Art Manufactures, The Linthorpe Pottery' in Jewitt, Llewellyn, ed. *The Reliquary* (1883–4), vol. 24, p. 113.

6. Bolitho, Hector, ed. *A Batsford Century* (London, 1943), pp. 16–19.

7. Dresser (1873), pp. 127–35.

8. 'Bretby Art Pottery' in Jewitt, Llewellyn, ed. *The Reliquary* (1883–4), vol. 24, p. 126; Lyons (1999), unpaginated [p. 49].

9. Durant (1993), p. 39.

10. 'The work of Christopher Dresser', *The Studio* (1899), vol. 15, pp. 104–14; reprinted in Durant (1993), pp. 132–5.

11. Starting with Nikolaus Pevsner, 'Minor Masters of the 20th Century: Christopher Dresser, Industrial Designer', *Architectural Review* (1937), vol. 81, pp. 183–6.

12. Dresser (1873), p. 13. Ruprich Ruppert, V.C.M. *Revue générale de l'architecture*, 20 (1862), quoted in Saboya, Marc. *Presse et architecture au XIXe siècle* (Paris, 1991), p. 147.

13. Watkin, David. *Sir John Soane, Enlightenment Thought and the Royal Academy Lectures* (Cambridge, 1996), p. 650.

14. 'John Buonarotti Papworth' in Colvin, Howard. *A Biographical Dictionary of British Architects 1600–1840* (London, 1995), pp. 729–34.

15. Ashbee, C. R. *Should We Stop Teaching Art?* (London, 1911), p. 100.

16. *From East to West, Textiles from G. P. & J. Baker* (Victoria and Albert Museum, London, exhib. cat. 1984), p. 30 (Haité and Hudson); Entwisle, E.A. *The Book of Wallpaper: A History and an Appreciation* (London, 1954), p. 113; see also Oman, Charles C., and Hamilton, Jean. *Wallpapers: A History and Illustrated Catalogue of the Collection of the Victoria & Albert Museum* (London, 1982), pp. 153 and 343 (Huntington).

17. Dresser (1862), pp. 148, 121 and 176.

18. Dresser (1873), pp. 3, 19–20 (nautilus), 117 and 120.

19. Dresser (1862), p. 8.

20. The fullest easily accessible accounts of Jones remain those by Michael Darby in Turner, Jane, ed. *The Dictionary of Art* (London, 1996), vol. 17, pp. 639–40, and Jervis, Simon. *The Penguin Dictionary of Design and Designers* (Harmondsworth, 1984), pp. 256–60. See also Darby, Michael. *The Islamic Perspective* (London, 1983), and Flores, Carol Ann H. *Owen Jones, Architect*, dissertation (Georgia Institute of Technology, 1996).

21. Dresser (1862), p. vii.

22. *Ibid.*, p. viii.

23. The Batley quotation is from Jervis, Simon. *The Penguin Dictionary of Design and Designers* (Harmondsworth, 1984), p. 48. For Batley, see also Soros, Susan Weber. 'Rediscovering H.W. Batley (1846–1932), British Aesthetic Movement Artist and Designer', *Studies in the Decorative Arts* (1999), vol. 7, pp. 2–41.

24. Dresser (1886), pls 43 and 47.

25. Dresser (1873), p. 14; Fuhring, Peter, and Bimbinet-Privat, Michèle. 'Le Style "Cosses de Pois", L'Orfèvrerie et la Gravure à Paris sous Louis XIII', *Gazette des Beaux-Arts* (2002), vol. 139, p. 84, no. 136.

26. Illustrated in *Art & Design in Europe and America 1800–1900* (Victoria and Albert Museum, London, exhib. cat. 1987), p. 110 (entry by Clive Wainwright).

27. Dresser (1874–6), pl. 32.

28. Hiesinger, Kathryn B. 'Ceramics and Glass' in *The Second Empire, Art in France under Napoleon III* (Philadelphia, 1978), pp. 179–80.

29. Durant (1993), p. 17.

30. Jervis, Simon. 'Introduction' in Daly, César. *Interior Designs of the 19th Century* (London, 1988), p. 5; Saboya, Marc. *Presse et Architecture au XIXe Siècle* (Paris, 1991), pp. 230–31.

31. Dresser (1862), p. 71.

32. Dresser (1873), pp. 142–3; Durant (1993), p. 25.

33. Dresser (1862), p. 40, slightly abbreviated and recast for clarity.

34. Dresser (1873), p. 73.

35. Atterbury, Paul, ed. *A.W.N. Pugin, Master of Gothic Revival* (New York, 1995), p. 373.

36. Dresser (1873), p. 74.

37. Saint, Andrew. *Richard Norman Shaw* (London, 1976), pp. 21–3, 58–63; Reed, Aileen. 'The Architectural Career of E.W. Godwin' in Soros, Susan Weber, ed. *E.W. Godwin, Aesthetic Movement Architect and Designer* (New York, 1999), pp. 139–45.

38. Dresser (1873), pp. 52–3.

39. *Ibid.*, pp. 53–8; Halén (1990), figs 58–63; Lyons (1999), [p.92]; Tilbrook, Adrian J., and

Fischer Fine Art Limited. *Truth, Beauty and Design: Victorian, Edwardian and Later Decorative Art* (London, 1986), pp. 26 (White chair) and 50 ('Granville' chair).

40. Dresser (1873), pp. 64–5.

41. *Ibid.*, pp. 145–51.

42. Crook, J. Mordaunt. *William Burges and the High Victorian Dream* (London, 1981), pp. 52–3 and 81–2.

43. Halén (1990), p. 36.

44. *Descriptive Catalogue of Japanese Enamels* (Liverpool, 1870); *Keramic Art of Japan* (Liverpool, 1875, London, 1881); *The Ornamental Arts of Japan* (London, 1882–4).

45. Stamp, Gavin. *Alexander 'Greek' Thomson* (London, 1999), pp. 60–61.

46. *Ibid.*, pp. 127 and 129; Stapleton, Annamarie. *John Moyr Smith 1839–1912: A Victorian Designer* (Shepton Beauchamp, 2002), pp. 7–11; *In Pursuit of Beauty: Americans and the Aesthetic Movement* (New York, 1987), pp. 414–16 (Cottier).

47. Oman, Charles C., and Hamilton, Jean. *Wallpapers: A History and Illustrated Catalogue of the Collection of the Victoria & Albert Museum* (London, 1982), pp. 346–8, 288–9, 329–30, 428–30, 297–313, 314–17; Eastlake, Charles Locke. *Hints on Household Taste* (London, 1878), 4th edn, pls XVI, XVII.

48. Smith, J. Moyr. *Ornamental Interiors Ancient and Modern* (London, 1887), has three brief references to Dresser (pp. 62, 72 and 215) as well as a presumed allusion: 'Many of these designs [by J. Moyr Smith], however, were done in the studio of a well-known ornamentist, and were given to the world as his work'.

49. Compare Talbert, B. J. *Gothic Forms Applied to Furniture Metal Work and Decoration for Domestic Purposes* (London, 1868), pl. 12 lower left, and Dresser (1874–6), pl. XXVII top right; MacDonald, Sally. 'Gothic Forms Applied to Furniture: The Early Work of Bruce James Talbert', *Furniture History* (1987), vol. 23, p. 57.

50. Quoted in part by Handley-Read, Charles. 'High Victorian Design: An Illustrated Commentary', in Thompson, Paul, ed. *Design 1860–1960, Sixth Conference Report* (London, n.d., [c. 1968]), p. 26, and in full by MacCarthy, Fiona. *William Morris: A Life for Our Times* (London, 1988), p. 182.

51. Durant (1993), p. 8.

52. Parry, Linda, ed. *William Morris* (Victoria and Albert Museum, London, 1996), p. 72; Durant (1993), p. 16.

53. Dresser (1873), pp. 53–8.

54. Halén (1990), p. 189.

55. Wakefield, Hugh. *Victorian Pottery* (London, 1962), p. 153.

SELECT BIBLIOGRAPHY

A full list of Christopher Dresser's writings can be found in Pasca and Pietroni (2001) or Halén (1990).

Anon. *Victorian and Edwardian Decorative Arts* (London, Victoria and Albert Museum, exhib cat 1952)

Anon. *The Aesthetic Movement and the Cult of Japan* (London, Fine Art Society, exhib cat 1972)

Anon. *Birmingham Gold and Silver 1773–1973* (Birmingham Museum and Art Gallery, exhib cat 1973)

Anon. *Minton 1798–1910* (London, Victoria and Albert Museum, exhib cat 1976)

Anon. *Christopher Dresser 1834–1904* (Arkwright Arts Trust, Camden Arts Centre, exhib cat 1979–80)

Bell, Quentin, *The Schools of Design* (London, 1963)

Bonython, Elizabeth and Burton, Anthony. *The Great Exhibitor : The Life and Work of Henry Cole* (London, 2003)

Burke, Doreen Bolger et al. *In Pursuit of Beauty, Americans and the Aesthetic Movement* (New York, The Metropolitan Museum of Art, exhib cat 1986)

Burton, Anthony. *Vision & Accident: the story of the Victoria and Albert Museum* (London, 1999)

Bury, Shirley. 'The Silver Designs of Dr. Christopher Dresser', *Apollo* (December 1962), pp. 766–70

Casteras, Susan and Parkinson, Ronald, eds. *Richard Redgrave 1804–1888* (New Haven and London, 1988)

Dennis, R. and Jesse, J. *Christopher Dresser 1834–1904* (London, Fine Art Society, exhib cat 1972)

Dresser, Christopher. *The Art of Decorative Design* (London, 1862)

Dresser, Christopher. *Principles of Decorative Design* (London, 1873)

Dresser, Christopher. *Studies in Design* (London, 1874–6; reprinted 1988)

Dresser, Christopher. 'The Art Manufacturers of Japan, From Personal Observation', *Journal of the Society of Arts* (London, 1878)

Dresser, Christopher. *Traditional Arts and Crafts of Japan* (London, 1882a; reprinted New York, 1994)

Dresser, Christopher. *Japan: Its Architecture, Art and Art Manufactures* (London, 1882b)

Dresser, Christopher. *Modern Ornamentation* (London, 1886)

Durant, Stuart. *Ornament. A Survey of Decoration since 1830* (London, 1986)

Durant, Stuart. *Christopher Dresser* (London and Berlin, 1993)

Faulkner, R. and Jackson, A. 'The Meiji Period in South Kensington. The Representation of Japan in the Victoria and Albert Museum, 1852–1912', *Treasures of Imperial Japan. The Nasser D. Khalili Collection of Japanese Art. Vol. I. Selected Essays* (London, 1995)

Gere, Charlotte and Whiteway, Michael. *Nineteenth Century Design from Pugin to Mackintosh* (London, 1993)

Halén, Widar. *Christopher Dresser* (Oxford, 1990)

Halén W., ed. *Christopher Dresser and Japan* (Koriyama, exhib cat, 2002)

Jervis, Simon. *High Victorian Design* (Woodbridge, 1983)

Jones, Joan. *Minton: The first two hundred years of design and production* (Shrewsbury, 1993)

Jones, Owen. *The Grammar of Ornament* (London, 1856, reprinted 1986)

Jones, Owen. *Examples of Chinese Ornament* (London, 1867)

Joppien, R. *Christopher Dresser, Ein Viktorianischer Designer 1834–1904* (Cologne, Kunstgewerbemuseum, exhib cat 1981)

Lyons, Harry. *Dresser: People's Designer, 1834–1904* (New Century, exhib cat 1999)

Pasca, Vanni and Pietroni, Lucia. *Christopher Dresser, 1834–1904. Il primo industrial designer. Per una nuova interpretazione della storia del design. Con testi allegati di : Henry Cole, Christopher Dresser, Owen Jones, Nikolaus Pevsner, Richard Redgrave , Gottfried Semper* (Milan, exhib cat 2001)

Pevsner, Nikolaus, *Pioneers of the Modern Movement from William Morris to Walter Gropius* (London, 1936)

Pevsner, Nikolaus. 'Minor Masters of the XIX Century: Christopher Dresser, Industrial Designer', *Architectural Review* (1937), pp. 183–6.

Pevsner, Nikolaus. *Studies in Art, Architecture and Design, II: Victorian and After* (London, 1968)

Rudoe, J. *Decorative Arts 1850–1950. A catalogue of the British Museum collection*, 2nd ed. (London, 1994)

Schmutzler, Robert. *Art Nouveau* (New York, 1962)

Soros, Susan Weber, ed. *E. W. Godwin: Aesthetic Movement Architect and Designer* (New Haven and London, 1999)

Stapleton, Annamarie. *John Moyr Smith 1839–1912: A Victorian designer* (London, 2002)

ABOUT THE CONTRIBUTORS

STUART DURANT studied at the Architectural Association and the Royal College of Art. He has written books on Voysey and on Ferdinand Dutert's Palais des Machines. His *Ornament: A Survey of Decoration since 1830* (1986) is considered to be a standard work on the subject. He is a contributor to the forthcoming Thoemmes Press' *Dictionary of Nineteenth-Century British Scientists*. He is the founder of the *International Design Yearbook*, and his writings on science and the arts have been widely translated.

CHARLOTTE GERE, nineteenth-century decorative arts specialist, has published extensively on design and historic interiors. Her publications include *Nineteenth-Century Decoration: The Art of the Interior* (1989) which won the Manuel Canovas Prize, 1989; *Nineteenth-Century Design from Pugin to Mackintosh*, with Michael Whiteway (1993); and *An Album of Nineteenth-Century Interiors*, for the Frick Collection in New York, (1992). Exhibition catalogues include *Morris & Company*, Fine Art Society (1978); *Architect Designers*, Fine Art Society (1982); *Gothic Revival: architecture et arts décoratifs de l'Angleterre victorienne*, Musée d'Orsay, Paris (1999); *The House Beautiful*, Geffrye Museum, London, on Oscar Wilde and aesthetic movement interior decoration (2000).

WIDAR HALÉN earned his doctorate at Oxford on Christopher Dresser and published the first monograph on him (Phaidon 1990, 1993). He was formerly director of West Norway Museum of Decorative Art in Bergen and is currently chief curator in the Museum of Decorative Art and Design in Oslo. He has published several books and numerous articles, particularly in the *Scandinavian Journal of Design History*. He was curator and editor of the catalogues of the recent exhibitions *Christopher Dresser and Japan* (Tokyo, 2002) and *Scandinavian Design Beyond the Myth*, which will tour European and U.S. museums in 2006.

SIMON JERVIS worked from 1964 to 1966 at Leicester Museums and Art Gallery, before moving to the Department of Furniture at the Victoria and Albert Museum. In 1990 he was appointed Director and Marlay Curator of the Fitzwilliam Museum, Cambridge. Simon Jervis moved back to London in 1995 to become Historic Buildings Secretary, subsequently Director of Historic Buildings of the National Trust, of whose Arts Panel he had been Chairman from 1987, and whence he retired in early 2002. He has published extensively; his books include *Printed Furniture Designs before 1660* (1974), *High Victorian Design* (1983), and *The Penguin Dictionary of Design and Designers* (1984).

HARRY LYONS is a student of Victorian design of household objects. He specializes in the designs of Christopher Dresser. His interest was first aroused by Dresser's simple philosophy of widening the circle of those who could afford good design, and he has subsequently spent twelve years researching the designer's life and work. He has frequently lectured and written on Dresser, and held an exhibition of the designer's work in 1999.

JUDY RUDOE has worked as a curator at the British Museum since 1974. She is an authority on jewellery and on nineteenth- to twentieth-century applied arts from Europe and America. Her publications include the two-volume *Catalogue of the Hull Grundy Gift of Jewellery to the British Museum* (as co-author, 1984), *Decorative Arts 1850–1950. A catalogue of the British Museum collection* (1991, revised 1994), and *Cartier 1900–1939* (1997), the catalogue of the exhibition shown in 1997 at the British Museum and the Metropolitan Museum of Art, and in 1999 at the Field Museum, Chicago. Her many articles on aspects of nineteenth-century design include contributions to the exhibition catalogue, *Whitefriars Glass. The Art of James Powell & Sons* (1996), and to the catalogue of the Gilbert collection of Micromosaics (2000).

DAVID A. TAYLOR is an expert on material culture and has researched and written about craftsmanship and the process of design for the past thirty years. His other areas of specialization include maritime culture, occupational culture, and field-research methodology. He is a senior staff folklorist at the American Folklife Center, Library of Congress, Washington, DC. He is the author of a number of scholarly books and articles, as well as the exhibition catalogue *Truth, Beauty, Power: Dr. Christopher Dresser, 1834–1904* (1998). As an adjunct professor, he has taught at the George Washington University and the University of Pennsylvania.

MICHAEL WHITEWAY has been at the forefront of the promotion of nineteenth-century British design for the past 30-plus years, advising museums on their collections and exhibitions on an international basis. He is the author of *Nineteenth-Century Design: From Pugin to Mackintosh*, with Charlotte Gere (1993) and *Christopher Dresser 1834–1904* (2001). He has also curated numerous exhibitions, including *Japonism: British Decorative Arts Influenced by the Arts of Japan 1860–1890*, Fine Art Society (1972), *Architect Designers: Pugin to Mackintosh*, Fine Art Society (1981), and *The Birth of Modern Design*, Sezon Museum of Art, Japan (1990).

INDEX